A Sentimental
EDUCATION
FOR THE WORKING MAN

A Sentimental
EDUCATION
FOR THE WORKING MAN

THE MEXICO CITY PENNY PRESS, 1900–1910

ROBERT M. BUFFINGTON

Duke University Press   Durham and London   2015

© 2015 Duke University Press
All rights reserved
Printed in the United States of America on acid-free paper ∞
Designed by Heather Hensley
Typeset in Warnock Pro by Westchester Publishing Services

Library of Congress Cataloging-in-Publication Data
Buffington, Robert
A sentimental education for the working man : the Mexico City
penny press, 1900-1910 / Robert M. Buffington.
pages cm
Includes bibliographical references and index.
ISBN 978-0-8223-5899-2 (hardcover : alk. paper)
ISBN 978-0-8223-5882-4 (pbk. : alk. paper)
1. Penny newspapers—Mexico—History.
2. Working class—Press coverage—Mexico—History.
3. Mexican newspapers—History—20th century.
4. Press—Mexico—History—20th century. I. Title.
PN4968.B844 2015
079.72'53—dc23   2014045005
ISBN 978-0-8223-7557-9 (e-book)

Cover art: Details from "¡Viva La Independencia!," *El Diablito Rojo,*
September 17, 1900 and "La Matraca de La Guacamaya,"
La Guacamaya, April 1905, (Número extraordinario).
Both courtesy of the Benson Latin American Collection,
University of Texas Libraries, The University of Texas at Austin.

CONTENTS

ACKNOWLEDGMENTS

Any naive thoughts I might once have entertained about the romance of writing for a living are long gone. But I do take real pleasure in thanking the wonderful people who made this book possible. I cannot adequately express my gratitude to my wife, Megan, whose patience and encouragement throughout the long gestation of this book was saintly—if not exactly boundless—and to my children (and now grandchildren) who provided the necessary inspiration for a reluctant author insufficiently motivated by reputation and career.

I remember reading somewhere that we academics are only as good as our intellectual communities. In this regard, I am fortunate to have very smart and very generous colleagues. Although I haven't always been able to measure up to their high expectations, my sincere efforts to stay in their good graces have made this book much better than it might otherwise have been. My longtime friend and sometime collaborator, Pablo Piccato, read through two different versions of the manuscript. His enviable ability to keep up on the latest scholarship helped me fill in gaps in my own, his unsparing commentary helped me avoid several serious errors of judgment, and his steadfast encouragement helped keep me on track while I fixed them as best I could. Another dear friend and collaborator, Eithne Luibhéid, gave me the courage, guidance, and support necessary to push beyond my disciplinary training while providing a fresh set of "undisciplined" eyes for what is still very much a history project. The first three chapters and much of the introduction to this book might never have been written in the first place if my friend and then colleague, Susana Peña hadn't agreed to a book-writing support group of two and committed to regular rigorous critiques of each others work from concept to comma. Finally, an anonymous reviewer for Duke University Press reminded me just how valuable a meticulous, thoughtful, demanding reader can be. Whatever its merits, this book owes a tremendous debt to the contributions of these terrific scholars. Its defects reflect the limitations of the author.

I also had a lot of help from a lot of people on various chapters of the book. These generous colleagues include Elisa Speckman Guerra, Lila Caimari, Donna Guy, Juan Pablo Dabove, Lyman Johnson, William Beezley, William French, Ricardo Pérez Montfort, Hai Ren, Deepti Misri, Donna Goldstein, participants at the Crime Narratives in Modern Latin America Conference at Columbia University, the Institute for the Study of Culture and Society Writing Group at Bowling Green State University, and the Women and Gender Studies Works in Progress Group at the University of Colorado Boulder. Thank you all!

Working with the editors and staff at Duke University Press has been a delight. My special thanks to Gisela Fosado, Valerie Millholland, Lorien Olive, and Sara Leone for their encouragement, good advice, and hard work.

Without archivists, historians would wither and die on the vine. In this case, my heartfelt gratitude goes to the archivists and staff at the Nettie Lee Benson Collection, University of Texas at Austin (especially Michael Hironymous); the Jean Charlot Collection, University of Hawaii (especially Bronwen Solyom); the Center for Southwest Research, University of New Mexico; Special Collections and University Archives, Stanford University; the Harry Ransom Center, University of Texas at Austin; and the Hemeroteca Nacional de México.

Major financial support for this project includes a National Endowment for the Humanities Fellowship, an Institute for the Study of Culture and Society Fellowship (Bowling Green State University), and an Associate Professor Growth Grant from the Leadership Education for Advancement and Promotion program (University of Colorado Boulder).

Last but never least, I would like to thank the wonderful staff at the University of Colorado Boulder's Women and Gender Studies Program, Alicia Turchette and Valerie Bhat, who not only helped with the book but covered for me while I finished it.

INTRODUCTION

Working-class Mexican men have hard lives. On that point at least, most everyone agrees. In a pioneering 1901 study of the "genesis" of crime in Mexico City, for example, lawyer-cum-sociologist Julio Guerrero expressed concern for the poor *jornalero* (day laborer): "moral instincts extinguished in the dark night of misery and an intimate acquaintance with cold; dignity spent in fruitless pursuit of work; the future turned into expectations of jail; and his suffering and desperation into a forced vagrancy, that many times ended with pulque or tequila."[1]

Even self-styled defenders of the working class couldn't resist portraying their protégés as miserable drunks. A 1904 issue of *La Guacamaya*— "whip of the bourgeoisie, staunch friend of the working class," and the most popular of Mexico City's penny press weeklies—featured a front-page illustration that could have served equally well for Guerrero's gloomy assessment (see fig. I.1).[2] Appearing under the title "La resurrección de Lázaro" (The Resurrection of Lazarus), the image depicts a prone, still groggy worker rousted by an erect, scowling policeman with raised nightstick. The poem beneath reads:

Se encontraba medio muerto
Lázaro José Trujillo
A consecuencia del pulque
que en la tarde había bebido,

Se encontraba medio muerto | cuando llegó un tecolote | y dándole garrotazos
Lázaro José Trujillo | con el ceño muy fruncido | de esta manera le dijo:
A consecuencia del pulque | y despertando al borracho | LAZARO. LEVANTATE Y ANDA ...
que en la tarde había bebido, | con las palabras de Cristo | Por ébrio sin domicilio

FIG. I.1 José Guadalupe Posada/Author Unknown, "La resurrección de Lázaro," *La Guacamaya*, March 17, 1904. Courtesy of the Benson Latin American Collection, University of Texas Libraries, The University of Texas at Austin.

cuando llegó ún tecolote
con el ceño muy fruncido
y despertando al borracho
con las palabras de Cristo

y dándole garrotazos
de esta manera le dijo:
Lázaro. Levántate y anda . . .
Por ebrio sin domicilio.

❧

[He was found half dead
Lázaro José Trujillo
Thanks to the pulque
He had drunk that afternoon,

When a cop arrived
With furrowed brow
And waking the drunk
With the words of Christ

And striking him
In this way said to him:
"Lazarus. Arise and walk . . ."
For being drunk and homeless.]

La Guacamaya editors might share Guerrero's apparent concern for the plight of a benighted worker like the homeless Lázaro.[3] But the similarity ends there. On page 2, the editors included a letter addressed to "the workers" with this expression of solidarity:

> Yo como vosotros he enervado mis fuerzas y agotado mis energias en los talleres para llevar, primero á mi querida madre y más tarde á nuestros idolatrados hijos el pan que nosotros los obreros amasamos con el sudor de nuestra honrada frente.[4]

❧

> [Like you I have drained my strength and exhausted my energies in the workshops in order to bring, first to my beloved mother and later to our idolized children, the bread that we workers knead with the sweat of our honored brow.]

While Guerrero too worried about the enervation of Mexican workers (and in similarly overwrought prose), he never pretended to share in their predicament. Nor did he find it amusing. And what are we to make of the decision of a penny press rival, *El Diablito Rojo*, to front the 1900 Independence Day issue with the image of a worker toasting *la patria* with a glass of pulque in one hand and a newspaper in the other (see fig. I.2)?[5]

Although more sympathetic than those of most of his peers, Guerrero's views on working-class men reinforced centuries-old stereotypes about their alleged lassitude, improvidence, promiscuity, and weakness for games of chance, intoxicating substances, and interpersonal violence. It can hardly come as a surprise, then, that the sentimental education for

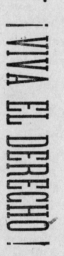

FIG. I.2 Artist/Author Unknown, "¡Viva La Independencia!," *El Diablito Rojo*, September 17, 1900. Courtesy of the Benson Latin American Collection, University of Texas Libraries, The University of Texas at Austin.

working-class men favored by elite social engineers sought to counter workers' loss of "moral instincts" with a range of modern institutions—schools, barracks, penitentiaries, and the like—designed to instill self-discipline and propagate up-to-date views on everything from politics to gender relations. While penny press editors often joked about the *vicios* (vices) of working-class men, they were up to something quite different. The sentimental education they proposed not only foregrounded the absurdity of bourgeois solutions to working-class problems; it sought, through social satire that mocked working-class and bourgeois sentiments alike, to construct for its protégés a way of being in the modern world that was every bit as complicated and contradictory as their day-to-day lives.

Historians—myself included—have written quite a bit about late nineteenth- and early twentieth-century disciplinary projects aimed at the Mexican working classes. But we have had less to say about the psychological impact of these projects on workers other than to note that they resisted as often as and as best they could under very difficult circumstances. This study thus seeks to fill in a small but crucial piece of a much larger puzzle through a reconstruction of an alternative sentimental education for working-class men produced by and through Mexico City's thriving penny press—a sentimental education that was less patronizing, less coercive, more realistic, and more comprehensive than anything proposed by the authorities. As we might expect, it was more nuanced as well.

In order to convey the scope and nuance of this ambitious endeavor, I arrange this book in five chapters. The first three chapters address different aspects of working-class patriotism and the fraught issue of working-class (male) citizenship. The final two chapters shift focus from male citizenship to masculine subjectivity—the way penny press editors sought to make sense of working-class men *as men*—as reflected in their work, leisure, and relationships with women. Before we enter the complex, curious, and contradictory world of the satiric Mexico City penny press for workers, however, the rest of this introduction provides some essential background that should help us understand the stories to come.

Macho Men and Masculine Scripts

Machismo—the nearly universal term used to describe aggressively masculine behavior—is likely Mexico's best-known contribution to world language.[6] Although applied to male culture in general, by nearly all accounts machismo's most notorious practitioners are working-class Mexican men. For example, Octavio Paz's definitive work on national character, *The Labyrinth of Solitude*, casts the mestizo lower-class man as Mexico's dysfunctional male archetype: the mixed-race son of a denigrated (raped) Indian mother and a despised (rapist) Spanish father, Paz's *macho* resorts to a dizzying array of public and private "masks" to disguise his profound alienation and a consequent predilection for violence directed against himself, other men, all women, the world.[7] Derived from the work of turn-of-the-century Mexican criminologists and sociologists, including Guerrero, the macho, as codified by Paz and others, appears in social science literature as the masculinity of choice for "traditional" working-class men. This is so even in Matthew Gutmann's sympathetic ethnography *The Meanings of Macho*, where a carefully historicized machismo appears as the outmoded masculine script against which contemporary working-class men construct their own modernity.[8]

The ubiquitous deployment of the working-class macho stereotype by mass media, politicians, policymakers, social scientists, and anthropological "informants" obscures a complicated historical terrain. This book seeks to shed light on that terrain by reconstructing the complex, shifting, and contradictory ideas about manhood, especially working-class masculinity, in circulation in early twentieth-century Mexico City. By examining alternative masculine scripts at work or under construction in the capital's satiric penny press for workers during the first decade of the twentieth century, it challenges the reduction of working-class masculinity to the macho—much as Gutmann's ethnography does for the late twentieth century. Further, it argues that the penny press's satire-driven sentimental education for the working man, which directly engaged the contradictions of modernity in ways that bourgeois notions of manhood never did, played a defining role in the development of modern male subjectivity in Mexico and across the Mexican diaspora.

The Working Classes in Early Twentieth-Century Mexico City

Any historical investigation into changing notions of manhood in early twentieth-century Mexico City must begin with an attempt to recover the specific historical conditions that shaped working-class masculinity. Those conditions had changed dramatically by 1900. The intricate web of causes, effects, and articulations behind these changes is too complex to do justice to here, but the essentials look something like the following.

By 1900, Mexico's longest-serving president, Porfirio Díaz, had dominated national politics for over twenty-four years; he would continue to do so for another eleven. (In recognition of his dominating presence, historians refer to the 1876–1911 period as "the *Porfiriato.*") When he first seized the presidency in 1876, General Díaz promised to restore order to Mexico after more than six decades of political turmoil, including the wars for independence, two foreign invasions, several bloody civil conflicts, innumerable *pronunciamientos* (political uprisings), and endemic banditry. As President Díaz's reelection started to become routine, the "indispensable caudillo" and his acolytes reassured supporters, skeptics, and agnostics alike that the ongoing restoration of order by a strong central government was providing the secure foundation for a vibrant national economy, which would soon produce a modern society composed of industrious, patriotic, and peace-loving citizens, who could then be trusted to participate responsibly in a free democratic process.[9]

By the turn of the century, Porfirian modernization efforts had begun to have a significant impact—not all of it positive—throughout Mexico, especially in the capital. For a variety of reasons, ranging from land enclosures to incipient industrialization to expanding railroad networks (financed by foreign capital), Mexico City experienced a huge influx of migrants throughout this period, most of them from outlying rural areas and nearby states. This influx caused the city to more than double in population, from 230,000 in 1877 to 471,000 by 1910.[10] As migrants flooded in, the middle and upper classes deserted the central districts for newer residential areas along the capital's showcase boulevard, the Paseo de la Reforma. At the same time, housing shortages drove up downtown rents and forced many poorer residents into less reputable neighborhoods, like the notorious Tepito and the working-class barrios that sprang up around the new penitentiary in San Lázaro. The class differentiation that resulted from these demographic and geographic shifts, although incomplete and permeable, encouraged the development of a working-class consciousness of sorts grounded in shared social spaces and shared cultural practices (like reading the satiric penny press).[11]

Conscious of itself or not, the Mexico City working class was hardly the industrial proletariat envisioned by Marxist theorists. Although the number of factory workers rose nearly 355 percent between 1895 and 1910 to around 10,500 people, they represented only 4 percent of the city's workforce; nearly a third of that workforce was female. While many more did comparable labor in small and medium-sized workshops, Mexico City workers employed in manufacturing actually declined as a percentage of the workforce: from 37 percent in 1895 to 33 percent in 1910 (although the overall number of workers in manufacturing grew substantially). In fact, the bulk of the capital's labor force was unskilled; the majority worked in sweatshops or service jobs. Moreover, by 1910 women represented 35 percent of the capital's waged workers, with over 35,000 of them employed as domestic servants, more than three times the number of male and female factory workers. Workers' wages ranged from 10 centavos a day for children to 1 peso for most routine factory work to 2 to 5 pesos for semiskilled mechanics. Women were invariably paid less than men.[12]

But the Mexico City working class included a sizable and influential contingent of skilled craft workers, many of them self-identified artisans. And literacy rates for the general population were a remarkably high: 50 percent for the Federal District by 1910, despite the presence of large numbers of illiterate rural migrants. (The national literacy rate was closer to 20 percent.) As early as 1873, a report on eligible jurors for one city district (Cuartel Mayor 6, northwest of the city center) indicated that nearly 40 percent of its more than 1,200 adult male artisans knew how to read, including 100 percent of the printers and typographers.[13] To further complicate the "class" question, the literate and better-paid end of the proletarian spectrum often blended imperceptibly into Mexico City's financially precarious petite bourgeoisie.

This was especially true in an industry like printing, which had benefited tremendously from a spate of technological innovations that significantly increased productivity and quality in the newspaper trade. Bolstered by the rise of mass dailies, beginning in 1896 with *El Imparcial*, skilled printers remained among the best-paid craft workers.[14] Those with more traditional talents benefited less: journalists struggled with notoriously low salaries, and artisans, like master printmaker José Guadalupe Posada, faced an exhausting daily scrabble just to make ends meet.[15] Class status for members of this group was fluid rather than fixed, circumstantial rather than predetermined. Even the status-obsessed reporter protagonist of the Porfirian novelist Emilio Rabasa's *El cuarto poder* (The Fourth Estate; 1888), admits that "we worked as scribes, not as writers; we weren't artists, but workers."[16] From this marginally respectable sector of Mexico City life— nominally *gente decente* (decent folk) but self-identified as working class at least when it suited their purposes—the satiric penny press drew its editors, writers, printers, illustrators, and much of its audience. It was principally their struggles with the changing conditions of male subjectivity that were recorded in its pages.

The Satiric Penny Press for Workers

The Mexico City satiric penny press has a historical importance that belies its relatively brief appearance (roughly 1900–15), uneven quality, and erratic publication record.[17] With mastheads that openly proclaimed working-class loyalties—*La Guacamaya* (The Squawking Parrot), "newspaper of gossip and good humor, agile and a teller of truths, not puffed up or snobby, scourge of the bourgeoisie and defender of the <u>Working Class</u>"; *El Diablito Rojo* (The Little Red Devil), "of the people and for the people"; *El Diablito Bromista* (The Little Joking Devil), "organ of the working class, scourge of the bad bourgeoisie, and bogeyman of bad government"—the satiric penny press provided a forum for working-class issues, contributed to the formation of working-class consciousness, and facilitated the imagining of a Mexican national community grounded on the honest, productive, and patriotic toil of Mexico's working classes.[18] In exchange, authorities allowed editors to criticize political corruption, crony capitalism, and exploitation of the working class so long as editors did not personally attack President Porfirio Díaz or espouse overtly revolutionary ideas.

These qualities set the satiric penny press apart from the mass dailies like the government-subsidized *El Imparcial* and the pro-Catholic *El País* that dominated the Mexico City newspaper business during the late

BIBLIOTECA AL AIRE LIBRE

Los hijos del pueblo atorándole a la leitura.

—Mira, mamá, lo que dice
el faceto PERIQUITO:
que ya se trincó un tandero
un vale de por Tepito.

—Mira á mi hijo, que bien lee,
parece un subvencionado.
—No, hijito, mejor pelado,
San Dimas, no San José.

—Y á quién se debe, criatura,
que leas bien, y violentito?
—Al chistoso PERIQUITO,
pues me agrada su lectura.

Trae versitos, notas ciertas,
chismarajos, historietas;
anda por todas las puertas,
y conoce bien las tretas.

—¿Las tretas de los malditos,
de los rotos pretensiosos,
que nomás son titeritos
faroleros y chismosos?.........

—No, mamá, yo no hablo de eso,
me refiero al peladaje,
al pueblo que en su coraje,
aun preso quiere más queso.

—Haces bien, hijo querido,
estima á tus semejantes,
y aborrece ese partido
de locos y de farsantes.

Trabaja, sí, con empeño,
sé honrado por donde quiera,
y jamás la faltriquera
de tu honradez sea el diseño.

La ropa es el espantajo
de este mundo maldecido;
sé pobre...... pero querido;
sé obrero, y ama al trabajo.

El trabajo al hombre honrado,
lo enaltece, lo redime,
y es digno de que se estime
por ser su nombre sagrado.

FIG. I.3 José Guadalupe Posada/Author Unknown, "Bilbioteca al aire libre," *El Periquito*, August 8, 1895. Rafael Barajas Durán (el Fisgón), *Posada mito y mitote. La caricatura política de José Guadalupe Posada y Manuel Alfonso Manilla* (Mexico City: Fondo de Cultura Económica, 2009), image 129, p. 186.

Porfiriato. Penny press stalwart *La Guacamaya* might claim as many as 29,000 copies sold for its hottest weekly editions but could not begin to approach *El Imparcial*'s daily sales, which had soared to well over 100,000 by 1910.[19] Nevertheless, evidence suggests that the satiric penny press— purchased, borrowed, shared, stolen, or read aloud on the shop floor, in the *vecindad* (tenement) patio, or in the local *pulquería* or *cantina* (bars)—circulated widely among Mexico City workers and sometimes even among their provincial counterparts.[20] An 1895 print from *El Periquito*, for example, carries the title "Biblioteca al aire libre" (Open-Air Library) and depicts a group of working-class men (including a policeman) listening as the paper is read aloud and discussed (see fig. I.3).[21] The mass dailies used up-to-date news, sensational crimes, sports coverage, and homey advice columns to attract readers of all classes, but only the penny press actively promoted working-class concerns and openly encouraged reader submissions on everything from strike information to poetic sentiment. Moreover, unlike the government subsidized *El Imparcial* (which also cost a penny), the satiric penny press relied entirely on daily sales to finance operations, a constraint that forced editors to pay special attention to the everyday concerns of their mostly working-class readership.[22] Probably for the same reason, they were less inclined to propagandize than papers sponsored by workers' organizations like *El Hijo del Trabajo, El Socialista, La Internacional, La Voz del Obrero*, and *La Revolución Social*.[23] The continued popularity of penny press stalwarts *La Guacamaya, El Diablito Rojo*, and *El Diablito Bromista* suggests that successful editors understood and represented working-class concerns quite well—at least as far as their readers were concerned—whatever their own class status, which was never more than petit bourgeois in any case.[24]

The satiric penny press for workers has many obvious virtues: eye-catching graphics (Posada was a frequent contributor), acerbic political and social critique, and—in contrast to the didactic tone of many newspapers directed at the working classes—a wicked sense of humor. It is also loaded with stories, vignettes, and poems, many of them submitted by loyal readers. To contemporary scholars, the juxtaposition of social critique and literary pretension is a bit unsettling and most prefer to focus on graphic images or political analyses and to ignore the fiction and poetry. This sensible strategy has produced some thoughtful work on Posada's artistic innovations and on working-class political culture.[25] Still, it leaves important questions about the penny press's representations of other aspects of working-class life unanswered.

Working-Class Politics

To frame these unanswered questions, let us begin with the as yet unsettled scholarly debate over working-class politics. Indeed, labor historians have given us three distinct perspectives on the politics of Mexico City's working classes at the turn of the century. In the aftermath of the 1910 Revolution—the decade-long struggle to unseat Porfirio Díaz and to resolve the succession question after his surprisingly quick departure— scholars began to sort through a confusing tangle of prerevolutionary labor organizations and movements for traces of an incipient radicalism they assumed must have contributed to that epochal event. They uncovered those traces in a nineteenth-century anarchist tradition that would find its revolutionary voice with the 1900 appearance of *Regeneración*, the mouthpiece of the opposition *Partido Liberal Mexicano* (Mexican Liberal Party) and its founders, Ricardo and Enrique Flores Magón.[26] As for the radicalism of working men themselves (rather than that of their organizers), historians noted future president Álvaro Obregón's successful 1915 recruitment of Mexico City workers associated with the Casa del Obrero Mundial (House of the World Worker) into "red battalions"— militia units mobilized and deployed by the constitutionalist faction under "First Chief" Venustiano Carranza to fight against the rival insurgent forces of Pancho Villa and Emiliano Zapata.[27]

Other historians looked at the broad spectrum of Porfirian working-class organizations and came away with a much different view of workers' politics. In an important early article, Rodney Anderson argued that most industrial workers were not radical internationalists but liberal patriots "who took their inspiration from what they believed to be *Mexican* ideals, originating in their own Liberal tradition, not from any of the more militantly class-conscious European ideologies." For most workers, Anderson added, "there was no reason to believe that the liberalism of *La Reforma* had failed but rather that its promises had been subverted by powerful foreign and domestic interests."[28]

Other historians of Mexico's urban working class have supported Anderson's assessment of its politics. "Given half a chance," Alan Knight notes, "the organized working class opted for unionism and reformism (sometimes camouflaged under revolutionary rhetoric); only when it was brusquely and brutally denied the chance did it entertain risky thoughts of revolution."[29] In his study of Mexico City workers in the revolutionary period, John Lear argues that during the first decade of the twentieth century they forged a unique brand of "popular liberalism"—a working-class ideology that "equated the [liberal] struggle against tyranny in the political sphere with that in the workplace . . . [and that] selectively drew from liberal doctrine and invocations of past national struggles and heroes to condemn the role of monopoly and foreign capitalists and to reclaim the participation of the workers in local and national politics."[30]

While recognizing the power of popular liberalism to shape working-class politics, Mexican labor historians have been more inclined to acknowledge the influence of European socialist thinkers like Claude-Henri de Saint-Simon, Robert Owen, and Charles Fourier and to stress the role of artisans (as opposed to industrial workers) in formulating a distinctly Mexican brand of socialism.[31] Carlos Illades, for example, observes that prominent late nineteenth-century working-class newspapers like *El Socialista* (1871–88) and *El Hijo del Trabajo* (1874–84) and their affiliated organizations enthusiastically touted European ideas about the importance of social harmony, cooperation, and association. At the same time, he argues, Mexican socialists reworked these imported notions to suit local circumstances by integrating liberal imperatives like individual autonomy, democratic participation, and social equality, which made it much harder to mobilize and control workers organizations than had been the case under the colonial-era trade guilds. To distinguish themselves from more radical socialist, anarchist, and communist groups, many of these mainstream socialist workers organizations insisted on staying out of politics—at least with regard to the endorsement of political candidates—and echoed Fourier's proposal for an alliance between capitalists and workers in the battle against the unproductive members of society: politicians, functionaries, clergy, idle rich, and idle poor.[32]

One of the central sites for the development of working-class politics in the decade before the Revolution was Mexico City's flourishing satiric penny press. As expected, the political views of penny press editors, contributors, and (presumably) readers fall well within the parameters of popular liberalism/liberal socialism. In her pioneering study of penny press politics, María Elena Díaz concluded that "The political discourse of these penny journals . . . approached all the classic issues of nineteenth-century democratic liberalism, but gave these a popular twist. . . . Indeed, the republican notion of sovereignty residing in the people acquired literally a popular meaning: more and more 'the people' were defined as the popular and labouring classes."[33]

At the same time, she points out significant political variation among the three most successful papers, *El Diablito Rojo*, *La Guacamaya*, and *El Diablito Bromista*, with *El Diablito Bromista* the most radical (generally supportive of strikes), *El Diablito Rojo* the most conservative (generally opposed to strikes), and the more "commercial" *La Guacamaya* somewhere in the middle.[34] But these editorial differences were variations on common themes: authoritarian subversion of traditional liberal values, bourgeois exploitation of workers, distrust of foreign capitalists, and the need to redeem the oppressed working class. Editorial differences aside, Díaz concludes that the penny press fostered a "rather vigorous sense of working-class consciousness," firmly rooted in "the principles of democratic liberalism."[35] In an exhaustive study of José Guadalupe Posada's political cartoons—many of them featured in the satiric penny press for workers—Rafael Barajas Durán argues that "Posada reflects a characteristic position of the urban proletariat and other poor classes of the period: he defends liberal ideology, he advocates for the poor and working classes, he denounces the abuses of patrons, and, while he stays loyal to Don Porfirio, he criticizes some aspects of his government." As Barajas Durán explains, "the Posada of the workers' press is something of a popular artist-agitator . . . but he is a long ways from being a radical revolutionary."[36]

Despite their disagreements, labor historians from all sides of the working-class politics question seem to agree that some form of class consciousness, whether radical, liberal, or socialist, had begun to emerge among Mexico City's workers by the first decade of the twentieth century.[37] Díaz, Lear, and Barajas Durán contend that the satiric penny press played a central role in its emergence by articulating a popular/socialist version of liberalism with broad appeal for urban workers, an appeal compelling and comprehensive enough to constitute workers as a distinct "public" with shared interests and a sense of themselves as a community of readers and listeners.[38] Convincing as they are, these conclusions fail to explain *why* the satiric penny press for workers was so popular in late Porfirian Mexico City.

The answer to that question lies in a dramatic reimaging of the relationship of the state, civil society, and the "people"—mirrored by a dramatic reimaging of the relationship between writers and their readers—that had begun to coalesce, especially within the Mexican intelligentsia, during the last decades of the nineteenth century. Central to this reimagining was the formation of a public sphere predicated on the notion of a "universally accessible conceptual space where private citizens came together to discuss matters of common interest, on the assumption that reason, the only requisite, was evenly distributed, and that their voices would have an impact on public opinion."[39] Although the Mexican public sphere was dominated by bourgeois voices and characterized by exclusions, historian Pablo Piccato argues that its presence nonetheless meant that "multiple actors addressed the state and civil society, assuming (as a key part of their notion of citizenship) that they could be involved in dialogues in the public sphere . . . and that in it all rational voices counted."[40] Among these multiple actors were a number of "unexpected citizens"—including penny press editors and contributors—whose "vernacular use of the norms and laws" around citizenship challenged elite efforts to limit access to the public sphere.[41]

Seeing Like a State: On the Legibility of Working-Class Men

Participation in the public sphere came at a cost. By the late nineteenth century, working-class men in Mexico City had become the principal targets of three disciplinary projects: the first endorsed and sometimes enforced (albeit in a haphazard way) by a liberal authoritarian state, the second envisioned and sometimes carried out (through the auspices of the state) by elite social reformers, the third promoted and sometimes essayed (albeit in a modest way) by socialist-inspired workers organizations. Because many elite social reformers were also public officials and even presidential advisors, the difference between the first two disciplinary projects—policy initiatives proposed and carried out by the Porfirian state, on one hand, and reform proposals generated and debated in the public sphere, on the other—can often be difficult to discern (as it was for penny press editors at the time), but since elite reformers envisioned much more than the state was willing to take on, the distinction is important to maintain.

Differences aside, all three projects drew inspiration from classic nineteenth-century liberal notions of self-help, individual autonomy, and personal character—qualities seen as "natural" to the bourgeoisie but considered rare in the working class, especially in working-class men. Government officials, social reformers, and socialists alike believed that these qualities could be transmitted to the working class through training, education, and moral example. Once acquired, these quintessentially *modern* traits would transform recalcitrant, unruly, lazy, self-indulgent, irresponsible working-class men into good citizens in the public sphere, productive workers in the marketplace, and responsible sons, husbands, and fathers in private life. Although government officials focused on improving public order and labor productivity, liberal social reformers on promoting middle-class values, and socialists on fostering responsible collective action, the three groups shared an abiding distrust of traditional working-class culture, most especially working-class notions of manhood—usually defined in terms of "vices" like drinking, gambling, philandering, spousal abuse, parental negligence, fighting, and idleness—which they considered a serious obstacle to material, social, and spiritual progress for the working classes and, by extension, for the nation.

Because the Porfirian regime ended in revolution, historians tend to forget its revolutionary roots—and to dismiss as self-serving and hypocritical the progressive agenda that provided the ethical rationale for authoritarian governance. Although less radical than subsequent generations of revolutionary social engineers in Mexico and elsewhere, Porfirian progressives nonetheless shared their faith in the high modernist ideology that swept across western Europe and the Americas after 1830 or so. In *Seeing Like a State: How Certain Schemes to Improve the Human Condition Have Failed*, anthropologist James Scott defines high modernism as "a supreme self-confidence about continued linear progress, the development of scientific and technical knowledge, the expansion of production, the rational design of the social order, the growing satisfaction of human needs, and, not least, an increasing control over nature (including human nature) commensurate with scientific understanding of natural laws."[42] This "supreme self-confidence" in scientific progress and rational planning characterized Mexican social engineers both before and after the Revolution. Like their revolutionary successors, Porfirian social reformers, including Díaz's technocratic advisers, the self-styled *científicos* (men of science), sought to use the power of an authoritarian state "to bring about enormous changes in people's habits, work, living patterns, moral conduct, and worldview."[43] This was of course much easier said than done, given the ideological constraints of nineteenth-century laissez-faire liberalism and the practical difficulties involved in implementing even relatively straightforward (and much needed) infrastructure projects like modern drainage and transportation systems. Despite these very real obstacles, however, Porfirian social engineers made concerted efforts—albeit with limited success—to transform Mexico City workers into hygienic, industrious, well-trained proletarians and informed, loyal citizens.[44]

At the heart of high modernist social reform is the bureaucratic compulsion to produce a "legible" population "with precisely those standardized characteristics that are easiest to monitor, count, assess, and manage."[45] The transformation of illegible traditional societies into legible modern ones required that the state intervene in the everyday lives of its citizens. As Scott explains: "A thoroughly legible society eliminates local monopolies of information and creates a kind of national transparency through the uniformity of codes, identities, statistics, regulations, and measures."[46] Although state-driven efforts to render society legible, and thus manageable, generally take into account the entire population, including second-class citizens like women and children as well as non-citizens like immigrants and refugees, the target of its most coercive interventions are the (often racialized) lower classes and particularly working-class men.[47]

Efforts to render the people legible meant, as Scott notes above, the elimination of "local monopolies of information." In the case of Mexico City workers, these local monopolies of information included working-class cultural practices, especially the (presumably) illicit use of public spaces and the impenetrable local speech or *caló* that authorities worried might serve as a cover for criminal activities. As the term itself suggests, legibility relies heavily on visual cues in order to make sense of a complex, previously obscure social world, not just through ethnographic forays into the urban labyrinth by intrepid social reformers or bohemian flaneurs but also through the encouragement of proper (legible) behavior via public education and law enforcement practices. Thus those who refused to visibly conform to these new expectations by spitting on sidewalks, dressing improperly, squatting on street corners, hanging around outside bars, and so on could expect to be reprimanded, fined, and perhaps even jailed by police. While the new rules of comportment proved difficult to enforce despite daily police harassment, working-class men and women certainly understood (and often resisted) official efforts to eliminate these visible affronts to public order, which they interpreted as an assault on their persons and on their cultural practices.[48] This sense of resentment and resistance extended to most sectors of the previously segmented laboring classes—although the poorest suffered most—and spawned a uniquely Mexican brand of liberal populism that set a newly emergent working class against a corrupt, exploitative, and hypocritical bourgeoisie.[49]

Scott focuses his analysis on high modernist projects undertaken by authoritarian states, but the Díaz administration was not the only party vested in making working-class men more manageable. Even though elite social reformers served as spokesmen for the high modernist principles that underlay the regime's bureaucratic initiatives and often used their government positions to attempt to put those principles into play, their larger project was far more radical than anything the Porfirian state apparatus could have accomplished, limited as it was by political realities, class loyalties, inadequate institutions, and lack of resources. For example, public health advocates (*higienistas*), like the well-respected Dr. Luis E. Ruiz, director of the National Academy of Medicine and a member of Mexico City's Superior Sanitation Council, proposed a comprehensive public health campaign that ran the gamut from adequate drainage, sewers, city parks, and uncontaminated water supplies to clean people, households, markets, and streets.[50] Initiatives such as drainage, sewers, parks, water, and the like, that depended primarily on financial resources, technical expertise, and political will were within the state's means, at least for some sectors of the city. Other aspects of the *higienista* public health campaign, especially initiatives to enforce personal and household cleanliness, demanded a wholesale transformation of the material circumstances and cultural practices of the urban lower classes. These efforts failed miserably, even with the nominal support of an authoritarian state, and were mercilessly ridiculed in the penny press (see ch. 4).

A new generation of "scientific" criminologists and penologists faced similar challenges. Supported by statistical evidence of Mexico City's notoriously high crime rates, they had little difficulty convincing the Díaz administration to build a new penitentiary, improve police practices, and revise the criminal code. But as happened with comprehensive public health reform, the government lacked the capacity (and probably the desire) to address the structural causes of the crime problem, especially the alleged degeneracy of the lower classes. Sociologist Julio Guerrero warned against the danger posed by "unhappy men and women who lack a normal, secure means of subsistence," arguing that "they have lost all control of their lives; their language is of the tavern; they live in sexual promiscuity, they inebriate themselves daily . . . they quarrel and are the principal instigators of scandal . . . from their bosom petty thieves are recruited and they are the hidden perpetrators of serious crimes."[51] His distinguished colleague Miguel S. Macedo even called for a modification of "our entire social structure" in order to address the problem.[52] This radical proposal from the Porfiriato's most influential penologist and a prominent member of the president's cadre of *científico* advisors vividly demonstrates the distance between the idealistic vision of elite social reformers as articulated in the public sphere and the state policies that they were charged with developing and implementing. As state functionaries, they gathered data, provided expert analyses, formulated policies, and built institutions—all crucial components of high modernist statecraft. But outside their bureaucratic offices, they articulated a high modernist social reform agenda that transcended the mundane needs of the state. Their desire to transform unhygienic, criminally inclined lower-class men into modern proletarians was no more nuanced than statist demands for a legible working class, but it would prove far more influential in the ideological struggle to redeem working-class masculinity. It too was a target of penny press satire.

By the 1870s, socialist-inspired working-class organizations had also turned to high modernist ideals in their efforts to promote a legible working-class culture grounded in scientific principles of hygiene, labor productivity, specialized training, and responsible collective action. While more vocal than their elite counterparts in their critique of the exploitation suffered by previous generations of workers and strongly opposed to state-sponsored disciplinary strategies, such as the *leva* (forced

conscription), Mexican socialists nonetheless envisioned a wholesale reform of working-class culture that closely resembled the recommenda-
tions of elite reformers like Ruiz and Macedo.[53] In other words, despite
their insistence that the worst aspects of Mexican working-class culture
were the direct result of centuries of exploitation and abuse rather than
a sign of inherent (perhaps biologically inherited) deficiencies, socialist
organizers advocated its reform, supported state efforts to rehabilitate
workers, and developed educational programs designed to promote modern values like thrift, sobriety, and industry in their constituents. Only
a radical reformation of working-class cultural practices, they argued,
could redeem workers in the eyes of their employers, *gente decente*, and
the state.

Despite the failure to realize even a small fraction of their ambitious
goals, high modernist attempts by the Porfirian state, elite reformers, and
socialist organizations to inculcate "modern" practices in the city's working classes had a profound impact on the way many Mexicans, including
workers themselves, understood working-class culture. Projects aimed at
rendering populations more legible to the state and the dominant classes
require that social engineers develop schematics and categories that sim-
plify a situation which would otherwise be impossibly complicated and
thus unmanageable. Even when done with the best of intentions, these
high modernist simplifications inevitably misrepresent, distort, or obscure the complex cultural practices they hope to rationalize. And when
authorities attempt to put high modernist reforms into practice, they
often produce disastrous results by disrupting the deeply embedded,
"traditional" attitudes and behaviors that had previously governed social
relations, whether in the countryside or urban neighborhood.[54] These
disruptions in turn produced the conditions for the formation of populist movements—liberal populism in the case of Mexico—as previously
segregated working-class groups (*jornaleros*, proletarians, artisans, etc.)
joined forces to oppose the assault on their distinct cultural practices.

Bodies That Matter: Subjectivity and Citizenship

Penny press editors and contributors also understood that high modernist reform projects, whatever their provenance, presented a serious challenge to human subjectivity—the ways in which individuals make sense

of themselves and others make sense of them.[55] In *Bodies That Matter*, feminist/queer theorist Judith Butler develops an account of the formation of "culturally intelligible" subjects that provides three important insights into the impact of high modernist disciplinary projects on human subjects.[56] First, she argues that *representation is central to subject formation*. "The domains of political and linguistic 'representation,'" she insists, "set out in advance the criterion by which subjects themselves are formed, with the result that representation is extended only to what can be acknowledged as a subject. In other words, the qualifications for being a subject must be met before representation can be extended."[57]

Butler's contention that the domains of political and linguistic representation predetermine the criteria of subjectivity and that subjects must meet those criteria before they are extended representation is something that penny press editors and their collaborators understood only too well. Hence, their obsession with challenging the conventional representation of Mexican working-class men as an undifferentiated mass of improvident, apathetic, violence-prone nonsubjects, whose unintelligibility (as discreet individuals) disqualified them from full citizenship. In place of this negative stereotype, they offered up the positive image of a hardworking, energetic, responsible worker-patriot. At the same time, penny press editors and collaborators also grasped the coercive foundation of high modernist projects whose "regulatory power maintains subjects in subordination by producing and exploiting the demand for continuity, visibility, and place" and its implications for working-class men.[58] Further, they understood that marginalized subjects, working-class Mexican men in this instance, were especially vulnerable to the cruder forms of subordination precisely because their "continuity, visibility, and place" in Porfirian society was so precarious—because workers' participation as rights-bearing citizens was sporadic (discontinuous), often ignored (invisible), and mostly relegated to the social margins (displaced). But they knew too that regulatory power was only as strong as the domains of political and linguistic representation that perpetuated it. And they knew those domains to be vulnerable to challenges.

Second, Butler's account of *the subjection process begins with the gendering of the subject*.[59] She rejects the possibility of a recognizable self that might exist prior to its gendering, noting instead that "*regulatory practices* of gender formation and division constitute identity, the internal coherence of the subject, indeed . . . the 'coherence' and 'continuity' of 'the person' are not logical or analytical features of personhood, but, rather, socially instituted and maintained norms of intelligibility."[60] This formulation has important implications for citizenship. If, as Butler avers, coherent subjects with recognizable social identities emerge only through "the stabilizing concepts of sex, gender, and sexuality," then the classic liberal concept of citizen—the most coherent of modern political subjects—is gendered from the start and liberalism's signature phrases like "the rights of man and citizen" and "all men are created equal" mean precisely what they say.[61]

The gendered nature of liberal citizenship is obvious in penny press efforts to validate working-class men as *men*. Editors and contributors (almost all of them male) went out of their way to praise working-class women as workers, wives, and mothers but made little or no mention of working women's political or civil rights. Their frequent misogynistic attacks on bourgeois *feminismo* and its emasculating effects on bourgeois men suggest that this glaring omission was no accident but reflected deeply held patriarchal attitudes.[62] Indeed, as we will see, the penny press sentimental education of working-class citizens was all about manhood, premised as it was on the notion that writing working-class men into the national narrative and altering the conditions that determined their subjectivity would transform them from despised *pelados*—a term used disparagingly by Porfirian elites to identify members of the lower classes—into valued citizens in their own eyes and in the eyes of the *gente decente*.[63]

Third, Butler's theory directly *links subject formation to language*, the battlefield of choice in the penny press linguistic struggle against the regulatory power of bourgeois norms and the Porfirian state.[64] Two aspects of Butler's argument about the constitutive properties of language are of special interest here. The first, her understanding of language as "the condition of possibility for the speaking subject," highlights its role in the production (and subjugation) of intelligible subjects. This role is especially evident in censorship, a "condition of power" with which penny press editors had an intimate and painful acquaintance. Butler contends that censorship seeks to establish "implicit and explicit norms that govern the kind of speech that will be legible as the speech of a subject," a move that ties the social recognition essential to subjectivity to pre-determined acceptable speech.[65] Although her abstract language might seem worlds away from the harsh realities of Porfirian authoritarian governance or the daily struggles of working-class men, Butler's explanation of the way that subjects are constituted "through the regulation of the social domain of speakable discourse" and her acknowledgement of the risks involved in refusing "to embody the norms that govern speakability" express the tangible concerns of penny press editors, who fought a daily battle with government censors over the "domain of the sayable."[66] Given the stakes, it is little wonder that they routinely used the word *psicología* (psychology)—a snide reference to the legal rationale behind press censorship—in political cartoons to condemn government efforts to regulate speech.[67]

Another useful aspect of Butler's argument about the constitutive properties of language, her contention that the "historicity [of language] includes a past and future that exceeds that of the subject who speaks," is its emphasis on historical changes in the linguistic criterion of subjectivity. This historical emphasis not only acknowledges that "the norms that govern speakability" have changed over time, it also insists on the inevitability of future changes as the apparently mindless iteration of regulatory norms crosses over into "insurrectionary speech." Butler's contemporary example is the radical resignification of the word "queer" by the gay community. Her description of the resignification process, however, works just as well for other contested labels: "The name one is called both subordinates and enables, producing a sense of agency from ambivalence, a set of effects that exceed the animating intention of the call . . . a risk taken in response to being put at risk, a repetition in language that forces change."[68] Seen in this light, the penny press redeployment of *pelado*, a "word that wounds," as an instrument of resistance in their struggle against the conditions of subjectivity dictated by Porfirian bourgeois culture is revealed as "insurrectionary speech . . . a risk taken in response to being put at risk, a repetition in language that forces change."[69] This insurrectionary speech held out the possibility of a radical reversal of established hierarchies—a reversal in which *nosotros los pelados* (we the pelados) would become *nostros el pueblo* (we the people).[70]

Masculine Scripts and Working-Class Subjects

For working-class men in late Porfirian Mexico City, the repercussions of this radical reversal of established hierarchies went far beyond the issue of political inclusion. It also sought to reshape other central aspects of their lives, such as their understandings of work, leisure, and interpersonal relations with other men and with women. Thus chapters 1 through 3 address the linkages between working-class politics, manhood, and citizenship, while the following two chapters explore the less public—but no less political—side of working-class male subjectivity. The different aspects of the penny press sentimental education for workers that emerge in each chapter necessarily involve two intertwined initiatives: the rehabilitation of working-class culture and the reeducation of working-class men.[71] Rehabilitation required critical engagement with bourgeois norms of respectability and the production of working-class alternatives. Reeducation meant shaping, articulating, and transmitting those alternatives for working-class men. Both initiatives sought to transform workers' sense of themselves and their relationship to the nation—but in a much more subtle, much less unilateral way than the high modernist projects of state officials, liberal social reformers, and socialist organizers. Instead, the Mexico City satiric penny press sought to validate different aspects of working-class culture by exploiting the productive tension between the redemptive projects of the Porfirian state, elite reformers, and socialist-inspired workers organizations, on one hand, and the everyday trials and tribulations of working men, on the other. In this way, penny press editors and contributors offered up a sentimental education for workers that was an education more realistic about their situation, more responsive to their concerns, more respectful of their distinctive culture, and every bit as modern as anything the competition could propose.

The first chapter looks at penny press efforts to construct and disseminate an alternative national history intended to undermine the legitimacy of the official story. This counternarrative involved appropriating and resignifying liberal icons like Hidalgo and Juárez as working-class heroes whose vision of an egalitarian, democratic Mexico had been subverted by self-serving, power-hungry elites. The second chapter takes a close look at the construction of a distinctive working-class cult around Benito Juárez and penny press efforts to turn the controversy over Francisco

Bulnes's critical biography of the liberal hero into a belated martyrdom sanctifying the former president (who died in bed) and highlighting his differences with the Porfirian regime. The third chapter examines penny press attempts to insert working men into Mexican history as active participants whose past and present sacrifices entitled them to all the rights of "man and citizen" and thus effect the symbolic transformation of marginalized workers from *pelados* into *el pueblo*, the Mexican "people." On the surface, this transformation involved the relatively straightforward task of writing working-class men into the national narrative as vigorous, heroic participants in the struggle for nationhood rather than as the downtrodden, disloyal *populacho* (rabble) depicted in official historiographies. A closer look reveals a more complicated and much more revolutionary attempt to remake the subjectivity of working men in order to render them legitimate political subjects entitled to all the rights (and duties) of full-fledged citizenship. Taken together, the first three chapters illuminate the rhetorical strategies of a liberal populism that sought to bind working men together as patriotic Mexicans and put them forward as the "people," the collective heart, soul, and backbone of the imagined national community.

With chapter 4, the focus shifts from issues of patriotism and citizenship to the re-creation and reconstruction of working-class attitudes toward work and leisure. Work-related satire in the penny press exposed productive tensions between proper and improper male behavior—improper behavior that confounded the conventional image of the citizen-subject by confronting civic virtue with popular resistance to bourgeois prescription, which appears not as a natural quality of the *gente decente* but as a form of class privilege. Moreover, these satires represented working-class men (and sometimes women) as more self-aware, more adaptable, and better attuned to the changing times than their bourgeois counterparts, characteristics that social observers, then and now, have considered essential to modern subjectivity—a telling reversal of conventional historical interpretations (and Porfirian bourgeois attitudes), which have insisted on a top-down "civilizing process," as proper sentiments trickle down from the bourgeoisie to the lower classes.

Chapter 5 explores the shifting landscape of male honor, female shame, and a new kind of relationship based on romance, love, and intimacy rather than the older ideal of mutual respect and gender-specific responsibilities. To become modern lovers, working-class men needed a traditional male role model against which to construct their new, more "companionate" selves. Don Juan Tenorio, notorious seducer of women and killer of men, proved the perfect foil. Ubiquitous in Mexican popular culture then and now, Don Juan epitomized all that was wrong with traditional male scripts with his arrogance, impetuosity, misogyny, cruelty, and callous disregard for the well-being of others (male or female). For penny press writers, local *tenorios* were figures of fun, ridiculed for their absurd seductions and their prickly tempers. And while they also made fun of themselves and their clueless peers, more often than not this affectionate fraternal satire of working-class sentiment came out of their clumsy efforts to accommodate (rather than deceive and dominate) their female partners. As with working-class attitudes toward work and leisure, this modern approach to gender relations, described as an awkward negotiation rather than an inherent trait, puts working-class Mexican men at the forefront of a phenomenon that contemporary sociologists and anthropologists have labeled the "transformation of intimacy."[72] Altogether, these five chapters seek to unpack penny press strategies that extolled, joked about, and sought to produce the virtues of working-class men: patriotism, hard work, resilience, humor, loyalty, and hard-earned respect for their female partners. These strategies position workers as more self-aware, flexible, and companionable—as more *modern*—than their bourgeois counterparts. A brief conclusion hints at a few suggestive continuities in working-class masculinities.

Recalcitrant Subjects, Recalcitrant Sources

The Mexico City satiric penny press for workers is a remarkable primary source. As the chapters that follow show, it provides a wealth of cleverly wrought, often unexpected detail on early twentieth-century Mexico City popular culture, in particular its obsession with working-class masculinity. At the same time, for historians, this author included, it poses challenges of several sorts.

The challenges related to deciphering ephemeral texts intended for a working-class audience with a shared cultural background and often written in the tortured (if brilliantly reproduced) local vernacular led to long hours spent tracking down obscure references and poring over dictionaries of Mexican slang. Arduous work to be sure but straightforward enough. Challenges related to lack of information on the identity of penny press editors, the makeup of the penny press readership, and the influence of the penny press on working-class culture were less easily resolved. For the most part, these questions of identity and influence stem from the fact that we know little about the editors of the satiric penny press beyond what we can glean from their work. Even world-renowned illustrator José Guadalupe Posada remains an enigma, although in his case historians have managed to patch together basic dates, bureaucratic records, anecdotal references, and a grainy photograph into something like a credible biographical sketch. Thus, although penny press editors often self-identify as proud members of the working class, we have no way of proving, disproving, or qualifying their claims. And that means we have no definitive way to determine how much of their interpretation of working-class culture derives from lived rather than observed experiences.

At the same time, while their exceptional literary talents make it difficult to argue that penny press editors and contributors were *typical* Mexico City workers, it would be remiss (and patronizing) to deny their claims to working-class status for that reason. As noted earlier, Mexico City artisans, especially typographers, printers, and illustrators, had unexpectedly high literacy rates. Most historians agree that they retained a strong sense of their special position within and above the unskilled working classes, even after decades of declining social status and political clout.[73] Moreover, evidence suggests that this combination could produce "organic intellectuals" with first-rate literary skills. For example, Illades argues that working-class newspaper editors in the 1870s and 1880s were "modern, organic intellectuals [who] articulated working-class discourse in two directions, serving both as vehicles and intermediaries for dialogue within their class and with the State. In the first capacity, they spread and synthesized the dispersed experiences of artisans and workers. . . . In the second, they were able to present the demands of the workers to government officials in a coherent fashion."[74]

This was true of the next generation of worker advocates as well. One of Mexico's most prominent organic intellectuals, labor activist Jacinto Huitrón, cofounder of the influential Casa del Obrero Mundial (House of the World Worker) during the first years of the Revolution, was born a shoemaker's son and apprenticed as an ironworker as soon as he finished primary school. Despite these decidedly working-class origins, Huitrón's popular history of labor activism in Mexico recounts a long list of the books and poems (many of which he could still recite from memory) that he had read as a young man and devotes several chapters to the Porfirian working-class press.[75] An even better example is the printer Fernando Celada, the so-called minstrel of the proletariat, whose poetry on inspirational topics like noble workers and founding fathers was regularly published in the mainstream and penny presses and won him considerable acclaim among all classes of Mexican society.[76]

In *Proletarian Nights: The Workers' Dream in Nineteenth-Century France*, Jacques Rancière chides labor historians for their cavalier dismissal of the nonrevolutionary literary aspirations of worker intellectuals. The literary texts and diaries produced by nineteenth-century Parisian workers, he observes, made it clear

> that workers had never needed the secrets of domination explained to them, as their problem was quite a different one. It was to withdraw themselves, intellectually and materially, from the forms by which this domination imprinted on their bodies, and imposed on their actions, modes of perception, attitudes, and a language . . . to take back the time that was refused them by educating their perceptions and their thought in order to free themselves in the very exercise of everyday work, or by winning from nightly rest the time to discuss, write, compose verses, or develop philosophies.[77]

Although grounded in the experiences of urban French workers in the revolutionary 1830s and 1840s, Rancière's insight that many self-taught, working-class intellectuals had literary aspirations that often superseded their political activism helps explain apparent incongruities in the otherwise puzzling mix of politics, social satire, stories, and poetry (in more or less equal parts) offered up by Mexico City penny press editors and their contributors. While it is possible that some editors and contributors were the wayward sons of the educated petite bourgeoisie, the Parisian scenario in which worker intellectuals "wrenched themselves out of an identity formed by domination and asserted themselves as inhabitants with full rights of a common world" seems the more plausible explanation. Moreover, Rancière's claim that their "discreet and radical" acts of literary self-liberation would prove in the long run more revolutionary than the overt political activism of labor organizers finds considerable support in the pages of the Mexico City penny press (and in this book).

A closely related challenge with regard to using the penny press as a historical source is that we can only speculate about the relationship of editors, collaborators, and their readers. Certainly, editors addressed themselves directly to fellow workers, even if their attempts to shame or solicit support from public officials suggest that they aspired to attract a broader secondary readership. Moreover, frequent letters from disgruntled factory workers (some of them women), describing abusive bosses and poor working conditions, support the idea that many penny press readers were indeed proletarians in the classic Marxist sense. That doesn't mean, however, that editors, contributors, or their readers were *typical* Mexico City workers.

In a self-deprecating image from *La Guacamaya*, Posada depicts editor Fernando Torroella performing all the tasks associated with writing and editing the newspaper (see fig. I.4).[78] In the central image, Torroella is dressed not in the overalls or white cotton clothing associated with unskilled workers (including those in the penny press) but in a respectable suit, vest, collared shirt, and bow tie. The caption reads

> Aquí está el Director del semanario,
> Agente, Responsable y Redactor,
> él solo se lo guisa y se lo come
> y hace veces tambien de corrector.
>
> El soporta á la cruel Psicología
> Y en una cosa se parece á Dios:
> que son varias personas muy distintas
> y un solo y verdadero redactor.

> [Here is the Director of the weekly,
> Agent, Manager, and Editor,
> he alone cooks it and eats it
> and at times he corrects the proofs.

FIG. I.4 José Guadalupe Posada/Author Unknown, "Actual Cuerpo de Redacción," *La Guacamaya*, August 23, 1906. Courtesy of the Benson Latin American Collection, University of Texas Libraries, The University of Texas at Austin.

He tolerates the cruel Psychology
and in one thing resembles God:
that they are various, very distinct persons
and the one true editor.]

The image and caption evoke a certain categorical confusion reminiscent of Illades's description of late nineteenth-century artisan intellectuals who served "both as vehicles and intermediaries for dialogue within their class and with the State." Torroella's sympathies might lie with the oppressed, uneducated working classes, but he clearly understands and represents his own status as *gente decente*. We know from the work of Mexican labor historians that Mexico City artisans, disturbed at the steady decline in their status over the course of the nineteenth century, made concerted and repeated efforts to distinguish themselves from the capital's unskilled laborers, especially recent migrants from the countryside. By 1900, after decades of sporadic employment and eroded privileges, that distinction may have been lost on employers, government officials, and the middle classes, but it persisted among skilled artisans, even as they embraced their new proletarian status for purposes of political solidarity.[79] As we will see, this ambivalence about social status and working-class culture—sometimes sympathetic, other times contemptuous—permeated penny press efforts to rehabilitate working-class men and supplied the catalytic spark for most penny press satire. It also suggests that penny press editors and contributors spoke most directly to the specific attitudes and concerns of Mexico City's long-suffering artisan class rather than to those of the much larger and more amorphous working class, despite editors' repeated expressions of pan-worker solidarity.

Ambivalence about social status was hardly the sole province of penny press editors. In his analysis of "combat journalism" in Porfirian Mexico City, Pablo Piccato argues that "the lofty standards of journalists, as men of honor, collided with the negotiations in which, as producers of cultural and political goods, they engaged in order to advance their reputations and careers."[80] Although only a select few managed to escape genteel poverty, prominent combat journalists could and did aspire to public reputations as men of honor, a precarious status they often defended in duels, sometimes to the death. But if penny press editors bickered amongst themselves on occasion, perhaps in imitation or mockery of their more status-conscious peers, they rarely engaged in the risky, if potentially reputation-making, attacks on public figures and fellow journalists that resulted in violent *affaires d'honneur*.[81] And despite a shared appreciation of homosocial spaces like bars, cantinas, and *pulquerías*, penny press editors appear never to have broken through the social barriers that separated them from bourgeois bohemian journalists-turned-novelists such as Federico Gamboa (before he became a prominent diplomat), Heriberto Frías, and Emilio Rabasa or from the modernist poets who edited the avant-garde *Revista Moderna* (Modern Magazine), including Rubén Campos and the prickly Salvador Díaz Mirón, who allegedly dismissed the Mexico City proletariat as producers of "cherubs for the barracks and angels for the brothel."[82] For the most part, penny press editors and contributors wrote for a different kind of audience—less privileged, less full of itself, less Eurocentric—composed of literate artisans, workers, and petits bourgeois like themselves. Moreover, while penny press writers also wrote and even obsessed about masculine honor, they did it mostly in a self-mocking tone that made clear just how petty the stakes could be for men of their "inferior" social position.

Another related challenge to using the penny press as a primary source is that we have no reliable way to determine whether or not it represents an *authentic* working-class perspective. This may be a moot point if by "authentic" we mean a perspective shared by most Mexico City workers. As noted earlier, the Mexico City working class bore little resemblance to an industrial proletariat, even though labor historians agree that workers shared a sense of class consciousness, at least according to the loose definition provided by E. P. Thompson, who famously argued that "class happens when some men as a result of common experiences (inherited or shared), feel and articulate the identity of their interests as between themselves, and as against other men whose interests are different from (and usually opposed to) theirs."[83] The shared experience of collective oppression and a shared sense of common interests might well produce class consciousness, but shared experiences and interests don't necessarily translate into a homogenous or egalitarian working-class culture, especially in those places, like Mexico, that mostly lack a large-scale industrial workforce.

Indeed, the Mexico City working classes ran a wide gamut, from unskilled, illiterate *jornaleros* (day laborers) to well-trained, innovative artist-artisans, like José Guadalupe Posada. So while *El Chile Piquín*'s editor went to the trouble to dedicate his paper "to the proletarian class, to the working class, to which we have the honor of belonging" and Antonio Negrete, editor of the short-lived *El Papagayo*, identified himself as a factory worker in poems written for other newspapers, for the most part penny press editors, contributors, and readers seem unconcerned about the authenticity of the editorial voice.[84] Further, even though penny press political editorials expressed special solidarity with the humblest of workers and though underemployed or idle *jornaleros* appear as regular protagonists in much of its fictional social commentary, it is doubtful editors saw unskilled workers as their primary readership. Instead, they sometimes channeled the personas of their backward brethren in order to mark themselves (and their readers) as modern subjects capable of self-awareness, self-improvement, and self-esteem despite their humble circumstances. In this instance, satire often proved a double-edged sword, on the one hand, ridiculing illiterate, superstitious, gullible workers while lauding their wit, resourcefulness, and endurance and on the other setting educated, rational, discerning workers apart while mocking their pretensions, probity, and self-pity. This was especially apparent in the penny press "satire of sentiment," which took aim at the affective aspects of both working-class and bourgeois cultural practices, something high modernist projects took very seriously, the former as a condition in desperate need of reform, the latter as a model of healthy social relations. As a result, penny press efforts to reenvision working-class masculinity—whether intended for ordinary workers, educated workers, the *gente decente*, social reformers, or government officials—revel in a sense of ambiguity, nuance, and contradiction largely absent in other historical sources from the period. It is these traits, so antithetical to high modernist disciplinary projects, which gave penny press engagements with working-class masculinity their distinct character and ensured their enduring popularity in Mexican popular culture.

Truth be told, the authenticity problem, which has haunted labor historians at least since Karl Marx's brilliant histories of the French Revolution, is something nineteenth-century English penny press satirist William Cobbett liked to call a "red herring"—a logical fallacy deployed by partisans, including historians, in their ideological battles over the moral right to speak for the working class *as a class*. In other words, as is the case with so many "natural" attributes (femininity and masculinity or race and ethnicity, for example), authenticity of class is produced and maintained through discourse. As the sociologists would have it: "authenticity is social construct." And as a social construct, authenticity plays a crucial role in the construction of subjectivities, especially in the production and maintenance of marginalized subjects like working-class men who must struggle to become legible to themselves, to others, and to the state. To search, as many labor historians do, for the authentic working class doesn't just miss this important point; it also reproduces a high modernist logic that seeks to distill the complications and contradictions of class consciousness into a manageable (reified) thing, more accessible to political manipulation and scholarly inquiry. Seen in this light, the satiric penny press for workers is not so much an interpretive quagmire for historians as it is an ideal (though certainly not definitive) source for getting at the messy realities of working-class consciousness in late Porfirian Mexico City and beyond. Or to paraphrase Torroella's poem on the editorial trinity, the satiric penny press reveals a working-class consciousness that is various, distinct, and the one true thing—all at the same time. This, I think, is what working-class consciousness *really* looks like.

In *Sentimental Education*, Gustave Flaubert sought to write "the moral history of the men of my generation—or, more accurately, the history of their *feelings*."[85] Despite the revolutionary times (1848), Flaubert's protagonist, Frédéric Moreau, is too caught up in self-exploration and bohemian lassitude to have much interest in epochal events. As the author explains: "It's a book about love, about passion; but passion such as can exist nowadays—that is to say, inactive." Penny press editors would have had no trouble recognizing Frédéric as a prototypical *catrín* (dandy) sleeping off his debauchery while working men celebrated national independence. They too understood the modern obsession with desire and its debilitating effect on the fatuous sons of the bourgeoisie, a generation or two removed from their forefathers' revolutionary moment. But the sentimental education for the working man portrayed in their pages was something altogether different, something altogether unexpected, something altogether more radical. The nature of that unexpected radical difference is the subject of this book.

❦

CHAPTER 1

WORKING-CLASS HEROES

Forging the Ties That Bind

As we saw in the introduction, most early twentieth-century Mexico City workers subscribed to a shifting constellation of interrelated ideas, attitudes, and notions that historians have labeled "popular liberalism." Although derived from mainstream liberalism with its emphasis on citizenship—civic responsibilities, political rights, respect for the rule of law, respect for the dignity of the individual—popular liberalism grounded that citizenship, not in the newly emergent middle classes (often allied in Mexico as elsewhere with traditional elites), but in the historical resentments, patriotic sentiments, and productive toil of marginalized working-class men (and to a much lesser extent women). Mexico City's thriving satiric penny press for workers played a key role in establishing popular liberalism as an oppositional discourse committed to challenging the exploitation, corruption, cronyism, and authoritarian tactics of the Porfirian regime.[1]

These are fundamental insights. Nevertheless, historians have only just begun to scratch the surface of what social theorist Raymond Williams calls the "structures of feeling"—"meanings and values as they are actively lived and felt"—that underlay popular liberalism and the emerging class consciousness of Mexico City workers.[2] This chapter thus examines the concerted efforts of satiric penny press editors and contributors

to link these structures of feeling to working-class political consciousness by constructing popular alternatives to the official story propagated
by liberal elites and Porfirian ideologues. These alternatives embraced
many of the same liberal icons featured in official histories but resigni-
fied them as working-class heroes and then deployed them to undermine
the regime's claims to legitimacy. An essential component of this time-
honored tactic of symbolic subversion was the forging of deep affective
bonds between popular figures—especially independence martyr Miguel
Hidalgo and liberal statesman Benito Juárez—and their working-class
admirers in an effort to bind workers to a utopian vision of a liberal,
democratic Mexico no longer in thrall to special interests and responsive
to all its citizens, however humble their circumstances. The oppositional
discourse that emerged from this process worked to split the liberal political spectrum into two distinct camps and transform popular liberalism into liberal populism, a move with revolutionary implications (see
ch. 3).

This was hardly the first manifestation of working-class support for
liberal heroes, especially Benito Juárez. In 1876, just four years after his
death, the Gran Círculo de Obreros de México (Great Circle of Mexican
Workers) staged the first of many Juárez commemorations sponsored by
working-class organizations.[3] But deepening fractures among Mexican
liberals after Porfirio Díaz's 1884 reelection, exacerbated by government
crackdowns on the independent press, provided an opening for an alternative liberal history that stressed the special bonds between liberal
heroes and workingmen (rather than fractious political elites).[4] The success of these late Porfirian efforts to link popular structures of feeling to
working-class politics proved remarkably durable. But the waging of this
symbolic "war of position" for the hearts and minds of Mexican workers
was no simple thing.[5]

The Art of War

In recent years, art historians have begun to explore the intimate links
between the production of images and the construction of national histories. As Tomás Pérez Vejo explains, "images, in addition to reflecting reality, are also . . . a sophisticated way of constructing reality, a powerful in-

strument in the production and control of collective imaginaries."[6] Given this remarkable power to produce and control collective imaginaries, it should come as no surprise that ideologues of all stripes—penny press editors included—made frequent use of graphic images in the struggle to develop a national narrative that promoted their different conceptions of the nation-state as an "imagined and imaginary community" and their different constituencies as central to that community.[7]

Two front-page illustrations from *La Guacamaya* provide a useful entry point into the intricacies of working-class politics in late Porfirian Mexico City. The first image, "En Honor de Juárez," from the cover of the July 18, 1907, issue, celebrates the anniversary of Benito Juárez's death (July 18, 1872). The second image, "¡VIVA la LIBERTAD!," from September 12, 1907, anticipates the upcoming Independence Day celebrations of September 15 and 16 (see figs. 1.1 and 1.2).[8] The images are unsigned but in the graphic style of master printmaker and frequent contributor José Guadalupe Posada.[9] Although close examination reveals some nice touches—the confrontation between a policeman and a newspaper boy in the second image, for example—neither illustration seems particularly inspired, at least in any conventional artistic sense. Despite these aesthetic shortcomings, the basic message is hard to miss: working-class Mexican men are true patriots; upper-class Mexican men are self-absorbed sycophants and slackers.

Although the main point is relatively straightforward; the complex web of symbolic and historical referents deployed in its service is not. Neither were its implications for working-class Mexican men. Before tackling these complications, however, we need first to examine the ways in which these graphic images and the short verses that accompany them work as *texts*, setting aside for a moment important questions about the historical circumstances and cultural context in which those texts were produced, circulated, and read. Only a close reading of image and text can properly convey the subtle art behind their creation and deployment: the deft manipulation of spatial conventions, the sly play with visual and linguistic signs, the meticulous fitting of graphic mortise to literary tenon. For all its fussing over picayune details and obsession with everyday tricks of the trade, a nuts-and-bolts analysis of this kind is in fact essential to our understanding of the penny press "war of position"

Tomo V, Época II.   México, Julio 18 de 1907,   Año V, Número 40.

DEL PUEBLO Y POR EL PUEBLO.

SEMANARIO INDEPENDIENTE DEFENSOR DE LA CLASE OBRERA.

Director Propietario: **FERNANDO P. TORROELLA**

En Honor de Juárez.

Mientras el pueblo patriota
sus ofrendas deposita
en la tumba del gran Juárez,
los rotos en la cantina

echándosela de lado
por el patriotismo brindan
y todo por estar bien
con el que les da..... propina.

FIG. 1.1 Artist/Author Unknown, "En Honor de Juárez," *La Guacamaya*, July 18, 1907. Courtesy of the Benson Latin American Collection, University of Texas Libraries, The University of Texas at Austin.

Tomo V. Epoca II.   Mexico, Septiembre 12 de 1907.   Año V. Número 48

DEL PUEBLO Y POR EL PUEBLO.

SEMANARIO INDEPENDIENTE DEFENSOR DE LA CLASE OBRERA.

Director Propietario: **FERNANDO P. TORROELLA**

¡VIVA la LIBERTAD!

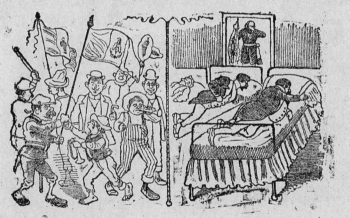

El pueblo entusiasmado vitorea	En cambio los catrines, los patriotas (?)
á aquellos que nos dieron Libertad,	se entregan á dormir la borrachera
y mientras tanto el gendarme arrea	y se olvidan de Hidalgo, cuyas gotas
al que grita y que toca y que...¡la mar!	de llanto caen sobre la patria tierra

FIG. 1.2 Artist/Author Unknown, "¡VIVA la LIBERTAD!," *La Guacamaya*, September 12, 1907. Courtesy of the Benson Latin American Collection, University of Texas Libraries, The University of Texas at Austin.

with Porfirian bourgeois culture. This is so, because without a solid appreciation of the *art* of that war, we would find ourselves hard pressed to explain its subtle but powerful ideological effects. Although compelled by disciplinary training to select, sort, and synthesize, in their heart of hearts historians, like moralists, know that the devil—little, red, joking, or otherwise—resides in the details. This inquiry, then, begins there.

The image beneath the July 18 headline, "En Honor de Juárez," depicts six well-to-do men in formal attire—top hats, frock coats, starched collars—holding champagne glasses. The central figure in the group is an older man with white whiskers, walking stick, and the erect posture of a former soldier, who bears a more than passing resemblance to longtime president Porfirio Díaz. A younger man with an umbrella tucked under one arm offers up a toast to the "indispensable caudillo" as the other men look on.[10] In the background, a campesino in traditional white cotton work clothes, serape over his shoulder, bare head bowed, sombrero in hand, back to the reader, sets a garland of flowers at the foot of Benito Juárez's tomb, with its signature marble statue of a woman—the personification of mother Mexico—cradling the hero's prone body in the pathetic style of Michelangelo's famous statue of Mary and Jesus, *La Pietà*.[11]

The short poem beneath the image reads:

Mientras el pueblo patriota
sus ofrendas deposita
en la tumba del gran Juárez,
los rotos en la cantina
echándosela de lado
por el patriotismo brindan
y todo por estar bien
con el que les da . . . propina.

❧

[While the patriotic people
place their offerings
at the tomb of the great Juárez,
the *rotos* [sycophants] in the cantina
tossing it aside
toast to patriotism

and that all be well
with he who gives them . . . gifts.]

As expected, the poem interprets the actions depicted in the illustration. This interpretation holds no big surprises. Juárez's mausoleum was a well-known pilgrimage site for his many admirers, and photographs from the period show it decked in floral *ofrendas* (offerings), the secular manifestation of a much older and still common religious practice associated with both the veneration of saints and respect for the family dead.[12] The contrasting patriotic styles of the upper-class men with their European fashions and drinking habits and the campesino with his emphatically Mexican dress and demeanor are identified with sycophantic *rotos* (literally, "the broken ones") on one hand and the humble *pueblo abnegado* (self-denying people) on the other. The Spanish word *propina*—translated here as "gift"—is more precisely a gratuity or tip for services rendered. Set off by ellipses in the text, it reveals the venal meaning behind the toast. More subtle is the news, not apparent from the image, that the elite men are drinking in a cantina, a behavior and a site (along with the less classy *pulquería*) more often associated with working-class men, at least in the mind of the Porfirian bourgeoisie.[13]

The September 12 image, "¡VIVA la LIBERTAD!," is divided in two equal frames. In the left-hand frame, six members of the urban popular classes—variously dressed in suits, loose jackets, overalls, bowler hats, felt fedoras, and fronted by a barefoot paperboy—celebrate the anniversary of Mexican independence with shouts, salutes, noisemakers, and flag waving. Contemporary readers would have understood these actions as popular responses to the annual *Grito* given by the president at 11 PM on September 15 to crowds gathered in front of the National Palace.[14] Two policemen harass the revelers. One wields a truncheon, the other jerks a flag from the hands of the protesting paperboy. In the right-hand frame, three well-dressed men in open frock coats sleep on a row of soft, frilly beds. A portrait of Miguel Hidalgo y Costilla, the "father" of Mexican independence and the source of the original *Grito*, hangs on the wall above the beds. The hero's right hand holds his famous battle standard emblazoned with the image of the Virgin of Guadalupe (another allegorical figure associated with mother Mexico); his left shields his eyes from the shameful sight of the sleeping men.

The poem that serves as caption reads thus:

El pueblo entusiasmado vitorea
á aquellos que nos dieron Libertad,
y mientras tanto el gendarme arrea
al que grita y que toca . . . ¡la mar!

En cambio los catrines, los patriotas (?)
se entregan á dormir la borrachera
y se olvidan de Hidalgo, cuyas gotas
de llanto caen sobre la patria tierra.

❦

[The enthusiastic people cheer
those who gave us Liberty,
and meanwhile the policeman rounds up
those who shout and toot and [sound] . . . the alarm!

In contrast, the *catrines* [dandies], the patriots (?)
dedicate themselves to sleeping off their drunkenness
and forget about Hidalgo, whose tears
of grief fall on the fatherland.]

As before, the poem's juxtaposition of the patriotic exuberance of ordinary men (identified as *el pueblo*) and the apathetic dozing of the privileged *catrines* clarifies the meaning of the image. Most of these clarifications are relatively straightforward: the people are celebrating Independence Day; the policemen are harassing them; the sleeping men are dandies; the dandies are sleeping off a drunk; the portrait depicts Hidalgo; Hidalgo is weeping tears of grief for the fatherland; and so on.

In this instance, however, the poet adds a more subtle touch in the form of an *albur*—a play on words. Especially popular among the working classes, *albures* could take many forms, including puns, double entendres, circumlocutions, and euphemisms.[15] As part of the wordplay, practitioners often elided syllables, inverted letters, and truncated words to reflect popular usage and to open up different interpretive possibilities.[16] Here, for example, the substitution of "la mar" for "la alarma" sets up a double meaning. In the original Spanish text, the phrase "toca . . . ¡la mar!" (literally: "touch . . . the sea!") refers to the unruly crowd and stands in for "toca . . . ¡la alarma!" ("sound . . . the alarm!"). At the most obvious level, the poet's use of the phrase "to sound the alarm," in reference to the celebrants graphically represented by the two bugles, works to portray the common people as alert citizens quick to respond to any threats to national sovereignty. At a more subtle level, the *albur* mocks officialdom's concern over disorderly public festivals and its perception of the crowds gathered in the Zócalo (Mexico City's main square) on the night of September 15 as a stormy "sea" of humanity, especially as seen from a balcony or rooftop, the preferred vantage points of the Porfirian elite.

If that weren't enough, in "¡VIVA la LIBERTAD!" the poet pushes the social critique even further than in the previous poem by advancing the notion, counterintuitive to Porfirian authorities and bourgeoisie critics, that the drunken sprees of self-absorbed elites pose a much greater threat to national well-being than the raucous but patriotic carousing of the popular classes. The absence of visible signs of alcohol consumption in the artist's depiction of the popular celebration—an absence unsubstantiated by most contemporary accounts, including those of *La Guacamaya*'s editor and his penny press counterparts—supports the poet's idealized version of events.

The striking class differences depicted in the two illustrations are revealed as full-fledged class conflict by *La Guacamaya*'s prominent masthead. Set within the newspaper's logo is a dramatic face-off in which a whip-wielding bourgeois *cacique* (boss man), dressed in frock coat, vest, and top hat, advances threateningly toward a stalwart blacksmith. The smithy, in shirtsleeves and leather apron, hammer resting on an anvil, stands fast with his chest thrust forward and feet firmly planted on the ground. In the center, slightly behind and above the two men, an angry parrot representing *La Guacamaya*—wings outspread, mouth open, tongue protruding—takes the blacksmith's part. The newspaper's motto, "OF THE PEOPLE AND FOR THE PEOPLE//INDEPENDENT WEEKLY DEFENDER OF THE WORKING CLASS," appears at the bottom of the masthead and leaves little room for misinterpretation.[17]

Formal iconographic elements present in all three images further reinforce and deepen the basic message as articulated in the pictorial content and accompanying texts—an especially important supplementary effect given the uneven educational backgrounds of *La Guacamaya*'s mostly working-class readership. Long-standing iconographic conventions in Western culture have used spatial relations within visual fields—left/right, up/down, foreground/background, big/small—as a way to represent inequalities of power and status.[18] These formal conventions set up expectations, whether conscious or unconscious, on the part of viewers; expectations that the artist manipulates in order to reinforce, nuance, or even contradict an image's specific content. The three images from *La Guacamaya* do all of these things.

The most prominent spatial deployment in these particular images is a horizontal axis, for which the left-hand side of the frame (from the viewer's perspective) represents active power, while the right-hand side represents passive weakness.[19] As just noted, however, these conventional expectations are suggestive rather than definitive and are thus open to artistic manipulation. Art historian Patrick Frank emphasizes the importance of directional movement across the horizontal axis, noting that "passionate or impulsive deeds or persons in Posada prints move from left-to-right, an orientation that is more natural to the eye for Western readers, and right-to-left motion characterizes deeds that are halting ᴄ 'complicated.'"[20] Frank's emphasis on movement rather than spatial location and his characterization of right-to-left motion as "complicated" underscores the potential for ambiguity that lurks behind conventional graphic binaries—active/passive, strong/weak, high status/low status, and the like—however deeply ingrained they might be.

In order to offset, exploit, disguise, or expose these lurking ambiguities, artists typically supplement spatial conventions with other kinds of markers. Thus, in the *La Guacamaya* images, the fundamental active/passive logic of the horizontal axis is overdetermined by three additional signifiers of active power: right-facing profiles, right-handedness, and hats. The first two follow the spatial logic of the horizontal axis. The right profile looks from active left to passive right; the right hand moves from active left to passive right. The third indicator of active power, hats, is more specifically Mexican and is deployed in these images in order to distinguish between active and passive groups of men.[21] These additional indicators are especially important here because of the absence of women and children—so often used to signify passivity and powerlessness. The allegorical figures of mother Mexico on Juárez's monument and of the Virgin of Guadalupe on Hidalgo's banner are the only obvious female presences and their considerable symbolic power complicates the gender conventions.

Keeping the horizontal axis and supplementary signifiers in mind, return to the images to see how iconographic conventions work either to overdetermine or complicate their meaning. In the first image, powerful upper-class men, all wearing top hats, appear left, front, and center. The older man (probably President Díaz) is shown in right profile, front and center within the group. His walking stick is in his right hand. He looks down his nose at the younger man who toasts him from the right. Taken together these markers—left frame, right profile, right-handedness, top hat, front and center within his group, looking down from left to right on a subordinate—leave the viewer with no doubts about the older man's considerable power and status. Although the younger man speaks the toast and raises his champagne glass in his right hand, he stands to the older man's right and the gesture is from right to left—the direction Frank identifies as complicated. Thus the positioning of the younger man signifies his relative subordination: despite elite social status, an active role, and a central position in the image, he is clearly a less important and less powerful "actor" than the older man.

In stark contrast to the men in the elite group, the humble campesino enters from the right with bowed head and back to the viewer. His right (active) hand offers up the wreath, while his left (passive) hand clutches his sombrero. Unlike the other images under consideration here which maintain a certain balance between left and right, foreground and background, "En Honor de Juárez" uses perspective to push the campesino and Juárez's tomb into the background and further to the right—an effect which both divides the image along its horizontal axis and emphasizes their marginal status in relation to active power as represented by the elite men.

The artistic manipulation of iconographic convention to send mixed messages is even more apparent in the second image. In "¡VIVA la LIBERTAD!," representatives of the *pueblo* occupy the left-hand (active) frame despite their lower social status.[22] The two policemen enter aggressively from the far left, a direction (left to right) which marks their action as impulsive or passionate. The foregrounded policeman is shown in right (active) profile, shouting down angrily at the protesting paperboy and seizing the flag with his right (active) hand. The boy looks up at the policeman holding his idle bugle in his left (passive) hand. In order to highlight their active roles in the celebration, everyone in the frame wears or waves a hat, even the boy. In the right-hand (passive) frame, three hatless dandies nap. Their backs are turned to the center line that divides the two frames, right profiles buried in their pillows—a formal violation of classical notions of symmetry, which favor face-to-face confrontations along the lines depicted in the masthead. Here the formal violation conveys the irregularity of the *catrines'* position: powerless, passive, and feminized (by the frilly bed) despite their privileged and powerful position in Mexican society.

La Guacamaya's masthead follows the same iconographic conventions as the two featured illustrations. The *cacique* is depicted in right (active) profile with clenched left fist, a whip in his raised right (active) hand, and wearing a top hat. He advances from left to right toward the hatless blacksmith. The smithy stands immobile (albeit firm) with right hand on his waist and left hand on his resting hammer. The shadows cast by the two figures indicate that the light source (another signifier of power) emanates from the left toward the right, an effect that heightens the left-to-right movement of the menacing *cacique*.

Less prominent but crucial to the iconographic meaning of the three *La Guacamaya* images is the vertical (up/down) axis with its strong hierarchical connotations. On this axis, up/above represents superiority, while down/below represents subordination, as they do in traditional European representations of heaven, earth, and hell or of God, monarch, and subjects. In a religious context, up/above most often signifies moral and spiritual superiority, while down/below can signify either humility or degradation. In secular terms, up/above signifies domination while down/beneath can signify either submissiveness or powerlessness. As with the horizontal axis, these expectations are subject to artistic manipulation.

In "En Honor de Juárez," the hero's statue occupies the visual high ground, with the deferential campesino in the appropriate subordinate position. Its obvious similarity to *La Pietà* and other representations of Mary cradling the body of the crucified Christ encourages a religious reading with implications of moral rather than temporal authority. As a result, the campesino's deference seems more respectful than demeaning. Other spatial relations within the image, however, produce two apparent anomalies. First, the location of the Juárez/Mexico statue behind and to the right of the *rotos* places moral superiority in a position of weakness vis-à-vis temporal power, symbolized here by the Porfirio Díaz look-alike. This discordant reading is compounded by the statue itself, with the female figure of Mexico cradling the dead body of the prone male hero. Second, while the deferential campesino is farther back in the frame and smaller in stature than the *rotos*, he is otherwise on their level—a spatial positioning that hints at equal status despite his obviously lower socioeconomic position. The deprecatory term *rotos*, or "broken ones," was commonly used among Mexico City workers to describe men who sought to deny their own modest origins by putting on "airs," especially fashionable clothes and upper-class mannerisms, or by fawning over their "betters," most often in pursuit of attention and favors.[23] The *rotos'* presence in this image thus vividly portrays the moral bankruptcy of the Porfirian bourgeoisie. Since despite his smaller size and marginal location, the campesino is morally superior to the *roto*, the image's leveling effect refers to the promise of legal or civil equality—a position very much in keeping with Juárez's reputation as a liberal lawmaker and *La Guacamaya*'s often stated commitment to full working-class citizenship, as guaranteed by the 1857 constitution.

The vertical axis in "¡VIVA la LIBERTAD!" follows a similar logic. In the left-hand frame the Mexican flags flutter over policemen and celebrants alike, signaling their subservience to the nation. As with the campesino in the first image, this subordination to a national symbol is appropriate and carries no hint of degradation or abasement (except perhaps as an ironic comment on policemen's brutality toward their fellow citizens). In the right-hand frame Hidalgo's portrait looks down on the sleeping men in the subordinate position; they display not the respectful deference of the campesino, as in the first image, but the disrespectful (their sleeping faces are turned away), moral degradation of apathetic, feminized *catrines*.[24] As in the first image, an allegorical female personification of Mexico—the Virgin of Guadalupe in this instance—is in the active position (to Hidalgo's left), conferring moral power on the male hero (via his right hand).[25] Here too, the protagonists are situated on the same level along the horizontal axis despite their distinct social and moral positions, again suggesting their equal rights under the Mexican constitution.

The masthead upholds the spatial conventions for the horizontal axis found in the two feature illustrations and, as before, shifts the context from suggestive class differences to outright class conflict. The squawking parrot as the worker's voice/conscience occupies the upper center of the logo, the position of moral superiority; its outraged posture and open beak speak moral truth to brutal power while the *cacique* and the blacksmith confront each other as equals on the horizontal plane. In this instance, the parrot's head is only slightly elevated, and the subservience of the two men seems minimal, although the fact that the parrot must speak for the blacksmith suggests subordination (but not degradation) of a different sort. More significant, perhaps, is the parrot's unique position astride the vertical axis: it responds aggressively in left profile, against the iconographic grain, to the *cacique*'s impending assault on the resolute smithy. *La Guacamaya* is thus depicted as a disruptive force, *actively* challenging the status quo, as represented by iconographical convention—something the dead heroes, despite their considerable moral authority, are no longer able to do.

As this reading suggests, the iconographic conventions at work in these images do much more than overdetermine the pictorial content of the two illustrations and their accompanying poem-captions. They allow the artist to inject a visible moral dimension into an otherwise routine critique of social inequality: first, by using the horizontal axis to reveal the workings of masculine power in contemporary Mexican society; second, by using the vertical axis to establish a moral/spiritual hierarchy capable of challenging that power. The images also reflect (and construct) a neat bifurcation of the political sphere into a corrupt regime overrun with *rotos* and *catrines*, on one hand, and patriotic workers committed to the democratic principles of the founding fathers, on the other—a discursive strategy that marks the potentially revolutionary transition from popular liberalism to liberal populism (see ch. 3).

Close reading of isolated texts, however, can take us only so far. Still unanswered are important questions about the historical moment and the cultural context in which these texts were produced, circulated, and read. Only by addressing these broader questions can we begin to get at the potential symbolic power embedded in them.

Secular Saints

Despite their seemingly marginal status in the two feature illustrations (smaller than the other protagonists and situated in the upper right-hand corners), the figures of Hidalgo and Juárez dominate their respective images. On the surface, the explanation for this apparent imbalance is simple: without the dead hero's presence there would be no holiday to commemorate. This symbolic potency obviates the need for visual dominance. But this straightforward explanation also raises an important question: why were penny press editors, contributors, and (presumably) readers so taken with these two particular heroes?

A close reading of the *La Guacamaya* images and their accompanying texts gives a feel for the art involved in promoting patriotic figures. However, as any good publicist knows, a well-crafted promotional campaign isn't enough. As potential "consumers"—whether of material goods, services, images, sentiments, or ideas—the public must be receptive to the product in the first place. Put simply, the public must *want* what the publicist has to offer, whatever it might be, even if they don't yet know what "it" is. Although penny press promotions excited and, to a certain extent, produced working-class patriotism (as an aspect of working-class consciousness), its seeds had been planted at least as early as the democratic experiments of the independence era.[26] From that vantage point, we can begin to reconstruct the penny press "war of position" that transformed official liberal icons like Hidalgo and Juárez into working-class heroes, historical figures of mythic proportions whose personal integrity and empathy for the workingman stood in stark and subversive contrast to the venality and selfishness of the Porfirian ruling class.

In the years leading up to and following independence, patriotic holidays became an indispensable part of Mexico City's rich tradition of civic festivals.[27] As annual celebrations of historical events like the founding of Mexico City and the promulgation of the Plan de Iguala (which led to independence), these early state-sponsored festivals supplemented traditional religious celebrations with civic commemorations that "would recognize individual participation in history, men who stood out for their civic virtues, and would thus give birth to the cult of the national hero."[28] This secularization of the ritual calendar intensified after the 1867 liberal victory over the conservative forces tainted by their alliance with French invaders, the imperial interloper Maximilian, the Mexican Catholic Church, and the reactionary Pope Pius IX who had publicly threatened to excommunicate anyone who dared to purchase confiscated church property or pledge allegiance to the liberal 1857 constitution.[29] Once firmly in power, liberal ideologues set about the crucial task of writing a victor's history, a history that would construct the nation's collective historical memory around the inevitability and rightness of liberal triumph. These efforts culminated in the 1888–89 publication of *México a través de los siglos* (Mexico across the centuries), a five-volume history, written by six prominent liberal historians, that began in the preconquest era and ended with the consolidation of liberal power.[30] The fundamental tenets of this liberal historiography were reflected and refracted across a spectrum of "liberalisms" that supported everything from the official stories of the Porfirian regime to the oppositional discourse of the *puros* ("pure," or "traditional," liberals) to the satirical subversions of the penny press.[31]

Eager to counter the moral authority of the conservative Catholic Church and to sanctify the nation on their own terms, liberal ideologues of all stripes proffered a secular trinity composed of Cuauhtémoc, Hidalgo, and Juárez to complement and, for some, subsume its religious counterpart.[32] The last Aztec emperor, courageous young Cuauhtémoc, symbolized Mexican resistance to Spanish conquest, and his torture and death at the behest of conquistador Hernán Cortés exposed the greed and cruelty at the heart of the imperial project.[33] Father Hidalgo, whose 1810 *Grito* had roused the slumbering spirit of resistance, personified the early nineteenth-century struggle for independence from Spain. Juárez, whose remarkable rise from humble Indian origins demonstrated the transformative power of enlightened education, represented the triumph of liberal ideas over the forces of conservatism as well as the symbolic resurrection of indigenous Mexico.[34]

Along with the secular trinity—Cuauhtémoc (Holy Spirit), Hidalgo (Father), and Juárez (Son)—liberal propagandists populated the historical field with a host of major and minor secular saints. The most important of these figures was undoubtedly Father José María Morelos y Pavón, the insurgent leader who took up Hidalgo's banner after his execution and began the work of translating liberal ideas into constitutional precepts before he was overtaken by his own martyrdom. One admirer went so far as to elevate Morelos into the liberal trinity by casting him as the principal character in a "Patriotic Creed":

> I believe in one God, Miguel Hidalgo y Costilla Almighty, creator of Independence and Liberty. I believe in José María Morelos, worthy son of these principles, our protector; incarnate by the power of the Siege of Cuautla and born of the virgin Santa Valladolid, he suffered under the Jesuitical Dominicans, was shot, died, and buried in San Cristóbal Ecatepec, descended to the hells of the inquisition, came to life among the dead of the State of Guerrero, ascended to the heavens of Cuauhtémoc, and is seated at his right hand. I believe that he will come again in glory to judge the liberals and the *mochos* [conservatives, religious hypocrites]. I believe in the Holy Spirit of the Reform, in the progress of liberals, in the punishment of traitors, the resurrection of Don Benito Juárez, and the fulfillment of the Constitution of 1857. Amen.[35]

Lesser saints in the liberal firmament included Hidalgo collaborators Ignacio Allende and Juan de Aldama (his principal generals), *La Corregidora* (who warned the conspirators that their plot had been exposed), *El Pípila* (the fearless miner who according to legend led the attack on the Spanish-held fortress/granary, Alhóndiga de Granaditas, in Guanajuato); insurgent leaders Guadalupe Victoria and Vicente Guerrero (both later presidents); the *Niños Héroes* (military school cadets who had died rather than surrender to the invading Americans during the U.S.-Mexican War, including Juan Escutia, who allegedly wrapped himself in the flag and jumped from the parapet of Chapultepec Castle), and Cinco de Mayo hero Ignacio Zaragoza, commander of the Mexican army that defeated the invading French forces at Puebla in 1862.[36] Awaiting seemingly inevitable canonization—at least in the eyes of mainstream liberal ideologues—was President Porfirio Díaz himself, a brigadier general in Zaragoza's army; his heroism on that symbolically momentous day had thrust him into the national limelight (see fig. 1.3).[37]

Noteworthy here is the near total absence of women. As is the case with the *La Guacamaya* illustrations examined earlier, the female figures in the liberal myth of nation tend to be allegorical rather than historical: Mexico is most often represented as a generic young woman or linked explicitly to the Virgin of Guadalupe—a popular symbolization that only the most extreme anticlerical liberals chose to ignore. Both representations

FIG. 1.3 José Guadalupe Posada, "¡2 de abril de 1867!," *La Guacamaya,* March 31, 1904. Courtesy of the Benson Latin American Collection, University of Texas Libraries, The University of Texas at Austin.

are virgin mothers, a condition that distinguishes them from their earthly counterparts.[38] One of the few exceptions to the men-only rule seems to be *La Corregidora*. Yet even she is most often identified in patriotic accounts as the wife of the former *corregidor* (mayor) of Querétaro, *la corregidora*, rather than by her proper name, Josefa Ortíz de Domínguez. Another exception, Agustina Ramírez, a poor indigenous woman from Sinaloa who allegedly lost a husband and twelve sons during the French Intervention (1861–67), may never have existed outside the imaginations of the men, including historian Vicente Riva Palacio, who promoted her story of willing sacrifice for Mexico and the liberal cause.[39] This extreme gender imbalance distinguishes the roster of liberal saints from its Catholic counterpart and illustrates the increasingly rigid separation of public and private spheres that characterized the liberal nation-building project in Mexico, Latin America, and beyond.[40] For example, article 15 of the 1859 Civil Marriage Law, drafted by liberal statesman Melchor Ocampo, promulgated by then exiled President Benito Juárez, and subsequently read at civil marriage ceremonies, advised newlyweds that "the woman, whose principal attributes are abnegation, beauty, compassion, insight, and tenderness, must give and shall give her husband obedience, pleasantness, assistance, solace, and advice, treating him always with the veneration that is to be given to the person who supports and defends us, and with the delicateness of someone who does not wish to irritate the brusque, irritable, and hard part of oneself."[41] While few working-class women had the luxury of attending solely to the maintenance of the private sphere or managing not "to irritate the brusque, irritable, and hard part" of their husbands, they were often held to bourgeois standards of chastity and comportment, especially by elite social critics who used their failure to live up to those standards as evidence of their inherent inferiority.[42]

Noteworthy too, is the ubiquitous use of religious imagery in patriotic iconography, despite the unabashed anticlericalism of many penny press editors and contributors. The apparent contradiction is not as unexpected as it might seem at first glance. For example, liberal statesman, *letrado*, and journalist Guillermo Prieto—a primary architect of the anticlerical Reform Laws, which sought to strip the Catholic Church of its colonial-era *fueros* (legal privileges)—achieved literary renown for *both* patriotic and religious poetry.[43] An 1895 collection, for example, coupled the nationalistic epic "Invasión Norteamericana," about the mid-nineteenth-century U.S. invasion of Mexico, with the more intimate "La confianza del hombre en la religion" (the trust of man in religion), which began with the following lines:

Cuando la juventud despavorida,
víctimas, delirios y pasiones,
vaga entre incertidumbres y aflicciones,
errante en el desierto de la vida,

¡Sublime religion! Le das asilo,
consuelas su existir desesperado,
en tus brazos el hombre reclinado
no teme el porvenir, duerme tranquilo.[44]

❧

[When terrified youth,
victims, delirious and tormented,
wander amidst uncertainties and afflictions,
at sea in the desert of life,

Sublime religion! You shelter them,
console their hopeless existence,
in your arms a reclining man
fears not the future, sleeps tranquilly.]

As Prieto's influential example demonstrates, while many committed liberals attacked the Catholic Church as an obstacle to progress, their objections to the institution did not necessarily undermine their religious faith.

Moreover, Church partisans and opponents, conservatives and liberals, believers and nonbelievers, alike drew on Catholic language and imagery to articulate their ideas and concerns. In *Democracy in Latin America*, historical sociologist Carlos Forment argues that "Catholicism was the language of public life" in nineteenth-century Latin America and that "citizens used its narrative resources to create new democratic meanings from old religious terms, thereby fusing the two to create an alternative vocabulary—call it Civic Catholicism."[45] This was certainly true in Mexico even among anticlerical socialist organizations and mutual aid societies, which often "found a certain inspiration in the gospel" even though they weren't "strictly speaking Catholic."[46] Moreover, according to Forment, "by the closing decades of the [nineteenth] century . . . in urban areas, newspaper writers used Civic Catholicism terminology and phrases to develop a new theory of Mexican history based on the changing nature of associative life and to develop a set of standards by which citizens could evaluate each other's actions in public."[47] In this context and despite their contentious relationship with the institutional church, secular heroes such as Hidalgo and Juárez played a central role in the new history of Mexico. As historian Rogelio Jiménez Marce explains: "The hero as archetype was inscribed in a profane sphere that without seeking to contradict religious models sought to share the same space of worship among the people. The identification of heroes as new saints in the popular imagination could help set them apart as role models in future histories and, in so doing, put them to the task of gradually replacing religious saints."[48]

As we saw earlier, graphic images also reflected, perhaps even more clearly than written words, the Catholic foundations of public discourse in Mexico, especially its insistence on "associate life" rather than personal autonomy, an idea more amenable to advocates of working-class solidarity than to bourgeois individualists. While the satiric penny press for

FIG. 1.4 José Guadalupe Posada, "Situación de la clase obrera,"*La Guacamaya*, August 11, 1902. Courtesy of the Benson Latin American Collection, University of Texas Libraries, The University of Texas at Austin.

workers never demonstrated the unrelenting anticlericalism of its counterpart *El Padre Padilla* ("founded to combat bad governments, popular ignorance, and clerical corruption") or opposition "combat" journalists like Ireneo Paz (*El Padre Cobos, La Patria Ilustrada*), Daniel Cabrera (*El Hijo del Ahuizote*), Jesus Martínez Carrión, and Federico Pérez Fernández (*El Colmillo Público*), its editors used much of the same religious imagery to illustrate their critiques of the bourgeoisie, the regime, and the institutional Catholic Church.[49] As historian of Mexican political caricatures (and political cartoonist) Rafael Barajas Durán points out: "In the liberal society of that time, to be at the same time a good Catholic and a hard-nosed Jacobin is not a contradiction in terms, but an act of Christian consistency: many notable liberals . . . criticize the hypocrisy of the conservatives and the Church, grounding their arguments in the teachings of the New Testament."[50]

This was certainly the case with the penny press. For example, a 1902 *La Guacamaya* cover, "Situación de la clase obrera: De Herodes á Pilatos" (Situation of the Working Class: From Herod to Pilate), conveys the tragedy of a destitute working-class family forced to pawn their clothes (to Herod) to buy bread for their hungry children (from Pilate) in explicitly New Testament terms (see fig. 1.4).[51] Equally explicit is another 1902 *La*

CALVARIO MODERNO

Un salvario moderno te presento,
Lector, si quieres contemblar un poco,
Ved al Burgues que lleno de contento
Vierte la sangre del martir, poeo á poco.

La clase obrera llega hasta el suplicio,
Del Longines recibe la lanzada,
Como un martir recibe el sacrificio
En medio de estruendosa carcajada.

Entretanto el Burgues, con ansia loca,
Recoge de su herida el santo fruto,
Y de su pecho más duro que la roca,
No siente compación en lo absoluto.

Vierte su sangre, y al vertirla deja,
De la miseria en lo más profundo,
A la familia que sufre y no se queja;
Que es la palanca que moviera al mundo.

FIG. 1.5 José Guadalupe Posada/Author Unknown, "Calvario moderno," *La Guacamaya*, December 5, 1902. Courtesy of the Benson Latin American Collection, University of Texas Libraries, The University of Texas at Austin.

Guacamaya cover, "Calvario moderno" (Modern Calvary), which depicts a crucified worker, identified as the working class, with coins pouring from the wound on his side into the top hats of two laughing bourgeois gentlemen (see fig. 1.5).[52] The second verse of the poem reads:

La clase obrera llega hasta el suplicio,
Del Longines recibe la lanzada,
Como *un* martir recibe el sacrificio,
En medio de estruendosas carcajadas.

[The working class arrives at the place of execution,
From Longinus he receives the spear thrust,
As a martyr he accepts the sacrifice,
Amidst roars of laughter.]

Whatever their personal religious beliefs, then, penny press editors and contributors routinely used religious concepts, language, and images to convey their righteous indignation at the exploitation of Mexican workers even as they lampooned the venality and corruption of the Catholic Church.

Working-Class Heroes: The Father of Independence

From among the crowded liberal pantheon of national heroes, penny press editors, contributors, and their readers exalted two men above all the others: Father Hidalgo and Benito Juárez. Of the two heroes, Hidalgo was represented as more remote in terms of both historical time and immediate relevance. Venerated for his catalytic role in sparking the wars that would lead to Mexico's independence from Spain in 1821, Hidalgo is most often portrayed in the penny press as having successfully completed his appointed task, however much he might rue the current state of the nation he so courageously fathered. In contrast, Juárez comes across as very much of the contemporary moment. Juárez had been dead for only twenty-six years in 1900, and his presidency fell well within the memory of many working-class Mexicans. Some doubtless remembered, and a few had even participated—like Porfirio Díaz himself—in the long struggle against conservatives, the French occupation army, and Maximilian that marked Juárez's first two terms. Furthermore, for penny press editors and readers, Juárez's most important legacy, "respect for the rights of others" as enshrined in the 1857 constitution, was as yet unfulfilled.[53]

In keeping with this ideological division of labor, penny press editors generally depicted Hidalgo as the personification of the enlightened "spirit" of independence rather than as a political thinker with a clearly defined political program.[54] This was a sensible enough solution to the representational dilemma—also a problem for official ideologues—posed by the disparate, often mutually antagonistic military, political, and ideological struggles that characterized Mexican independence.[55] Thus the familiar figure of Hidalgo served first and foremost as an object of veneration for services already rendered, well deserving of the accolades and honors of a grateful people.

Only on rare occasions does he participate (figuratively speaking) in the penny press's running critique of social problems. In this regard, his grieving image in "¡VIVA la LIBERTAD!" is something of a fluke. So

FIG. 1.6 José Guadalupe Posada/Author Unknown, "Después de las fiestas," *Don Cucufate*, September 25, 1906. Courtesy of the Benson Latin American Collection, University of Texas Libraries, The University of Texas at Austin.

is José Guadalupe Posada's cover illustration for *Don Cucufate*'s 1906 post–Independence Day issue, "Después de las fiestas" (After the Fiestas; see fig. 1.6).[56] Like "¡VIVA la LIBERTAD!," this print depicts a weeping Hidalgo—the poet tells us that "anguished and sad, he cries over our decadence"—cradling the Virgin of Guadalupe battle standard with his right arm.[57] Here, however, the cause of the hero's distress, shared by a sword-bearing female liberty seated on the lower right-hand side of the frame, is not bourgeois self-indulgence but the Porfirian regime's repression of the independent press, represented at the lower left by a seated woman, head bowed, bound hand and foot with ropes. As befits his iconic status as Father of the Country, Hidalgo and his "attributes"—flag, rosary, bible, declaration of independence clutched in his right hand— dominate the image: the hero's physical stature dwarfs the two women and he occupies the powerful upper center of the frame much like God the Father in traditional representations of the Trinity.[58] In the frame's upper left is a representation of the Dolores church in front of which Hidalgo delivered the *Grito*; as a symbol of outspoken ("shouted") liberty, it stands in stark and ironic contrast to the figure of the shackled, silenced woman. In the upper right are the famous volcanoes Popcatépetl and Iztaccíhuatl; as indigenous symbols of Mexican identity, they serve to nationalize the generic female liberty (with her French Phrygian "liberty" cap) seated just below.[59] The female figures on either side portray virtue as a feminine trait, morally superior but powerless in the face of masculine (state) power: "liberty" (on the passive right) is too discouraged to wield her sword, while the "independent press" (on the active left) is openly oppressed by government censors (represented here by the shackles). Although the image succeeds in conveying Hidalgo's anguish at the current state of affairs, it holds out little hope for change. Remote in historical time and with his primary mission accomplished, Father Hidalgo, like the women who share his table, can only weep for Mexico.

More common were the Independence Day issues that penny presses published each year on or around September 16.[60] The typical cover illustrations for these commemorative issues feature a formal head-and-shoulders portrait of Hidalgo, instantly recognizable with the bald crown of his head above shoulder-length white hair, broad forehead, aquiline nose, clerical collar, and frock coat with broad lapels in typical French post-revolutionary style. Several Independence Day cover images also include

Hidalgo "attributes": the bell towers of the Dolores church, the "liberty" bell that he rang to assemble his followers on that fateful day, and a laurel crown to symbolize his (posthumous) victory over the Spanish overlords.

The deliberate formality of these stock images suggests that editors expected them to double as wall posters or to occupy honored spaces in home altars after the fashion of the patriotic and religious broadsheets commonly sold on the Mexico City streets—a decorative, devotional use of patriotic icons in the domestic sphere that reflected and reinforced their intimate place in workers' hearts.[61] *El Diablito Rojo*'s 1910 pre–Independence Day issue even ran an advertisement for "two very beautiful patriotic allegories, obtainable at low cost to commemorate the Centenary"; one of the lithographs was "crowned by the figures of Hidalgo and Juárez, breaking the chains of slavery."[62] Penny press commemorative covers may not have qualified as "beautiful patriotic allegories," but they served much the same function and addressed similar themes. For example, *La Guacamaya*'s September 13, 1906, cover illustration (signed by Posada) depicts a sword-wielding Hidalgo severing the chains of a kneeling man held in bondage by a *cacique* wearing a beret. The sword is labeled "liberty"; the kneeling man, "Mexican people"; the *cacique*, "Spanish domination" (see fig. 1.7).[63]

The commemorative portraits were generally accompanied by poems and essays in praise of the hero, some written by the editors, others by contributors. In keeping with the formality of most portraits, the cover poems took on pseudoreligious overtones, with titles like "Hymn to Hidalgo" and "Excelsior."[64] The inside pages provided more variety; editorials, essays, and poems on historical themes taken from Hidalgo's career mixed with more standard patriotic fare.[65] This mix of history and patriotism was especially notable in issues that commemorated the anniversary of Hidalgo's execution (July 30, 1811). *La Guacamaya*'s July 30, 1902, issue, for example, included a Posada illustration of Hidalgo before the firing squad, the text of Hidalgo's execution order, a historical account of Hidalgo's betrayal by "the infamous Elizondo," two separate editorial statements, poems by five different authors, and a collection of "thoughts" on Hidalgo by yet another contributor (see fig. 1.8).[66] If that weren't enough, in conjunction with the 1904 Independence Day celebrations, *La Guacamaya*, in collabo-

¡LIBERTAD!

El pueblo mexicano yacia opreso
bajo el dominio del feroz hispano
y aquella esclavitud, rompióseal peso
del denodado arrojo de un arciano.
Fué el Cura Hidalgo, quien con firme mano

supo marcar del pueblo la igualdad
disipando la negra oscuridad
y el yugo de los fieros opresores
proclamando en el pueblo de Dolores
la augusta y sacrosanta *Libertad*.

FIG. 1.7 José Guadalupe Posada/Author Unknown, "¡Libertad!," *La Guacamaya*, September 13, 1906. Courtesy of the Benson Latin American Collection, University of Texas Libraries, The University of Texas at Austin.

ration with the Sociedad Mano Amiga Hidalgo (Hidalgo Hand of Friendship Society), staged a benefit, solicited subscriptions, and arranged for a "pilgrimage" to present a "magnificent clock" at Hidalgo's house in Dolores.[67] This elaborate public performance "on behalf of the workers of the Federal District" tied penny press literary offerings to the patriotic pilgrimages and offerings undertaken regularly by "humble" workers. An act of solidarity with those popular practices, it served to complement and perhaps even co-opt the affective bonds that already bound many workers to the father of Mexican independence.

It is hardly surprising, then, that penny press patriotic literary offerings would feature many reader contributions, especially poems written by self-identified workers, modeled for the most part on the patriotic poems of liberal *letrados* such as Guillermo Prieto. Editors often solicited worker contributions in advance. For example, *La Guacamaya*, in the

FIG. 1.8 José Guadalupe Posada, "Fusilamiento de Don Miguel Hidalgo y Costilla," *La Guacamaya*, July 30, 1902. Courtesy of the Benson Latin American Collection, University of Texas Libraries, The University of Texas at Austin.

issue that preceded the one just mentioned, included a request "to the workers who have honored us with their compositions, that they submit them as soon as possible."[68] This particular solicitation produced a "poetic essay to the immortal Hidalgo" by Antonio Negrete, a "former worker at the Linera Factory." Written in the high romantic literary style considered appropriate to patriotic sentiments, Negrete's poem included references to the traitorous Elizondo and the "sublime *Grito*," along with "eternal praise for the noble elder [*anciano*] who understood how to free my *Patria* [homeland] from the iron yoke of the cruel tyrant."[69] In a similar vein, Elena F. Montero, a young woman from the Loreto Factory in San Angel, writing in to *La Palanca* lauded the "sublime elder" for his "holy *Grito* of Dolores which, overthrowing viceroys and tyrants and oppressors, gave us liberty and honors, gave us independence and laws."[70] Even more high-toned was a poem by "Pascual Mendoza, Worker" that was "read by the author on the night of September 15 [1904] at the literary evening in honor of our liberator that took place in the Factory 'El Molina de Enmedio.'" The first of Mendoza's twelve stanzas conveys something of the respect, bordering on religious veneration that many workers felt for the independence hero-martyr:

¡Ave Hidalgo! á tus altares
vengo á abrir el áureo broche
para enzalsarse [sic] esta noche
con mis sencillos cantares,
no vengo á ofrecerte azahares
de románticos olores
pero te traigo las flores
más puras del corazón
que te ofrece esta reunión
de obreros trabajadores.[71]

[Hail Hidalgo! to your altars
I come to open the gilded clasp
that I might extol you this night
with my simple songs,
I come not to offer you
sweet smelling citrus blossoms
Instead I bring you the heart's
purest flowers
those that this gathering of hardworking laborers
offer up to you.]

Here, as in the celebrations sponsored by *La Guacamaya* and the Sociedad Mano Amiga Hidalgo, popular veneration of Hidalgo becomes a
"live" public performance, very much in the tradition of the floral offering
depicted in "En Honor de Juárez" and hinted at in the poem, but much
bolder—and decidedly literate, with its formal deliberation and elaborate vocabulary. While not all worker-poets had access to a public venue
or could match Mendoza's linguistic virtuosity, this profusion of poetic
homages from self-identified workers testify to a sincere, deeply felt affective bond with Hidalgo, often expressed in openly religious language,
that put to shame the "floral offerings" of their professional counterparts,
to say nothing of the officially endorsed secular patriotism of liberal ideologues. As one "humble worker" put it:

Soy Mexicano, y el deber me obliga
que en esta fecha con amor ardiente,

agradecido el corazón te diga
el regosijo [*sic*] que mi pecho siente.[72]

[I am Mexican, and duty obliges
that on this date with burning love,
my thankful heart tell you
the joy that my breast feels.]

On the face of it, penny press veneration of liberal icons Hidalgo and Juárez played directly into the hands of official ideologues. Still, the fervor with which editors and contributors embraced these two national heroes suggests that there was more to the story than naive nationalism, false consciousness, or an understandable desire to portray workingmen as committed patriots. In fact, these most beloved of national heroes presented serious ideological problems for the Díaz regime. From the regime's perspective, for example, Hidalgo was an abject military failure whose heroism, however inspiring to later generations, led ultimately to his ignominious defrocking and execution at the hands of Spanish loyalists.[73] This tragic fate made any effort to closely identify the failed father of Mexican independence with the regime, especially with war hero Porfirio Díaz, more than a little awkward.

For penny press editors, however, the equanimity and courage of Hidalgo, in the face of bitter betrayals by his fellow countrymen working in collusion with imperialist forces, resonated with the press's own oft repeated criticism of the Porfirian administration, especially the much reviled *científicos* (technocrats), for its unseemly courting of foreign interests at the expense of Mexican sovereignty. The poem beneath Posada's cover illustration for the September 20, 1909, issue of *El Diablito Rojo* makes the connection explicit (see fig. 1.9).[74] Similar in composition to the *Don Cucufate* cover analyzed earlier, the image is a seemingly innocuous representation of Mexico and Spain, depicted as women seated next to their respective national symbols, the Mexican flag and the Spanish coat of arms, and joining hands across the water under the benign gaze of Father Hidalgo; a Phrygian cap surmounted by the word "liberty" floats over Hidalgo's head like a halo, and the hero is flanked by the two volcanoes, Popcatépetl and Iztaccíhuatl, which serve as before to Mexi-

FIG. 1.9 José Guadalupe Posada/Author Unknown, "Después de un siglo," *El Diablito Rojo*, September 20, 1909. Courtesy of the Benson Latin American Collection, University of Texas Libraries, The University of Texas at Austin.

canize the scene. But if the image holds no hint of critique, the poem makes clear that "after a century of struggle" Mexico is reduced to nothing more than a "mother lode" for foreign millionaires. For penny press editors and contributors, official efforts to channel the primal force of Hidalgo's historic *Grito* had floundered in hypocrisy. Instead, Hidalgo's cry had become the "*grito santo*" (holy cry) of Mexican workers, as they called out for new leadership and a new independence in which "progress affectionately opens its wings to give them shelter."[75]

Civic Catholicism and the Liberal Tradition

The compelling image of a Catholic priest who sacrificed his social position and institutional privilege to free an oppressed people from the colonial yoke, whose *grito santo* ignited the spirit of a new nation, whose martyrdom transformed him into the spokesman for a still unrealized dream of social justice, testifies to the power of so-called Civic Catholicism to transform patriotic discourse into secular scripture. As noted earlier, Civic Catholicism's emotional appeal and its insistence on the primacy of collective responsibility over personal autonomy resonated with considerably more force for advocates of working-class solidarity, including penny press editors and contributors, than it ever could for bourgeois proponents of scientific politics and enlightened self-interest. This elective affinity between Civic Catholicism and appeals to working-class solidarity gave the penny press editors a decided advantage in their ideological struggle with the Porfirian official story for the hearts and minds of Mexico City workers.[76] Moreover, Catholicism's penchant for moral dichotomies further reinforced the populist tendencies implicit in the penny press critique of the Porfirian regime. Whatever that advantage, the penny press appropriation of Father Hidalgo's story presented few serious challenges for Porfirian liberal ideologues. The story of Benito Juárez, however, was their Achilles heel, as the next chapter shows.

CHAPTER 2

THE ONE TRUE JUÁREZ

El Benemérito

Even more troublesome for official ideologues than Father Hidalgo's military failures was Díaz's personal history of strained relations with liberal icon Benito Juárez, especially over the issue of reelection. Díaz, a fellow Oaxacan and a liberal hero in his own right, had considered Juárez's decision to run for a fourth presidential term in the 1871 elections to be unconstitutional and had presented himself as an opposition candidate. When Congress declared Juárez victorious after a three-way split in the vote failed to produce a majority for any one candidate, Díaz led an unsuccessful military coup d'état against the newly elected government. Thus despite the regime's strong push to canonize Juárez as a liberal saint in preparation for Díaz's own ascension, the well-known historical facts about their troubled relationship and the obvious hypocrisy involved in the latter's turnabout on presidential succession—he would be elected president eight times—complicated the situation quite a bit.

For Díaz's political opponents, however, the canonization of Juárez proved the perfect means to subvert official patriotic discourse, to turn one of the regime's principal ideological initiatives—the conflation of liberal politics with national patriotism—against its perpetrators. Fearful of the regime's willingness to jail newspaper editors who crossed the line into personal attacks on the president, penny press editors for the most

MÉXICO, LUNES 21 DE JULIO DE 1902.   NÚM 10.

LA GUACAMAYA

DEL PUEBLO Y POR EL PUEBLO.

Periódico hablador y de buen humor, revalsador y decidor de verdades, no papero ni farolero, azote de los burgueses y defensor de la CLASE OBRERA.

derecho ageno

El respeto al   ES LA PAZ.

C. BENITO JUAREZ,
Benemérito de las Américas.

FIG. 2.1 Artist Unknown, "El respeto al derecho ageno es la paz," *La Guacamaya*, July 21, 1902. Courtesy of the Benson Latin American Collection, University of Texas Libraries, The University of Texas at Austin.

part left overt comparisons between the two men to the imagination of their readers or made nominal efforts to disguise their intent, as happens in "En Honor de Juárez," where the presidential central figure sports a full beard when the president himself generally favored a bushy moustache.[1] So rather than tackle Díaz head on, penny press editors preferred to exalt Juárez and let the implicit contrast between the two men speak for itself—perhaps helped by a strategic hint or two to ensure that their readers got the point. Whatever care they took not to incur presidential displeasure, they nevertheless knew Juárez to be the regime's Achilles heel, and they exploited that weakness at every opportunity.

As was the case with Hidalgo, commemorative issues were the most obvious and least provocative way to render due homage to the hero. More overtly patriotic than the other presses, *La Guacamaya* ran a Juárez commemorative edition each year on or around July 18, the anniversary of his 1872 death.[2] The 1902 issue, published in the paper's first year, set the standard for subsequent commemoratives (see fig. 2.1). The cover illustration—most likely an artist's rendition of an official presidential photograph—features a formal head-and-shoulders portrait of Juárez wearing a black suit, waistcoat, white shirt, starched collar, and bow tie. His skin is dark, and his features distinctly Indian (albeit conventionally dignified). The caption underneath reads "C. Benito Juárez, Benemérito de las Américas." The "C" stands for "Ciudadano" (citizen) and highlights Juárez's adamant refusal of military or quasi-aristocratic titles. the acceptance of which was a particular failing of the notoriously vain liberal antihero Santa Anna and the liberal war hero General Porfirio Díaz. The honorific "Benemérito de las Américas" alerts readers to the hero's status as the "worthiest of Americans," a posthumous distinction that extended recognition of his merit and influence to the entire Western Hemisphere. Framing the portrait on the top and sides is Juárez's well-known motto: "Peace means respect for the rights of others."[3]

Although less consistently than *La Guacamaya*, other penny presses also devoted commemorative covers to Juárez. A Posada illustration for the 1904 anniversary issue of *El Pinche* (The Scullion) proved a particular favorite, appearing on the cover of penny press competitor *El Chile Piquín* (The Hot Little Chile) twice the following year—in honor of Constitution Day (February 5) and the anniversary of Juárez's death (July 18; see fig. 2.2).[4] The image depicts the bust of Juárez floating above a pile

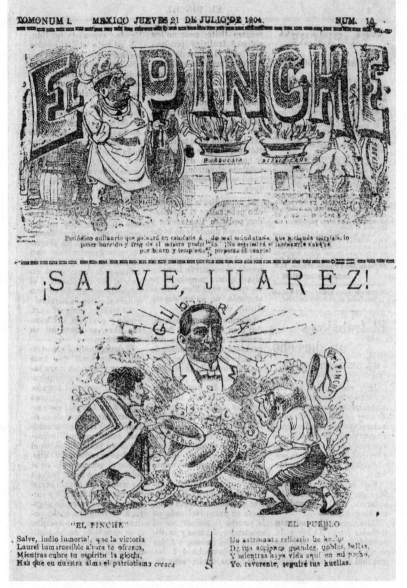

FIG. 2.2 José Guadalupe Posada/Author Unknown, "¡Salve Juárez!," *El Pinche*, July 21, 1904. Courtesy of the Benson Latin American Collection, University of Texas Libraries, The University of Texas at Austin.

HOMENAJE

Recibe ¡oh! Juárez, esta humilde ofrenda
que el pueblo deposita en tu ataúd;
en ella representa su cariño,
su respeto ó inmensa gratitud.

Aun cuando algun tirano te ofendiera
y tu nombre intentara mancillar,
los patriotas y nobles mexicanos
en su pecho te forman un altar.

FIG. 2.3 José Guadalupe Posada/Author Unknown, "Homenaje." *La Tranca*, July 22, 1906. Courtesy of the Benson Latin American Collection, University of Texas Libraries, The University of Texas at Austin.

of wreaths in the upper center of the frame; rays of light emanate from behind the hero's head, and the word "GLORIA" serves him as halo or crown. On the lower left, a serape-clad campesino doffs a sombrero labeled "pueblo" (people); on the lower right, an apron-wearing cook follows suit with a chef's hat labeled "El Pinche." The title translates as "Hail Juárez!," an honorary greeting traditionally used to address religious figures like the Virgin Mary but also common in patriotic poetry (as we saw with Hidalgo). Although less formal than *La Guacamaya*'s commemorative covers, the various elements of this popular Posada image add up to the same unambiguous message of popular respect for the "immortal Indian." So do the elements of yet another of Posada's patriotic illustrations, this one for the cover of *La Tranca* (The Truncheon; see fig. 2.3).[5] The image depicts a scene already familiar to us from "En Honor de Juárez": a bareheaded worker, wearing a leather apron and work boots, doffs his hat respectfully and places a wreath labeled "gratitude" at the foot of the hero's tomb. In contrast to the discordant elements that constitute "En

Honor de Juárez," here everything is harmoniously balanced: the carefully drawn wreath of gratitude dominates the center frame, the worker appears prominently on the same horizontal plane as the hero's reclining figure (although smaller in stature), and a rather voluptuous-looking Mexico in the upper center gazes suggestively toward heaven. The accompanying poem offers up only the slightest of subversive possibilities:

> Recibe ¡oh! Juárez, esta humilde ofrenda
> que el pueblo deposita en tu ataúd;
> en ella representa su cariño,
> su respeto é inmensa gratitud.
>
> Aun cuando algún tirano te ofendiera
> y tu nombre intentara mancillar,
> los patriotas y nobles mexicanos
> en su pecho te forman un altar.

> [Receive, oh Juárez! this humble offering
> that the people place on your coffin;
> it represents their affection,
> their respect and immense gratitude.
>
> Even if some tyrant should offend you
> and should seek to tarnish your name,
> patriotic and noble Mexicans
> will make an altar of your breast.]

The poem's vague reference to "some tyrant," however, is hardly enough to disturb the respectful tranquility of the scene.

Reasons for Juárez's special appeal to workers are readily at hand. Unlike Father Hidalgo, whose well-to-do creole origins marked his racial and class privilege, Juárez had risen from humble Indian beginnings to become "the dominant figure in the History of our Patria."[6] *La Guacamaya* described the process for its readers: "our great Juárez, pure-blooded Indian, born in the small town of Ixtlán, amidst the common people [*masas populares*], grows, develops himself, to the extent that his intelligence takes on gigantic proportions, in order afterward to occupy the place reserved for him by the Creator's hand, and like the phoenix he rises up from nothing to spread his doctrines and to shake off the yoke of tyranny."[7] This remarkable individual achievement warranted the upmost respect, especially from workers. Addressing the hero personally, a *La Guacamaya* contributor explained: "Men like you, who raise themselves up from the most debased social class [*la más ínfima clase social*] to where you raised yourself, deserve the respect, admiration, and affection of all their fellow citizens, most of all, when they execute and put into practice the laws that have come to establish progress and civilization."[8] Here, the use of the informal *tú* for "you" in the Spanish original—typical of prayerful dialogue between supplicant and saint—conveys a sense of intimacy and veneration (rather than casual disrespect) that suggests the presence of a deeply felt affective bond between writer and hero.

Although writers make frequent note of Juárez's Indian origins, these references serve most often to emphasize his remarkable ability to transcend Mexico's deeply entrenched and highly racialized class divisions. Like the volcano images in the Hidalgo covers, penny press references to Juárez's Indian blood work to "indigenize" the hero, to make him a "worthy son of Mexican soil"—something a Creole like Hidalgo, enlightened or not, could never quite manage. This rootedness was certainly important to the mostly mestizo (mixed-race) working class, which suffered daily from the racial prejudices of its social "superiors." And racial solidarity doubtless played an important role in Juárez's popularity despite the persistence of deep-seated racist attitudes toward Indians in general, even among the very mestizo workers who nevertheless idolized "our little Indian."[9] Still, for penny press editors and contributors, Juárez's greatest feat was having overcome his *class* origins, having risen by sheer strength of character from "the most debased social class" to the presidency of Mexico and thus having become in every sense of the word a true working-class hero.

Like Hidalgo commemoratives, *La Guacamaya*'s 1902, 1903, and 1904 Juárez editions featured poems and essays by both the editors and a diverse group of outside contributors. Here, too, the paper actively solicited contributions, especially from "our brothers, the workers."[10] The outpouring of literary affection for Juárez was apparently greater than the paper could accommodate. An editorial note in the 1903 edition explains to two contributors that their poems could not be included in the commemorative due to lack of space but would appear in the next issue.

While none of the other penny press followed *La Guacamaya*'s example in producing commemorative editions devoted entirely to Juárez, most regularly ran reader submissions extolling his many virtues.

Poems and essays by self-identified workers were even more common for Juárez than for Hidalgo.[11] The prolific Antonio Negrete, writing in 1902 as an ex-worker at the Linera Factory and in 1903 from La Indianilla workshops, made regular contributions.[12] His 1903 Juárez poem even allows a rare (if circumspect) critical note to creep into an otherwise laudatory text. "Mexico, oh my Patria!" he laments, "if only the great Juárez lived; your fate would be different!"[13] Fernando Celada, the best known of Mexico City's worker-poets, went so far as to assemble his many Juárez poems into a book and took out advertisements for it in the penny press.[14] Along with a reprint of the popular Posada cover, the two cited *El Chile Piquín* commemorative editions include Juárez poems from Celada's book.[15] The following excerpt gives a sense of the seriousness, quasi-religious zeal, and literary virtuosity with which the poet—like most of his peers—approached his favorite subject:

Veo tu sombra cruzar por el desierto
Como la sombra de Moisés errante
Que condujo á su tribu por lo incierto;
Pero más que á Moisés, te veo gigante,
Soberano, divino,
Abriendo con tu fé nuevo camino
Y á la Patria diciéndole: ¡adelante![16]

[I see your shadow cross the desert
Like the shadow of wandering Moses
Who brought his tribe through the unknown;
But more than Moses, I see you as colossal,
Sovereign, divine,
Opening a new road with your faith
And saying to the Patria: Forward!]

Given Juárez's bitter battles with the Catholic Church over the reform laws and the 1857 constitution, the prominence of religious motifs in this and similar poems might seem out of place.[17] For cult adherents like

Negrete and Celada, however, their hero's near-miraculous intercession had converted religious fanaticism into patriot fervor. Given the prominence of Civic Catholicism in Mexican public language, comparisons to Moses and Christ were inevitable. "Jesus is a symbol, a holy vessel / And you are the Patria converted into Man!" Celada wrote in another of his poems to Juárez, "The church curses you . . . [but] you are no criminal, / You are no wretch, no atheist, / You are a reflection of God and of his glory!"[18] Thus the "immortal" Juárez had almost singlehandedly transformed the traditional emotional ties that bound good-hearted (but deluded) workingmen to superstitious doctrines and repressive overlords into the affective bonds that joined patriotic Mexican citizens to each other and to the "Patria" *of their own free will.*

As noted earlier, outright criticism of the current president and overt comparisons of Diáz and Juárez were relatively rare in the penny press. Crass political critique would have seemed out of place in the laudatory poems of Negrete, Celada, and their compatriots. But aesthetic considerations aside, editors and contributors understood and usually played by the unwritten rules of the censor's game.[19] At times, however, the veil of enforced civility slipped, allowing implicit criticism to blaze forth in all its vituperative glory. Take, for example, this "diabolic" 1908 *El Diablito Rojo* editorial in honor of Benito Juárez's birthday, written in the wake of a devastating economic recession and bloody government attacks on striking workers at Cananea and Río Blanco:

> These days it is said of me that I know so much not because I'm the Devil, but because I am old, and that's the truth. I have seen the great work of that illustrious Indian nearly destroyed in less than half of a century, and I assure you that if I were to bring Juárez into the world, he wouldn't recognize the famous Constitution. Consider that today even minor Municipal Presidents have their miniature palaces; the Political Bosses, forget about it; the Governors believe themselves to be direct descendents of some Divinity, and those on top . . . they believe themselves nothing more nor less than demigods.
>
> Newspapermen take bribes.
>
> The clergy grows.
>
> Americans take over.
>
> Money gets scarcer even in peace time.

Adulation triumphs . . . I don't want to continue, because I wouldn't finish in a year, and all the paper from the San Rafael Factory would not be enough to say what I have to say, and I need my Secretaries for other things.

What is certain is that the Father of the Patria is seen by certain Mexicans as a mythological being, and they don't remember as they should, because they're too busy burning incense to General Díaz, that on the 21st day of this month, was born the true Hero of the Peace.[20]

✻

[Ahora se me dirá que no sé tanto por Diablo, cuanto por viejo, y es la verdad. Yo he visto casi destruida en menos de medio siglo, la grande obra de ese ilustre indio, y aseguro que si yo llevara á Juárez al mundo, desconocería la famosa Constitución. Figúrense ustedes que hoy hasta los Presidentillos Municipales tienen sus palacios-miniatura; los Jefes Políticos, no se diga; los Gobernadores se creen descendientes en línea recta de alguna Divinidad, y los de más arriba . . . esos se creen ni más ni menos que semidioses.

Los periodistas son amordazados.

El clero se engrandece.

Los americanos conquistan.

El dinero escasea en plena paz.

La adulación triunfa . . . ya no quiero seguir, porque no acabo en un año, ni me alcanza todo el papel de las Fábricas de San Rafael para decir lo que yo quiero, y tengo que ocupar a mis Secretarios en otras cosas.

Lo cierto es que al Padre de la Patria los ven ciertos mexicanos aduladores como un ser mitológico, y por eso no se acuerdan como debieran, por quemar incienso al Gral. Díaz, de que el día 21 de este mes, hace años que nació el verdadero Héroe de la Paz.]

While this sarcastic screed stops just short of personal attack on the president—blaming instead the Mexicans who treat him like a demigod—the comparison of Díaz and Juárez is deliberate—and damning to Díaz.

As was so with this editorial, unflattering comparisons most often surfaced in conjunction with the 1857 constitution, a document closely associated with the mid-nineteenth-century liberal "reform" movement and its greatest statesman, Benito Juárez. A 1909 *El Diablito Rojo* cover illustration, for example, vividly depicts the betrayal of Juárez's constitutional legacy by the Porfirian regime (see fig. 2.4).[21] The image features three male figures. On the lower left a ragged young man (*pueblo*) with no pants stands in front of a wooden desk clutching a tattered copy of the 1857 constitution. Behind the desk, at the center of the image, sits a well-dressed, bearded older man with a family resemblance to Díaz's *científico* advisers (some of whom appear in the paper's masthead); his eyes are covered by a blindfold that reads "justice"—an obvious play on classical representations of justice's impartiality. Most often, "blind justice" is depicted as a woman holding the scales of justice in one hand and a sword in the other, ready to weigh the offense and administer punishment without regard to influence, wealth, or social position. In this instance, however, the bearded man consigns the constitution to a bookshelf labeled "Museum of Antiquities" with an imperious gesture of his right hand while his left rests protectively on a sheaf of open documents with such damning titles as "circumstantial law" and "favoritism." In the image's upper right—the "location" of moral superiority—the ghost of Benito Juárez appears in a burst of glorious light; his left hand covers his eyes in disgust, and his right points accusingly at the bearded man's heinous act. The accompanying poem's first strophe explains that the ragged young man has gone from "one potentate to another," hoping to exchange the tattered book for some pants, only to be denied at every turn because he is already *pelado*—literally stripped of his clothing and figuratively stripped of his constitutional rights. The second strophe expresses Juárez's posthumous anger and sadness at the ignoble fate of his great work of liberal reform, with its constitutional guarantee of equality under the law.

Although directed at a broad range of contemporary targets—*caciquismo*, press censorship, religious privileges, Yankee encroachment, repression of strikes—most constitutional critiques made only oblique reference to President Díaz, preferring instead to remind authorities that "there is a Constitution that protects and favors all citizens, regardless of class or category."[22] Less discreet than most of his colleagues, *El Diablito Bromista*'s editor, Antonio P. de Escárcega, sometimes pushed the limits of accepted practice, a tendency that landed him in jail on occasion.[23] A 1904 cover features a bowing devil—Escárcega's editorial persona—who holds a placard labeled "1857" in his left hand and gestures with his right

FIG. 2.4 Artist/Author Unknown, "Al Museo de Antigüedades," *El Diablito Rojo*, February 8, 1909. Courtesy of the Benson Latin American Collection, University of Texas Libraries, The University of Texas at Austin.

FIG. 2.5 Artist/Author Unknown, "Al Sr. Presidente de la República Mexicana General Porfirio Díaz," *El Diablito Bromista*, February 7, 1904. Courtesy of the Benson Latin American Collection, University of Texas Libraries, The University of Texas at Austin.

to an open appeal addressed to "His Honor, the President of the Mexican Republic, General Porfirio Díaz" (see fig. 2.5).[24] The appeal calls the president's attention to "the unconstitutional attack on the rights of six workers from the 'La Colmena' Factory who were arbitrarily consigned to military service by the Political Boss (*Jéfe Político*) of Tlalnepantla" and ends with a sardonic comment: "Will justice be done? We hope so." Penny press editors resorted to these sorts of appeals on a regular basis, most often to alert national authorities to the abuse of workers by factory

FIG 2.6 José Guadalupe Posada, "Un matrimonio desafortunado," *El Diablito Bromista*, November 26, 1905. Courtesy of the Benson Latin American Collection, University of Texas Libraries, The University of Texas at Austin.

managers or local political bosses, but only on occasion did they address the president directly and only rarely with such obvious disrespect.

An *El Diablito Bromista* cover from November 1905 goes further still (see fig. 2.6).[25] Under the heading "an unfortunate marriage," the feature illustration presents before-and-after views of a marriage between Porfirio Díaz and a woman whose wedding dress identifies her as the "Constitution of 1857." In the "before" image, a tuxedoed Don Porfirio, shown in distinctive right profile, gallantly offers his arm to his beautiful, elegantly dressed, and stylishly coiffed young bride—a reflection of his earlier status as a liberal hero and constitutional champion.[26] In the "after" image, the couple appears disheveled and at odds: General Díaz, in shirtsleeves, striped uniform trousers, and riding boots, angrily wields his cavalry saber and clenches his fist; the bride, in a shredded gown and veil and with stooped posture, frizzy hair, hook nose, protruding ears, and spindly arms, cowers in fear. The tatters at her feet read "laws of reform," "individual guarantees," and "Article 7"—specific references to the constitutional precepts most often violated by the president and his minions.[27] By casting the constitution as a beautiful young woman and Porfirio Díaz as a wife beater, the image renders the abuse of power at the heart of the regime's constitutional violations in the most graphic possible way: a violent beating that the sword (as a phallic symbol of the first order) and ripped dress (as a symbol of a woman's ruined reputation) suggest is also a rape.[28] Although, as with *El Diablito Rojo*'s satanic rant, frankness of this kind was rare, it gives yet another unadulterated peek at an otherwise hidden transcript—aimed this time at Díaz himself—a transcript reflected and nurtured in the penny press (and elsewhere) by countless subtle innuendos and furtive winks but nevertheless threatening at the propitious moment to throw off its disguises and openly avenge Porfirian affronts to the national honor.

Indeed, the public humiliation implicit in this symbolic rape of the constitution did nothing to diminish the ardor of Escárcega, his penny press colleagues, and other true believers. A 1910 *El Diablito Rojo calavera* addressed to "The Constitution of 1857" noted reassuringly that no matter how much "they sweat, fret, and push they can't kill you . . . they [can only] squeeze you or pull out some of your pages!"[29] But even if "his" constitution was beyond reproach, the same could not be said of the great Benito Juárez himself. At least, not without some timely help from an unlikely source.

The Belated Martyrdom of Benito Juárez

Despite his remarkable popularity, Juárez's preeminent position in the working-class roster of hero-martyrs was troubled by the historical record: *El Benemérito* had died of a heart attack in the early days of his fourth presidential term—just as Díaz's short-lived revolt against Juárez's "unconstitutional" reelection was winding down. While death from coronary complications at the relatively advanced age of sixty-six might seem a fitting end for one of Mexico's few civilian presidents—especially one who steadfastly declined military honors and titles—it was hardly the glorious act of self-sacrifice expected of national hero-martyrs.

Into this ideological breech stepped Francisco Bulnes, prominent *científico* and professional polemicist. His highly publicized attacks on Juárez's legacy would ironically secure (at least in the eyes of regime opponents) *El Benemérito*'s position in the national pantheon.[30] Already a court favorite, Bulnes had further ingratiated himself with the "good dictator" at the 1903 National Liberal Union convention by nominating Díaz for an unprecedented sixth presidential term.[31] His provocative nomination speech took great pains to distinguish the current regime from its liberal predecessors, condemning radical "Jacobins," like Juárez, for having destabilized the country in their ill-advised attempts to impose artificial and inappropriate notions of governance on an unready and unreceptive nation.[32] In two subsequent books, *El verdadero Juárez y la verdad sobre la intervención y el imperio* (The True Juárez and the Truth about the Intervention and the Empire, 1904) and *Juárez y las revoluciones de Ayutla y de reforma* (Juárez and the Revolutions of Ayutla and of the Reform, 1905), Bulnes elaborated and publicized these heretical ideas, alleging that Juárez was not a true liberal and stalwart statesman but a political opportunist and mediocre leader with authoritarian tendencies, who had at one point contemplated exchanging Mexican territory for U.S. support in the war against Maximilian.[33] In the face of Juárez's many failings—which Bulnes attributed in no small part to Indian blood—*El Benemérito*'s veneration as the personification of liberal ideals made no sense. "Juárez is certainly an idol of liberal veneration," he argued,

> but a false idol, formed piece by piece from political subterfuges and the stuff of legend extracted from the volcanoes of our illusions, always lit, never to illuminate us but to calcify our spirit. The mold into which we have poured the figure of Juárez is the immense vacuum of our ignorance and consequently the sculpture has turned out to be colossal. Juárez is on the road to being a lay Zapotec Buddha, imposing and marvelous, an emanation of the intellectual chaos, ever shrouded by lack of critical judgment on the part of our enlightened classes, by the exuberant vanity of our masses, by the demands of our residual Catholicism, which always seeks an image, a cult, a grounding for the social emotion unleashed by religious sentiment.[34]

Given Juárez's stature as a popular liberal icon and the slanderous nature of Bulnes's attack, it is hardly surprising that the 1904 publication of *El verdadero Juárez*—on the eve of Independence Day—triggered a contentious debate in Mexican political circles and in the Mexican press.[35] Factions within the regime, the liberal opposition, and conservatives all entered the fray. With the exception of the conservative Catholic press, which had little use for Bulnes but agreed with his assessment of Juárez, most commentators took issue with some or all aspects of his critique. This included regime proponents such as the subsidized mass daily *El Imparcial*, prominent *científico* intellectuals like Justo Sierra and Genaro García, liberal *letrados* like Hilarión Frías y Sota (who had opposed Juárez's reelection efforts), foreign minister Ignacio Mariscal, and even the president's nephew, Felix Díaz, newly appointed Mexico City Police Chief and head of El Comité Patriótico Liberal (Patriotic Liberal Committee). Regime opponents—who ranged from supporters of the former presidential favorite and ex-minister of war Bernardo Reyes to longtime critics in the opposition press—seized on the Bulnes polemic as a golden opportunity to undermine the legitimacy of the regime and its adherents, especially the president's *científico* advisers (which included Bulnes).[36] Writing from exile in San Antonio, Texas, the editors of the opposition journal *Regeneración* blamed Bulnes's attacks on the "Great Democrat" squarely on the Porfirian regime and its leader. "It's not just the product of a demented mind and corrupted spirit;" they insisted: "It is the product of tyranny; it is the flowering of abjection; it is an abortion of Porfirian despotism, which after having insulted the rights and persons of Mexicans, insults their affections, their venerations, their cheers."[37] Not content with blaming Porfirian despotism in general, they attributed "the libel of Francisco Bulnes" directly to a personal vendetta on the part of Porfirio Díaz himself:

> The autocrat who always hated Juárez; who rebelled against him and was vanquished; who hoped to rise up and was humiliated; who harbored in his soul the bile of his resentments and his defeats, couldn't suffer that the man he detested was so enthusiastically glorified, nor could he sit by as national gratitude heaped the brow of the immortal Benemérito with laurels, while he, Díaz, could only count on the homages bought with gold and with the acclamations of well-compensated lackeys.[38]

Far from the reach of Porfirian police (although not its secret agents), *Regeneración* editors could afford to speak their mind more openly than their Mexico City counterparts, but it seems likely that many regime opponents, especially opposition journalists, shared their view that the president's minions (and very possibly the president himself) had encouraged Bulnes's assault on Juárez's reputation.

While not as openly critical of the president as *Regeneración*, the satiric penny press response was nonetheless vitriolic. *La Guacamaya*'s featured illustration for September 15, 1904, "El Verdadero Bulnes y 'El

FIG. 2.7 Artist/Author Unknown, "El verdadero Bulnes," *La Guacamaya*, September 15, 1904. Courtesy of the Benson Latin American Collection, University of Texas Libraries, The University of Texas at Austin.

Verdadero Juárez,'" replaced the paper's traditional Independence Day cover portrait of Hidalgo with the image of an enraged mob of working-class men and women who chase after a fleeing Bulnes—dressed in suit and top hat, book tucked under his right arm—as they shout insults and pelt him with cobblestones (see fig. 2.7).[39] As in the "En Honor de Juárez" illustration examined earlier, the hero's famous statue occupies the upper right-hand corner of the image; this time, however, the prone hero has turned on his side and points his right arm accusingly at his detractor as mother Mexico covers her face in shame after the fashion of Hidalgo in "¡VIVA la LIBERTAD!" The editorial comment below the image advises readers that men like "the denigrator Francisco Bulnes . . . are unworthy of walking on National soil, [and] we should pierce [nail] them with the hurtful darts of our scorn and damnation."[40] Nor was the popular response confined to literary rebuttals. A letter to the editor of *La Palanca* alerted him to a "public demonstration" by workers from the factories of Río

LIMPIA DE CIUDAD

Arre, mula, arre mula,	Pero le apesta muy feo	Otro que sea mas conejo
Cansada de caminar,	Su inmunda literatura.	Por que yo aunque probecito
Ya muy poquito te falta	Para el Norte me los llevo	No pelo de esas cotorras
Para llevarte á cenar.	Y ahi en la frontera dejo	A ya á ver si el tio Samuel
Eléctrico me parece	Bestia y carro con basura	Se encarga de darle sopas
Este carro de basura	Y que venga de carrero	A esta malota furriel.

FIG. 2.8 Artist/Author Unknown, "Limpia de ciudad," *La Guacamaya*, September 29, 1904. Courtesy of the Benson Latin American Collection, University of Texas Libraries, The University of Texas at Austin.

Blanco, Nogales, and Santa Rosa de Necoxtla to "protest against the infamous libel, written in an evil hour, by the Deputy Don Francisco Bulnes."[41]

The Bulnes-as-traitor trope was a favorite. In the September 11 issue, *El Diablito Bromista*'s editor referred to him as "the future Yankee Bulnes."[42] A later *La Guacamaya* cover illustration, "Limpia de Ciudad" (City Cleanup), depicts Bulnes as a swaybacked mule hitched to a trash wagon (see fig. 2.8).[43] The wagon, filled with copies of *El verdadero Juárez*, is driven by a whip-wielding muleskinner identified as the *pueblo* (people). The welcoming figure of Uncle Sam looms on the horizon—the upper right-hand corner of the image standing in for *la frontera* (the border). In the poem that follows, the muleskinner tells the reader that

> [. . .] Este carro de basura
> Pero le apesta muy feo
> Su inmunda literatura.

Para el Norte me los llevo
Y ahí en la frontera dejo
Bestia y carro con basura [...]
Aya á ver si el tío Samuel
Se encarga de darles sopas
A esta malota furriel.

🌟

[...] This trash wagon
Well it smells really ugly
From its filthy literature.
So I'm taking them North
And leaving them there on the frontier
Beast and trash wagon [...]
There to see if Uncle Sam
Takes charge of feeding [giving soup to]
This despicable scoundrel.]

Over two months later, a *La Guacamaya* contributor was still suggesting to "Pancho Bulnes" that "you pack your book in a sack and go off to
New York with Uncle Sam."[44] The editor of *El Diablito Bromista* looked
improbably to Mexico's other frontier. "They say that Bulnes is Guatemalan," he noted, "and if that's true we should tell him no, don't berate [our
heroes], please go berate your own motherland."[45] On the surface, connecting Bulnes's anti-Juárez polemic with foreign interests seems a bit off
since the stakes were so decidedly Mexican and concerned the United
States and Guatemala not at all. The connections begin to make sense,
however, once we consider the symbolic significance of the two countries
in the working-class imaginary.

For the penny press and its public, Bulnes and other *científicos* were
the driving force behind the Díaz administration's unseemly preference
for American capital at the expense of Mexican interests. Grievances
on this score were many, but the regime's continued tolerance of wage
discrimination against Mexicans employed by American-run companies was especially galling to workers and their advocates. "To what does
[Yankee investment in Mexico] come?" an *El Diablito Bromista* editorial
asked; "to take charge slowly but surely of the best businesses, establish

more factories, and further reduce salaries in order to dominate us more easily."[46] By extension, they associated any and all *científico* malfeasance, in this instance Bulnes's attack on Juárez, with selling out to a predatory Uncle Sam.

Although much less common than anti-U.S. sentiments, editorial complaints about Guatemala appeared from time to time in most penny presses. Because the country was less powerful and less developed than Mexico, the Guatemalan connection was strictly a political critique, with the rule of presidential strongman Manuel Estrada Cabrera standing in for the despotism and corruption of an ancien régime untouched by modern liberal ideals. For example, the author of the *La Guacamaya* poem "Guate . . . mala" asserts that "it touches and exasperates the universe / the expectant and resigned attitude / of such an esteemed Nation / [a nation] that tolerates the government of Cabrera."[47] The poem itself is a more or less respectful critique of Guatemala's lamentable political situation. However, the ellipses in the title, in addition to highlighting the "bad" (*mala*) in Guatemala, produce the suggestive *albur* "cuate mala," which translates loosely as "bad buddy" or "bad ball [testicle]." Both possibilities hint at a close friend turned bad. In a similar spirit, *El Diablito Bromista*'s editor portrays Bulnes's polemic as a surreptitious attempt to undermine the strong liberal heritage that distinguished Mexico, whatever the authoritarian tendencies of its current government, from a truly benighted country like Guatemala. In the face of such betrayal, exile seemed the best solution. As a poet-contributor to *La Guacamaya* put it, "the one who intends [to insult Juárez] is a scoundrel and ought to quit the homeland."[48]

Along with stigmatizing Bulnes as a *científico* sellout and political reactionary, penny press editors sought to portray him as the quintessential *roto*—the sycophantic hypocrite who would serve as model for subsequent stereotypical representations, like the toasting gentlemen in "En Honor de Juárez." To support this accusation, they had only to turn to Bulnes's published recollections: an 1897 article for *El Mundo*, a prominent government-subsidized newspaper, in which he publicly confessed and then repented his earlier sins against President Díaz. As a journalist for the middle-class opposition newspaper *La Linterna*—which he described in his later confession as "a horribly trashy newspaper, defamatory, and perhaps slanderous"—around the time of the 1876 coup d'état that brought Díaz to power for the first time, Bulnes had viciously criticized "the current president, his friends, his Generals, his Magistrates, [...] everyone." As punishment for this "slanderous" act, he was beaten, stoned, shot at, and nearly strangled by Díaz supporters. Twenty years later, he willingly admitted that "all those that attacked me were right: if they had killed me, they would have done a good thing."[49] To drive home the point about Bulnes's inconstancy, El Diablito Bromista's editor also included a particularly obsequious passage from a recent speech in which he had praised Díaz as "the man of the future, man of peace, our glory, our idol!"[50] For penny press editors, both the initial attack on Díaz and the subsequent repentance stank of opportunism: "that puppet that moves by hidden hands, despite his talent and his clever [filigreed] pen, is nothing more than a cynic and a coward, who in his weakness and lack of civility, insults the dead and licks the feet of the living."[51] Or in the more colloquial terms of the anti-Bulnes poem that followed this editorial: "He that is born in a sheepskin ends up stinking of goat!"[52]

The stinking sheepskin in the popular saying and the reeking trash wagon from the "Limpia de Ciudad" illustration engage a less refined trope, Bulnes-as-filth, which adds a strong dose of visceral revulsion (or abjection) to the traitorous act.[53] "Bulnes has sunk into the mud, stirred in with others of his ilk" remarked La Guacamaya's editor in the caption to "El Verdadero Bulnes."[54] Contributors to the "Limpia de Ciudad" issue elaborated further: for one poet, Bulnes was "a cowardly reptile lashing around in the filthy cesspools of the swamp"; for another, "the dirtiest, pettiest reptile [...] of the mud hole, of the cesspool, of the garbage heap."[55] The September 11 cover illustration for the less well known La Palanca was even more explicit: the image depicts an angry blacksmith booting a surprised Bulnes into a smelly toilet surrounded by the torn pages of El verdadero Juárez, intended no doubt to be used as toilet paper (see fig. 2.9).[56] The accompanying editorial insists that "only a deranged or malevolent brain is capable of aborting such false concepts [producing such abortions]"—a particularly graphic combination of abject images given the common association of public latrines with urine, excrement, and aborted fetuses.[57]

As in so much of Mexican popular culture, there was also the inevitable connection between abjection and death. True to form, the 1904 Day of the Dead editions of El Diablito Bromista and La Guacamaya include

FIG. 2.9 Artist/Author Unknown, "BULNES—Su entrada triunfal al país de la Fama," *La Palanca*, September 11, 1904. Courtesy of the Benson Latin American Collection, University of Texas Libraries, The University of Texas at Austin.

calaveras (literally, "skulls")—short illustrated satirical poems mocking the rich, famous, powerful, or familiar by reminding them of the futility of all human achievement—directed at Bulnes.[58] Under the figure of a dancing skeleton, *La Guacamaya*'s *calavera* jeers that "in the end, caught up in his haughty disdain, death laid him low, and on his tombstone we read 'here hides a traitor.'"[59] As late as 1909, *El Diablito Bromista* was still at it, with a caricature of a bucktoothed Bulnes on the run and a *calavera* that read: "In punishment for the audacity of bruising [making gold and blue] the one who gave us democracy, they gave him a seat in Congress! . . . There he died in disgrace!"[60]

Anticlerical tendencies may have discouraged penny press editors themselves from exploiting yet another popular trope, Bulnes-as-Judas. Their contributors, less doctrinaire, made the obvious religious connection for them. Borrowing the form of a traditional Catholic prayer of praise, the poet of "Ave, Juárez" (Hail, Juárez) compared Bulnes to infamous traitors from antiquity, Brutus and Judas, and suggested that the "reptile" be condemned to wander eternally like the "dishonored Jew" or that he hang himself from a "foreign tree," as Judas had done.[61] Another contributor manipulated poetic form to reinforce the link between Bulnes and Judas:

En verdad eres muy prisco
   Francisco
Que á un grande hombre impugnes
   Bulnes
Con la sotana te escudas
   Judas
Solo las almas desnudas
de amor a los patrios lares
Puedan insultar á Juárez
Francisco Bulnes y Judas.[62]

[In truth you are quite a peach
   Francisco
To impugn a great man
   Bulnes
You hide behind your cassock
   Judas
Only souls devoid
of love for the homeland
Are capable of insulting Juárez
Francisco Bulnes y Judas.]

The ideological effect of all this Bulnes bashing was to complete the secular sanctification of Juárez. Before the controversy, Juárez had been a liberal hero of the first rank. But despite many sacrifices for the nation, he still lacked the martyr's crown—a trait he shared with liberal saint-in-waiting Porfirio Díaz. After his well-publicized literary crucifixion by the *roto* Bulnes, however, Juárez could ascend to his rightful place in the Mexican pantheon of hero-martyrs alongside Cuauhtémoc, Hidalgo, Morelos, and the *Niños Héroes*—and to his rightful place in the liberal trinity as the sacrificed son (of the "Holy Spirit" Cuauhtémoc and the "Father" Hidalgo)—who had died to redeem a nation's sins. Sanctification complete, Juárez became an even more potent weapon in popular liberalism's ideological battle against the Porfirian regime. In the hearts and minds of penny press editors and their public, the greatest of Mexico's hero-martyrs stood ready to do battle with the great pretender and his *científico* minions for the national soul.

Street Talk

Along with the sanctification of Juárez, the penny press response to the Bulnes controversy reveals other ideological effects more specific to the working class. That response, provenance aside, was not especially different from the indignation and scorn that middle-class liberal opposition journalists heaped on Bulnes and *El verdadero Juárez*. What set the penny press counteroffensive apart was its treatment of the Bulnes scandal in the "street talk" columns. Appearing under different rubrics— "Contesta callejera" [street talk], "Desde la estaca" [from the stake], "Entre valedores" [between buddies], "Entre cotorras" [between gossips]—these columns were a regular feature in all of the major penny press newspapers. They were clearly one of the keys to the remarkable success of long-running papers like *La Guacamaya*, *El Diablito Bromista*, and *El Diablito Rojo*. *La Palanca* and similar penny press hopefuls that failed to include street talk columns or refused on principal to resort to the popular vernacular because it demeaned workers rarely lasted more than a season or two.[63]

The street talk formula was invariable: an informal exchange between two lower-class acquaintances that happen to run into each other on the street as they're going about their daily business. Most often the acquaintances are two men, sometimes two women, on rare occasions a man and a woman. To lend verisimilitude to these casual encounters, penny press editors went to great lengths to reproduce the colorful vocabulary, fractured syntax, subtle inflections, raucous rhythms, and intricate wordplay that characterized the everyday speech of Mexico City's working class. The street talk columns thus gave voice to the concerns of the capital's working poor in a language that mimicked—and through mimicry validated—their own. More than any masthead declaration, it was this gesture of linguistic inclusion and solidarity, undertaken in the mocking spirit of popular speech, which marked the penny press as the true "organ of the working class."[64]

The following commentary on the Bulnes controversy from *La Guacamaya*'s "Desde la estaca" column for September 15, 1904, conveys some sense of the editor's considerable skill at manipulating popular speech in order to constitute a working-class public that he appears to address (as already constituted):

—¡Mexicanos al grito de Guerra!

—¿Pero que te asucede [ha sucedido] manís que vienes gociferando con mucha marcialidá?

—Pos nada manario, se la vengo mentando al siñor del diente fino. Sino que como vitoquié [ví] al choco [policía] dije, no me vaya á cargar por inmoral y por eso comienzo á cantar el Indio [Himno] Nacional.

—Oye, oye valedor: corrémela más despacio ¿quien es ese siñor del diente fino?

—Pues es un siñor D. Pancho Rebusnes que sea puesto á escribir un librote, en que lecha [le echa] muchas fraudas y muchas cacayacas á nuestro sublime indito el Sr. Juárez.

—¡Ah, vaya! quedrás [querrás] decir Búlnes.

—Eso mero, pero como yo ya sabes, que no soy tan deslustrado [ilustrado] cómo tú, por eso le dije Rebusnes.

—¿Pos que? oye manario con la mesma letra se pone güey y burro, por eso mesmo te dije ansina: pero entre parientes, que dice en su librote tú que los has leído.

—Pos no te lo sabré dicir todo, porque el día que agarré el libro pa lerlo no pude, porque había dejado las antiparras que conocen las letras, pero al día siguiente que llevo las que saben ler y entonces si que nos pusimos á darle á ver manito que le decía ese jijo de la ... mala palabra, le decía muchas cosotas al gran reformador y entonces adigo [he dicho]: esto vá pa su lugar y que lo meto mano ¿á que no sabes en donde?

—¡Pos no manito!

—Pos al comú, depósito de la giña, pues dije hay [ahí] quedan al pelo el libro y su autor.

—¡A que al pelo estuvo eso valedor! pero oye déjate de Don Empacho Vulvo y acuéntame que sucedió con la jarana [muchacha] de la Soledad.[65]

[—Mexicans to the call of war!

—Hey, what's up with you my friend [literally, "peanut"] that you're running around vociferating with such martiality?

—Well it's nothing brother, I'm just going along thinking about that Mister Good Tooth. But when I spotted a cop I said to myself, he's not going to get me for immoral conduct, so I started singing the National Indian [Anthem].

—Hey, hey, comrade: run it past me a bit slower. Who is this Mister Good Tooth?

—Well he's one Mister Don Pancho Rebusnes who sees fit to write a nasty book in which he hurls a lot of slander and boastful bullshit at our sublime little Indian Señor Juárez.

—Oh, I get it! You mean Bulnes.

—That's right, but you know me, I'm not as tarnished [enlightened] as you, that's why I said Rebusnes.

—Why shouldn't you? Listen, buddy, with the same word you get guy and donkey, that's why I asked about it: but between friends [among family], what does he say in his nasty book?—since you've read it.

—Well I can't tell you everything, because the day I got hold of the book to read it I couldn't, because I had left behind the glasses that know the letters, but the next day I took the ones that know how to read and then, my friend, we really began to figure out what that son of a . . . bad word had to say, he said many ugly things about the great reformer [Juárez] and then I say: this is going where it belongs and that's where I'm going to put it brother. Bet you don't know in where?

—No clue brother!

—Straight into the crapper, where shit goes, because I said "that's right where this book and its author belong."

—That is right where it belongs, my friend! But hey, let's forget about Don Empacho Vulvo and you tell me what happened with the girl from the Soledad.]

The basic message in this excerpt—*El verdadero Juárez* is shit and so is its author—deploys less (apparently) polished and much wittier versions of two tropes mentioned earlier: Bulnes-as-traitor and Bulnes-as-filth.[66] In this instance, however, the author abandons the clichéd images of high poetic abjection—reptile, serpent, swamp, cesspools, mud—for a more improvisatory, "vulgar" style grounded in popular speech.

The opening line from the Mexican national anthem invokes a familiar image: the working-class man as enthusiastic patriot ready to burst into patriotic song at the slightest provocation (in this case the approach of a policeman). The tone is reminiscent of the celebrants in "¡VIVA la LIBERTAD!," and indeed the subsequent attack on the *roto* Bulnes shows that that image's binary opposition, patriotic workers versus apathetic bourgeoisie, is present in this text as well. There are, however, important differences. In the earlier illustration, the artist places the public outside the image so that its members can observe the two scenes, make the comparison, and draw the unavoidable conclusion. In the above excerpt, however, the author invites his public into a casual *and* intimate conversation between two men on the street—a chat between friends or, as one of them puts it, "among family."

The text marks this casual intimacy in several ways. The most obvious is the familiar form of address—*tú* for "you" singular in Spanish—used most often among close friends and family (and in talking down to social inferiors).[67] Playful permutations of *hermano* (brother)—*manís, manario, manito, mano*—along with the repeated use of *valedor* (comrade, buddy) further emphasize the familiarity or closeness of the two men. So does the closing query about a possible love interest ("tell me what happened with the girl from la Soledad") and the peculiar mix of open vulgarity ("Don Empacho Vulvo") and feigned fastidiousness ("that son of a . . . bad word") that so often characterize banter among friends.

Less obvious—as an inclusive linguistic strategy—is the writer's appropriation of the inflections, rhythms, and vocabulary of popular speech. The intimacy markers noted in the previous paragraph represent the closeness of the two men for the readers. This strategy draws the reader in— but only to the edge of the conversation, as casual listeners, not intrusive or threatening enough to stifle the dialogue (as a policeman or higher status person might) but not actively participating in it either. Implicit in the text is an affective bond between interlocutors and readers, a mutual recognition that allows for the open articulation of an otherwise "hidden transcript" even in the presence of apparent strangers.

Other linguistic games at play in the text—games not easily understood by "outsiders"—create a sense of solidarity through a shared lan-

guage that bridges this final gap between listener/onlooker and speaker/
participant. That shared language is decidedly working-class. Indeed, linguistic class markers distinguish the street talk columns from other regular
penny press features like political commentary, news, and poetry. The most
common of these class markers, all in evidence here, include (1) deliberate misspellings that mimic popular speech—*gociferando/vociferando*
(vociferating), *ler/leer* (reading), *lecha/le echa* (hurls at), *siñor/señor*; (2)
improper word substitution—*deslustrado/ilustrado* (tarnished/enlight-
ened), *hay/ahí* (there are/over there); (3) improper verb forms—*adigo/
he dicho* (have spoken), *asucede/ha sucedido* (has happened), *quedrás/
querrás* (you'll want); (4) fractured syntax—*¿a que no sabes en donde?*
(literally, bet you don't know in where?); (5) the use of pretentious or ar-
chaic words that sound more "important" or more colloquial than their
standard Spanish equivalents—*vitoquié/ví* (espied/saw), *gociferando/
gritando* (vociferating/shouting), *marcialidá* (in a warlike manner), *an-
sina/así* (thusly/so); (6) slang—*choco* (cop), *jarana* (girl, chick), *cacayacas* (bullshit); (7) popular idioms—*quedan al pelo* (fit to a T). Along
with marking for class, these linguistic tricks of the penny press trade
impart unique and compelling rhythms to the street talk columns, popular rhythms conducive to oral recitation and performance more than to
solitary reading. Like the front-page illustrations, this "folkloric" dimension greatly enhanced the penny press's appeal for all kinds of readers,
and greater appeal likely translated into increased sales and a broader
audience for the editor's political views.

While linguistic games were standard practice in street talk columns, a
few were tailored specifically for the column of the day. Here, for example, the improper word substitution *Indio Nacional* for *Himno Nacional*
(National Indian/National Anthem) draws attention to Juárez's indigenous roots in order to conflate hero and nation, a connection it secures
with the honorific title "our sublime little Indian Señor Juárez." Indianness in this context thus distinguishes authentic Mexican values from the
"foreign" ideas espoused by the despised *científicos*. Insulting nicknames
for the villain of the piece demonstrate a similar imaginative flair: "Siñor
del diente fino" (Mister Good Tooth) mocks Bulnes's protruding front
teeth and refined tastes, "D. Pancho Rebusnes" (The Distinguished
Mr. Frank Hee-Haw) plays off the Spanish verb *rebuznar* (to bray like a
donkey) in order to disparage both his buck teeth and his strident message,

and "Don Empacho Vulvo" (The Distinguished Mr. Impacted Vulva) adds a misogynistic touch with connotations of stillbirths and abortions, abject images often used to condemn failed "artistic" productions.[68] A particularly infamous villain like Bulnes might even enter the street talk lexicon as a symbol of slander and betrayal. In a subsequent "Desde la estaca" column, for example, Pitacio chides his friend who he thinks (or pretends to think) has insulted him with "listen here, buddy, don't go goading me with snide remarks or walking around talking bullshit, because you know that I'm me and I'm not at all like Bulnes."[69]

Although cast as the uneducated, improper speech of marginally literate *pelados*—a notion reinforced in the above dialogue by the joke about forgetting "the glasses that know the letters"—the street talk columns were in fact quite sophisticated even by the literary standards of the day.[70] Taken together with the superficially "crude" illustrations in the popular style that graced penny press front pages, these often brilliant literary constructs seem designed to draw together a diverse readership: *pelados* like the fictional Pitacio and Chema, who might find amusement and validation in their literary reflections; respectable workers, who could laugh at and with those just below them in the social hierarchy while still enjoying their own tenuous superiority; working-class (organic) intellectuals, who could appreciate the gesture of cultural solidarity; and literati, who could admire (from afar) the writers' wit, artistry, and bohemian street smarts. Whether or not readers responded in an "appropriate" way to these popular touches is impossible to determine. Regardless, the remarkable success of the penny press and the obvious popularity of the street talk columns make it a safe bet that editors did indeed succeed, by hook or by crook, in constituting their diverse readership as a "counterpublic" actively engaged in contesting "the exclusionary norms of the bourgeois public, [and] elaborating alternative styles of political behavior and alternative norms of public speech."[71] In other words, membership in the penny press counterpublic depended not on an individual's actual class status but on whether that person could appreciate the subtle art behind the feature illustrations and decipher the linguistic codes embedded in the street talk columns. To be a counterpublic member was to be "in on the joke."

Conclusion

The importance of nationalism—the quasi-religious cult of the modern nation-state and its secular saints—to working-class consciousness is indisputable. Certainly, for most Mexican working-class men during the first decade of the twentieth century, allegiances to nation and social class were slowly but surely being woven into a single (albeit densely textured and multicolored) tapestry—an always complex, sometimes contradictory, but nonetheless distinctive "structure of feeling" that bound workers and their advocates to each other and to an idealized vision of the *patria* as embodied in its great hero-martyrs Hidalgo and Juárez. As the first two chapters have shown, the editors of Mexico City's satiric penny press and their collaborators aspired to be the master weavers of this emerging working-class consciousness; their artistic vision, as popular as it was provocative, helped forge the affective bonds of a new national identity. Working-class men figured in this vision as the true patriots whose hard work and steadfast devotion would one day realize the nation's destiny and redeem the noble sacrifice of its immortal champions. From this perspective, "worker" and "patriot" were synonyms caught up in a tautology—all workers were patriots, all patriots were workers—that sought to reconfigure the conceptual borders of Mexico as an imagined community grounded in working-class values and bound together by working-class structures of feeling, even if the exact nature of those values and feelings were still open to debate.

Mexico City's satiric penny press thus provided a central site for the production and dissemination of popular liberalism's response to the foundational question that confronts every modern nation-state: "Who exactly are 'the people'?" For the adherents of popular liberalism—a group that included penny press editors, contributors, and readers—the answer was self-evident: "the working class." Arriving at that answer, however, required a thorough reworking of Mexican liberalism's bourgeois origins. In *Domination and the Arts of Resistance,* James C. Scott points out the righteous indignation that characterizes popular resistance (to domination). At the same time, he reminds us that "the anger born of a sense of betrayal implies an earlier faith."[72] It was this sense of betrayal and bitterness that drove popular liberalism's critique of the Porfirian regime throughout this period. The betrayed faith in this instance was *puro* liberalism with its intertwined and still unfulfilled promises of democratic participation and social equality. This explains the elaborate resignification of traditional liberal icons like Hidalgo and Juárez into working-class heroes and the quasi-religious insistence on tropes of betrayal and redemption that shaped that resignification. But popular liberalism did much more than pour old wine into new bottles, it produced a distinct ideological and discursive framework for working-class consciousness, something *puro* liberalism had done for the Mexican middle classes several decades earlier. On the surface, this new framework looked a lot like its predecessor with a proletarian twist, but the working-class structures of feeling that gave that framework its distinctive shape also transformed the "earlier faith" into something altogether different—a liberal populism as radical in its time as bourgeois liberalism had been in *its* heyday.

Discursive subversion of dominant ideologies is a time-honored tactic in the historic wars of position waged by the weak against the strong. In this instance, the reworking of Mexican liberalism, reflected in the penny press and elsewhere, grounded the concerns and complaints of oppressed workers in a particularly intense form of popular nationalism. Born of historic allegiances and practical necessities, this strategy enhanced the ability of oppositional discourse to challenge the official story (without drawing undue official attention) and thus facilitated its eventual emergence into the larger public sphere in the years following the Revolution. In other words, the painstaking resignification of liberal iconography allowed penny press editors and contributors (among others) to tap into deep-seated, albeit contested, political and ideological allegiances in order to constitute Mexican workers as a recognizable "counterpublic," capable of formulating and articulating "oppositional interpretations of their identities, interests, and needs" but nonetheless intensely loyal to the nation.[73] Moreover, the patriotic connection—as a political strategy that legitimized "oppositional interpretations" *and* deployed them to forge a deeply felt affective bond—enabled this newly constituted working-class counterpublic to make demands on governmental authorities and assert claims in the public sphere, including its "right" to be acknowledged as a public and to integrate popular liberalism into the official story or even supplant it. Such was the case in Porfirian Mexico with its fractured, competing liberalisms.

At the same time, Michael Warner alerts us that members of a counterpublic are "marked by their participation in this kind of discourse; ordinary people are presumed not to want to be mistaken for the kind of person who would participate in this kind of talk."[74] This marking or "setting apart" is essential to the construction and maintenance of group identity in the face of official apathy, disavowal, and repression. Aside from the rowdy celebrants in "¡VIVA la LIBERTAD!" (see ch. 1), these less savory aspects of working-class culture have not so far been much in evidence. But the formation of a working-class identity "set apart" from respectable bourgeois society was soon to take center stage in the more carnivalesque aspects of the penny press project.

CHAPTER 3

꽃鞭

THE APOTHEOSIS OF THE WORKING MAN

Working-Class Subjects

Chapters 1 and 2 showed how the Mexico City satiric penny press served as a central site for the development of a popular liberal version of Mexican history—an unofficial story that editors and their collaborators deployed in a literary "war of position" against the authoritarian regime of Porfirio Díaz. They showed, too, the powerful affective bonds between working-class readers and national hero-martyrs like Hidalgo and Juárez that penny press editors sought to forge in the process, bonds they hoped would reinforce workers' deep-seated loyalties to the Mexican liberal tradition, tie their interests to the nation, and legitimize their claims on the government. This chapter looks at penny press efforts to write working-class men into the national narrative as active participants whose humble but heroic contributions to nation building warranted their inclusion, not just as passive beneficiaries but as full-fledged rights-bearing citizens.

Penny press efforts at working-class redemption involved two related initiatives. The first initiative—the rehabilitation of working-class culture—sought to confer legitimacy on the vibrant popular vernacular of the Mexico City streets and to recast popular behaviors that the Porfirian bourgeoisie considered uncivilized or even dangerous as the patriotic exuberance of hardworking men. (We had a glimpse of this process at work in *La Guacamaya*'s "¡VIVA la LIBERTAD!")[1] The second initiative—the reeducation of working-class men—sought to construct a distinctly working-class "structure of feeling" around these new notions of popular culture and proletarian manhood. This cultural validation would empower workers on their own terms, allowing them to contest the three Ps of bourgeois political subjectivity—propriety, probity, property—built into classic liberal models of citizenship and used by bourgeois elites to justify the exclusion of *el pueblo inferior* from full participation in the nation's political life.[2]

Taken together, these two initiatives promised a radical transformation in the "conditions of regulatory power"—the social criteria that govern proper comportment and the institutional structures that enforce them—through which working-class men might emerge as viable political subjects.[3] In particular, this proposed remaking of the conditions of subjectivity envisioned fundamental changes in how workers thought of themselves as men and citizens. Indeed, penny press editors envisioned manhood and citizenship as the twin pillars of worker redemption, the double helix of a new working-class structure of feeling, grounded in the intimate recesses of selfhood and experienced as collective consciousness.

Working-Class Citizens

Effective citizenship for working-class men, however, required more than the emergence of a counterpublic constituted through shared structures of feeling and expressed in shared language. It also required public spaces, physical and symbolic, in which to rehearse new forms of working-class political subjectivity and from which to project that emergent class consciousness onto the larger Mexican society. In the final analysis, working-class citizenship required that workers be publicly acknowledged as legitimate political subjects. To that end, it needed working-class heroes, working-class festivals, and working-class monuments.

One promising avenue to effective working-class citizenship was voluntary military service, especially when it provided a public stage on which to perform, for themselves and for the *gente decente*, as patriotic citizens of the republic. In 1902, *La Guacamaya* devoted two covers and several columns to promoting the newly formed Second Reserve— brainchild of General Bernardo Reyes, one of the more progressive members of Díaz's inner circle.[4] The first cover depicts waves of workers (in

LA SEGUNDA RESERVA DEL EJERCITO NACIONAL.

Maniobras en La Vaquita.

LA CLASE OBRERA
Y LA
SEGUNDA RESERVA.

En las grandes fábricas, en los grandes talleres, en los centros de trabajo, desde los que regentean poderosas compañías, hasta

el humilde *clanchichol* de barrio, se ha visto al obrero, no como un ser útil á la sociedad, no como el factor importantísimo de esos centros de producción, no como el hombre que honradamente ofrece sus conocimientos, sus energías, su trabajo material á cambio de la justa retribución, sino como á la bestia de carga, como al escla-

vo que, tras ruda labor, se le arroja un mendrugo de pan, más que por retribución, por lástima.

Para muchos el obrero es el ser vicioso, que huye del taller los lúnes, que dilapida el pan de sus hijos en la taberna y esgrime el cuchillo por vaso más ó menos de pulque, nada más exacto: el grupo que se designa con el nombre

FIG. 3.1 José Guadalupe Posada/Author Unknown, "La Segunda Reserva del ejército nacional," *La Guacamaya*, August 18, 1902. Courtesy of the Benson Latin American Collection, University of Texas Libraries, The University of Texas at Austin.

civilian dress) drilling under the watchful eyes of regular soldiers and their officers with a crowd of admiring women looking on (see fig. 3.1).[5] A benevolent sun smiles down on the assembled throngs, flanked on the left by a cameo of Porfirio Díaz and on the right by one of Bernardo Reyes, both in dress uniform. Noting that many (presumably bourgeois) Mexicans hold the worker in low esteem, the accompanying article argues that patriotism has been his redemption: "For many, the worker is a depraved being, who spurns the workshop on Monday, who squanders his children's bread in the tavern, and bloodies his knife for a glass or two of pulque; nothing could be further from the truth [. . .] Today the worker goes to Juárez's tomb and leaves his humble offering; today the worker gives great proof of his civic pride by applying to the second reserve."[6]

The editor goes on to praise the reserve as "an extremely meritorious institution that seeks to make the citizen into a soldier, a dignified and honorable soldier who will know how to defend his beloved fatherland inch by inch, who will know how to die for his flag!"[7] Although technically correct—workers were already citizens in the legal/constitutional sense—the citizen-to-soldier formula works better in reverse (as the rest of the article implies): by becoming "dignified and honorable" soldiers capable of self-sacrifice for the nation, workingmen would become full-fledged citizens empowered to assert their rights in the public sphere. In the words of the Second Reserve anthem, published on *La Guacamaya*'s October 5 front page:

> Por nuestra enseña tricolor,
> Gloria debemos siempre disputar
> Y del guerrero Cuahtémoc,
> Su ejemplo hemos de imitar,
>
> Hidalgo, Juárez y otros más
> Desde la tumba donde están,
> Antes que esclavos nos dirán:
> Sucumban por la libertad.[8]

> [For our tricolor ensign,
> For glory we shall always strive
> And the warrior Cuauhtémoc,
> His example we must follow,
>
> Hidalgo, Juárez and the rest
> From the tomb where they lie,
> Before [rather than] becoming slaves, of us they'll say:
> They died for liberty.]

Grandiose sentiments like these, delivered in high patriotic style, demonstrated the importance of working-class sacrifice to fellow workers and to society in general. But to ensure that the message got through, editors supplemented them with "street talk," which provided a less pompous way to stoke workers' patriot fervor and address their potential concerns. In this instance, street talk supplied the requisite humor, wit, and sarcasm needed to balance out some of the more ridiculous aspects of the military experience. In the August 18 "Desde la estaca" column, for example, *La Guacamaya*'s editor has his stock *pelado* characters, Pitacio and Chema, discuss the merits of voluntary military service. The dialogue begins with

Pitacio loudly practicing his drills in the street: "One! Two! One! Two! Two! Forward, ar[ms] . . . Right face, Left face, Double time, ar[ms] . . . Line up on the right, Rest, ar[ms] . . . Port, ar[ms] . . . Present arrrr[ms]."[9] When Chema asks what he's doing, Pitacio explains that he has joined the Second Reserve in order to do his patriotic duty and because "well, you know us workers, we're not afraid of death on stilts or of cops on bicycles." When Chema makes excuses about not having joined himself— he's just lost four teeth in a fight over a woman and "without teeth you can't be a soldier"—Pitacio scornfully replies:

> Well what does the ace of spades have to do with the army reserves? Since they [the reserves] want men with chests on their hairs, I mean, hair on their chests, [men] who won't be chickens and who will know how to mix it up with the Yankees when they come to visit us, because at the end [of the training period] everyone gets a Mauser so we don't have to fight with our teeth, and because we are no longer living in the times of his serene highness [Santa Anna] when they had to bite the cartridges.[10]

The appeal to patriotism appears here as an in-your-face challenge to working-class manhood: Do you have hair on your chest? Are you chicken? Are you afraid of Yankees? Are you man enough to defend your country? The implication behind the challenge is that a worker like Chema might not respond to nobler sentiments like self-sacrifice, even if he could appreciate them in the great hero-martyrs Cuauhtémoc, Hidalgo, and Juárez. Upper-class Mexicans might assume that workers were willing to fight over trivial things like a woman or "a glass or two of pulque," but violent tendencies in workers' private lives didn't mean they were ready to lay down their life for their country. Pitacio's challenge to Chema suggests much the same thing but offers an opportunity for a patriotic alternative missing from the bourgeois stereotype. In other contexts, penny press editors often worried that years of oppression had made the working class too beaten down to fight. Either way, linking patriotism to manhood could only benefit workers and the nation. As properly gendered political subjects, worker-class men could be transformed in their own eyes and in the eyes of the *gente decente* (decent folk) into rights-bearing citizens.

In addition to challenging Chema's manhood, Pitacio also addresses long-standing worker concerns about military service. The dreaded *leva* (forced conscription) was one of the great banes of Mexican lower-class existence throughout the nineteenth and early twentieth centuries. Under the *leva*, unprotected men, almost always from the lower classes, were routinely rounded up by national and local authorities to fight in the period's many armed conflicts, which included everything from frontier protection to military insurrections, local uprisings, civil wars, and foreign invasions. To make matters worse, because the *leva* targeted vagrants and convicted criminals as well as the temporarily unemployed, workers rightly considered military service demeaning as well as discriminatory and dangerous. Thus Pitacio reassures Chema that joining the Second Reserve will not involve "fighting with our teeth"—a play on *mordidas*, "bites," the Mexican slang word for "bribes"—or "biting cartridges" for "his supreme highness" Antonio López de Santa Anna, a notorious abuser of forcibly conscripted cannon fodder in his many military campaigns.[11] In contrast to past practices, reserves would be properly trained, issued modern weapons (Mausers), and deployed only to defend Mexico against foreign aggressors, especially the United States.[12]

By dialogue's end, Pitacio has convinced Chema to join up. But in practice, the realities of soldiering for working-class men undermined penny press editors' optimistic efforts to link military service to responsible citizenship. Despite Pitacio's assurances, the Díaz regime continued to use the *leva* to supplement recruitment. As before, the burden of compulsory military service fell on lower-class men, their families, and their communities. Published four years after Díaz disbanded the Second Reserve, *La Guacamaya*'s featured illustration for April 11, 1907, "Obligatory Military Service," depicts a row of workers with shouldered guns, on one side of a city street, observing and being observed by two bourgeois gentlemen and their overdressed female companions, on the other (see fig. 3.2).[13] The poem-caption beneath the image complains that

Dentro de muy poco tiempo
verémos formar en fila
á todos nuestros obreros
cargando su carabina.

Y mientras que el pobre sirve
á la Patria tan querida

El Servicio Militar Obligatorio.

Dentro de muy poco tiempo
verémos formar en fila
á todos nuestros obrer s
cargando su carabina.

Y mientras que el pobre sirve
á la Patria tan querida,
vagará, aual de costumbre,
toda la ralea catrina.

FIG. 3.2 Artist/Author Unknown, "El servicio military obligatorio," *La Guacamaya*, April 11, 1907. Courtesy of the Benson Latin American Collection, University of Texas Libraries, The University of Texas at Austin.

vagará cual de costumbre,
toda la ralea catrina.

[In a very short time
we'll see forming lines
all our workers
carrying their carbines.

And while the poor man serves
the beloved fatherland
they will roam, idle as usual,
all the dandy breed.]

The image manipulates the active-left/passive-right iconographic convention of the horizontal axis to expose the shameful irony of armed manly patriots (on the passive right) going off to defend the homeland while privileged, effeminate men and their overdressed womenfolk (on the active left) continue to enjoy the capital city high life.[14] This ironic inversion is heightened by the poet's pointed use of the verb *vagar* (to wander) to describe the behavior of the *catrines*: the Spanish verb labels the upper-class men *vagos* (vagabonds, vagrants), whose upper-class status nevertheless protects them from military service, the likely fate of their lower-class counterparts. Such blatant inequalities rendered the notion of military service as an avenue to working-class citizenship less attractive than it might have appeared in the heady days of the Second Reserve. Voluntary service for civil defense against a future foreign aggressor was one thing; compulsory service in a national army used principally to put down strikes, suppress rural rebellions, and keep Mexico safe for Yankee capitalists was quite another. Nor was obligatory military service likely to elevate workers' status in the eyes of the Porfirian bourgeoisie.

If military service proved a troubled road to citizenship for working-class men, other possibilities for symbolic inclusion in the great national narrative remained. There was at least one precedent: independence-era hero *El Pípila*, the heroic miner who, according to legend, had led the final assault of Hidalgo's army on Spanish forces besieged in a well-fortified grain depository, the Alhóndiga de Granaditas, in Guanajuato. Still, urban workers had little in common with miners (other than the status of wage laborers), and the deed probably seemed too remote in time and place to resonate with the Mexico City working class. *El Pípila* does emerge from "the furious mob" (*la muchedumbre enfurecida*) brandishing a firebrand and bent on satisfying "his infinite yearnings" (*sus ansias infinitas*) in a *La Guacamaya* poem.[15] More often, however, editors and contributors ignored *El Pípila* despite his working-class origins and his close connection to the much-celebrated Hidalgo.

A more successful example of the symbolic inclusion of regular "folk" in the national imaginary was the cult of the *Niños Héroes*. The actual events are a bit murky but the official story runs something like this: On September 13, 1847, the final day of the bloody American assault on Mexico City, six teenage military school cadets charged with defending

Chapultepec Castle, site of the Colegio Militar (military high school) and the city's last fortified position, chose to die at their own hands rather than surrender to the enemy. One of them, Juan Escutia, wrapped himself in the Mexican flag and jumped from the castle ramparts to his death. The reputed suicide of these six courageous cadets, although they were not associated with the working class per se, represented a heroic collective act by "ordinary" people. Thus, while not exactly "unknown soldiers," the *Niños Héroes* served much the same symbolic function: opening up a space for "everyman" in the official story of the nation, a story otherwise dominated by great men like Hidalgo and Juárez.[16]

The ideological possibilities of this melodramatic, possibly apocryphal, and certainly much embellished story were not lost on liberal ideologues or Porfirian propagandists. In 1871, President Juárez decreed September 13 a national day of mourning. Porfirio Díaz added a few solemn ritual touches to the annual celebration and, in 1882, inaugurated a monument to the fallen cadets.[17] The *Niños Héroes* monument—like Juárez's tomb two years earlier—quickly became an important pilgrimage site and began receiving regular floral *ofrendas* (offerings), many of them no doubt from humble workers, like the campesino in the "En Honor de Juárez" illustration.[18] *Ofrendas* also took literary and musical form, with some of Mexico's best-known poets and musicians contributing to the glorification of "the martyred children of Chapultepec."[19]

As they had done with Juárez, penny press editors and contributors responded enthusiastically to this latest patriotic cult with poems and panegyrics of their own.[20] Also as before, they used the opportunity to promote the unpretentious patriotism of the working man. *La Araña*'s cover illustration for September 8, 1904, for example, shows a covetous Uncle Sam—depicted in classic anti-Semitic style with beady eyes and hooked nose—attempting to embrace a resistant female Mexico under the gaze of a shrouded sun, while American troops storm the battlements of Chapultepec Castle (see fig. 3.3). The editorial that accompanied the same image the following year in *La Guacamaya* accused the Yankees of having "sacrificed in a most bestial manner a handful of children who had just crossed the threshold of puberty."[21] To honor that sacrifice, the editors—self-identifying as "the lowliest representatives of the press"—pledged to make a "humble offering" on behalf of "a self-denying and

FIG. 3.3 José Guadalupe Posada/Author Unknown, "8 de Septiembre de 1847," *La Araña*, September 8, 1904. Courtesy of the Benson Latin American Collection, University of Texas Libraries, The University of Texas at Austin.

hard-working people who know how to respect, praise, and venerate those who discounting dangers, those who abandoning home, family, and livelihood, sacrifice their life on the altars of the homeland that oversaw their births, that gave them name and shelter."[22]

Attempts to link workingmen to the *Niños Héroes* persisted. The following year, *La Guacamaya* indignantly dismissed rumors in the American press that a tribute to the *Niños Héroes* planned by Mexican workers was nothing more than an anti-Yankee demonstration. To counter the suggestion that xenophobic sentiments rather than patriotic solidarity inspired workers' affections for the young martyrs, the cover illustration showed Uncle Sam surrounded by weapons and writing an angry letter while a pair of blacksmiths and a paper boy go peacefully about their work under an olive branch labeled "peace" wielded by the unlikely hand of Porfirio Díaz (see fig. 3.4).[23] Here, the artist emphasizes the active-passive/left-right horizontal axis (supplemented by other iconographic conventions) in order to contrast the bellicose bullying by the United States with Mexico's moral superiority, which is personified by its brave martyrs and

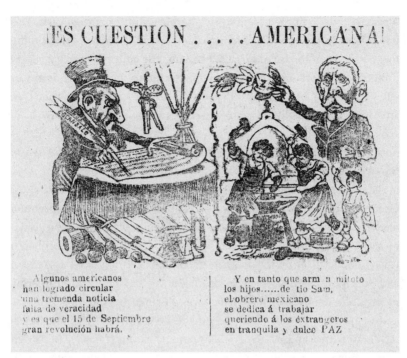

Algunos americanos	Y en tanto que arm n mitote
han logrado circular	los hijos......de tio Sam,
una tremenda noticia	el obrero mexicano
falta de veracidad	se dedica á trabajar
y es que el 15 de Septiembre	queriendo á los éxtrangeros
gran revolución habrá.	en tranquila y dulce PAZ

FIG. 3.4 José Guadalupe Posada/Author Unknown, "¡Es cuestión ... Americana!," *La Guacamaya*, September 6, 1906. Courtesy of the Benson Latin American Collection, University of Texas Libraries, The University of Texas at Austin.

peaceful, industrious working-class men.[24] "We pacific sons of a progressive nation," the editor explains, "rebutting alarmist claims, extend a hand to our neighbors [...] as a sign of brotherhood and [...] peace."[25] Here, too, as in the other image, Uncle Sam is portrayed as an archetypal Semitic villain, a figure linked in the imaginative language and iconography of Civic Catholicism—the prevailing public language in nineteenth- and early twentieth-century Mexico—to betrayal, blood sacrifice, and capitalist greed.[26]

The Apotheosis of the Mexican Worker

Teenage boys, like workingmen, may have been second-class citizens, but *La Guacamaya*'s efforts to link the heroism of cadets to the passivity of workers were a bit awkward. As the above examples imply, "peaceful," "industrious," "self-denying" workers might honor the heroism of other "ordinary" folk, but they seem to lack heroic impulses of their own. This last proposition was untenable, especially for *El Diablito Bromista*, the most militant of the three principal papers. The editor's response was to promote yet another patriotic event connected to the U.S.-Mexican war and the *Niños Héroes* celebration and close in time to Independence Day, an event that highlighted working-class heroism. The paper's August 16, 1903, issue included the following announcement: "*El Diablito*, which is no slacker when it comes to patriotism, invites you to come together on the twentieth of this month in the historic town of Churubusco at 10:30 in the morning, at which time a patriotic event organized by the Patriotic Group 'Gratitude' will take place in commemoration of the forgotten worker patriots who perished there, fighting vigorously against the gringo invasion."[27] On August 20, 1847, at the fiercely fought battle of Churubusco (then a small village on the outskirts of Mexico City), a quickly assembled and poorly supplied Mexican force fought the invading American army nearly to a standstill before being overwhelmed by superior numbers and weapons in vicious hand-to-hand combat. This battle, though better documented and nearly as melodramatic as the *Niños Héroes* story, also testified to inept military leadership and was thus less appealing to Porfirian propagandists (troubled enough by heroic failures like Hidalgo and Morelos) than the teenage cadets' heroic suicides.

For *El Diablito Bromista*, however, Churubusco represented the apotheosis of the Mexican worker. In a street talk–style "speech given by a comrade before the tomb of the heroes of Churubusco," the orator assures his "dear comrades of soft kidney [kind heart], shaved [affectionate] ladies of the barefoot brigade, plebes in general . . . [that] were it not for the fearless workers that met their deaths here defending the fatherland, our honor would have turned out like the tortoise's harp, rasping for lack of strings, and splitting from too much water."[28] Reiterated throughout the speech, the reference to national honor is notable because, as the speaker tells it, in an otherwise disgraceful war—most historians agree it was plagued by bickering, corrupt, and incompetent leaders—only the sacrifice of "fearless" workers had been able to redeem "our name as Mexicans." Ashamed perhaps of their ignominious predecessors, he continues, subsequent leaders have preferred to ignore Churubusco because "the gratitude of great men is nothing more than snores."[29]

In contrast, genuinely grateful workers knew how to express their thanks with respectful humility and boundless enthusiasm. "If I could shout out to my heart's content," he tells his audience, "I assure you all that I would overflow the banks of Pan's pool and have gas to spare."[30] To heighten the contrast, the speaker's garbled allusions to Greco-Roman mythology—the lyre (harp) fashioned by messenger god Hermes from a tortoise's shell and the pool beside which goat god Pan played his pipes—mimic and mock the "professional" orators whose pretentious rhetoric and presumed insincerity set the tone at most official patriotic events. Further, his pairing of the aristocratic lyre with dishonor, on one hand, and the plebian pipes with exuberant patriotism, on the other, recalls the famous mythological musical contest between Apollo (lyre) and Pan (pipes), which resulted in the jealous sun god transforming his rival into a goat-man—not exactly a *pelado* (literally, a peeled person) but like a *pelado* stigmatized by his "betters" as alcoholic, lascivious, and lazy.[31] Moreover, Pan is the god of "panic"—a role captured here in the image of an overflowing pool "with gas to spare"—yet another disturbing characteristic he shared with urban *pelados*, at least as reflected in the anxious eyes of the *gente decente*.[32] Whether marginally literate workers caught these classical allusions is debatable—it is not as unlikely as it might seem since less educated penny press readers (even illiterate listeners) might well have acquired some knowledge of classical mythology through popular theater and illustrated books, which often took stories from myths and traditional folk tales.[33] Regardless, better-educated members of the penny press counterpublic probably did understand them. And literate touches like these lent a subtle charm and intellectual intimacy to the street talk columns that compounded their subversive effects.

Not to be outdone, *La Guacamaya*'s editor featured the Churubusco celebration in successive "Desde la estaca" columns. In the first column—published just four days after the speech analyzed above—Pitacio informs Chema that he's been appointed by his fellow workers to take a wreath to Churubusco to honor "the memory of those brave comrades." Chema's candid excuse for failing to attend the August 20 celebration underscores its unofficial status: "there's no way I can go with you, because in the workshop where my job is, we have a worthless manager whose country is in his belly and if I'm absent, he fires me from my job and quarrels over my pay and then I won't have snot [food] to give my kids."[34] The following week's "Desde la estaca" column ends with Pitacio's brief memorial speech:

> Queridos conclapaches [compatriotas], jaños y jañas [caballeros y damas], al treparme en este lugar donde tantos siñores deslustrados [ilustrados] y más langüaricos [lingüisticos] que yo, an venido á endilgarles [divulgar] la palabra lo ago porque el contento me ase [hace] circo [círculo] a recordar que dentre nuestros parcias, los que le damos á la chamba salieron de sus talleres cambiando lerramienta [herramienta] por el fucil pa venir a enseñarles á los *gringos*, como saben morir los verdaderos Mexicanos, y por eso llego aquí á depocitar anteste monumento, esta corona de flores á nombre de mis parcias los peladitos como nos dicen los *rotos*. He dicho.[35]

❧

> [Dear accomplices [compatriots], guys and dolls, I climb up to this place where so many gentlemen, more tarnished [illustrious] and languorous [linguistic] than I, have come to divulge the word, because contentment has made a me a circus [circled around] to remind me that our compatriots, workers just like us, left their workshops, exchanging tools for rifles, to go and show the *gringos* how true Mexicans die, and for that reason I deposit before their monument this wreath of flowers in the name of my compatriots "los peladitos" as the *rotos* call us. I have spoken.]

Greek mythology aside, the linguistic strategies at work here are nearly identical to those in the *El Diablito Bromista* speech noted earlier. In that instance, the speaker put himself on equal footing with his presumably lower-class audience through the use of colloquialisms ("soft kidney" instead of the more conventional "kind heart"), improper word choice (*afeituosas*, "shaved," rather than *afectuosas*, "tender"), and by directly addressing the crowd as *plebes en general*. Pitacio's tactics are no different. The choice of *jaños y jañas*—gendered variants of *jaraneros*, "fun lovers"—translates the conventional greeting "ladies and gentlemen" into informal street vernacular with the same hint of playful insult evident in the *El Diablito Bromista* speech. The opening reference to accomplices—

conclapaches, "conclave of Apaches"—with its connotations of wild Indians, urban gangs, and whispered conspiracies, takes group solidarity
a step farther by linking the speaker and his listeners to an ongoing plot
against the established authority (*los rotos*) on the part of the socially
marginalized (*los peladitos*).[36]

Notable too is the sarcastic commentary on class differences implicit
in the verb *trepar* (to climb, creep up) used in connection with a *pelado*
who dares to speak up at a public function. The subversive effect of these
different class markers is compounded by other linguistic strategies, like
the apparently disingenuous substitution of *deslustrados* (tarnished) for
ilustrados (illustrious, enlightened); *langüaricos* (languorous) for *lingüis-
ticos* (linguistical); and *endilgar* for *divulgar* (to divulge)—strategies that
mirror in classic carnivalesque fashion the pomposity of elite orators.
Coming from the mouth of an uneducated and unauthorized speaker,
Pitacio's final "*he dicho*" (I have spoken), the conventional end for public
speeches, takes on satiric and even subversive overtones.[37] By definition,
pelados were deprived or shorn: of hair, clothes, money, education, de-
cency, and (for the men) manhood.[38] *Pelados* were thus categorically refused the right to speak publicly or, to be more precise, to speak to or on
behalf of a public. Understood in this context, Pitacio has not just "spoken"; he has publicly transgressed a centuries-old tradition of lower-class
deference and, in so doing, has slapped the collective face of the Porfirian
bourgeoisie—challenging its honor by declaring himself a social equal
across a previously unbridgeable chasm of class difference.[39]

These 1903 mock speeches predate "¡VIVA la LIBERTAD!," with its sleeping *catrines* and boisterous workers, by nearly four years, but the message is the same. Moreover, the annual Churubusco celebration, never
effectively co-opted by the regime, gave that much-repeated message a
symbolic place in the national narrative and a ritual space in which to
enact it. Street talk speeches, in turn, served to claim those spaces for
workers by mimicking and mocking the official discourses and oratorical
conventions that literally gave meaning to most patriotic rituals.

If annual reports and reader submissions from *El Diablito Bromista*
and *La Guacamaya* are any indication, workers responded enthusiastically to penny press efforts to promote Churubusco. *El Diablito Bromista*
took the lead with regular articles on the annual Churubusco celebration.

For example, a detailed accounting of the 1904 ceremony thanks the organizers and helpful local officials, laments the absence of some of the Mutualist societies, describes the festival (including an especially distinguished wreath from the operators of the municipal slaughterhouse), and concludes that "the people were greatly excited and with good reason, since this significant and patriotic festival had been previously relegated to oblivion."[40] These endorsements did not go unnoticed. *La Guacamaya*'s 1907 report notes the presence of several Mutualist societies, a military band, the poet Carlos Ezeta, a child speaker, one Ignacio López, and the "warmly applauded" editor-director of *El Diablito Bromista*, Antonio de P. Escárcega, along with an "infinity of workers and respectable families from the surrounding towns."[41] The editor adds that "the most complete order prevailed and demonstrated that [the Mexican] people, who have been judged illiterate and arrogant, with their newfound civilization and respect for authority, might serve as an example to many nations more cultured still than our own."[42] Readers would have understood this last comment as a deliberate critique of the extravagant and notoriously rowdy patriotic spectacles staged by the Porfirian regime—a rowdiness that penny press editors represented as patriotic enthusiasm in other contexts.

More telling even than annual reports were reader submissions in poetry and prose dedicated to the worker-heroes of Churubusco. Antonio Negrete, a regular contributor to *La Guacamaya*—here self-identified as an employee in the La Indianilla workshops—adopted a reverential tone in his prose paean to the fallen workers:

> You fought with superhuman valor against the invading hosts [. . .] you gave your lives on the altars of the Fatherland, out of love. Although victory did not choose to gird your brow with its laurels, the grateful Fatherland lovingly covers you with its cloak and softly sings celestial canticles that you might sleep tranquilly through the dream of immortality. Heroes of Churubusco! I salute you.[43]

Other contributors took a similar reverential tack. These lines from well-known working-class poet Fernando Celada—published in the same issue of *El Diablito Bromista* as the speech noted earlier and probably read aloud at that year's celebration—capture the popular spirit of Churubusco but without the satirical tone of the street talk columns:

Verás á la clase obrera
Que viste blusa de dril,
Luchar grandiosa y viril
Viendo al invasor de frente,
Y morir heróicamente
Embrazando su fusil! [44]

[You will see the working class
Dressed in shirts of drill,
Fighting with greatness and virility
Looking the invader in the eyes,
And dying heroically
Embracing his rifle!]

The combination of earnest sincerity and romantic sensibility that characterize Negrete's prose and Celada's poetry set the standard for subsequent homage to the worker-heroes of Churubusco. For example, the stirring poem "For the Dead," read by Carlos Ezeta at the 1907 celebration, elaborates on Negrete's point about victory denied by emphasizing the brave workers' transcendent heroism despite their betrayal at the hands of "Cains and Judases" in league with the American invaders:

No importa que el coloso haya triunfado
A merced de la infamia y los traidores;
Si en este heróico pueblo se ha enseñado,
Cómo se muere en México . . . Invasores.[45]

[No matter that the colossus won
Thanks to infamy and traitors;
If in this heroic town was shown,
How they die in Mexico . . . Invaders.]

As happened with the figure of Juárez in connection with the Bulnes controversy, the symbolic conflation of traitorous Mexican elites with biblical betrayers (including Jews in the New Testament) on the one hand and self-sacrificing workers with innocent victims on the other conferred moral authority on the working class and undermined the legitimacy of the privileged classes. In all these examples, the moral authority, derived from the sacrifices of the martyred workers of Churubusco and passed on to later generations of workers, more than compensated, on a symbolic level at least, for the greater political and economic power of the Porfirian bourgeoisie, compromised like its infamous predecessors by close ties to foreign interests—often caricatured as a Semitic Uncle Sam. A 1907 *El Diablito Bromista* editorial noted that "capital flees from armed conflicts, it doesn't recognize patriotic sentiments, it possesses no homeland: it is cosmopolitan." As a consequence, only the worker, despite being treated as "little more than a beast of burden [. . .] has undertaken and fulfilled the duties imposed by patriotism, abandoning interests and family to spring to the nation's defense."[46]

Under these circumstances, effective citizenship for working-class men was not just a hard-won right to respect and political representation based on past sacrifice but a historical imperative essential to the nation's future well-being. "Wake up! the future is yours," another *El Diablito Bromista* editorial urged workers, "yours is the powerful arm that our beloved Mexico counts on to fulfill its aspirations, you that have always shown courage and greatness in painful times, give us yet another demonstration of your heroism and grandeur, bring us through your work and energy, to the grand banquet of civilized Nations: to Liberty, to Progress, and to the free exercise of your indisputable Rights."[47] Behind this rousing call to arms, however, was a widespread concern among penny press editors that Mexican workers—ground down by years of fruitless self-sacrifice and cruel exploitation, "bound by the chains of apathy and the inability to live up to their duties as citizens"—might not be up to the task, might not be man enough to claim their rights.[48]

Of the Rights of Men

The various penny press strategies for rehabilitating working-class culture and reeducating workers examined thus far were relatively uncontroversial. To be sure, editors disagreed over an issue like the use of the popular vernacular in the street talk columns, but such disagreements tended to occur on the penny press fringes rather than among mainstays like *La Guacamaya*, *El Diablito Bromista*, and *El Diablito Rojo*, which recognized its potential for marking working-class belonging.[49] This strategic consensus fell apart, however, as the moralistic tendencies of *El Diablito Rojo* came up against the bohemian permissiveness of *La Guacamaya* over the nature of popular participation in patriotic celebrations. Of special concern to both papers were less "respectable" manifestations of working-class patriotism such as drinking in public and shouting xenophobic slogans. The disagreement over the meaning of those manifestations reflected very different visions of working-class manhood and set very different conditions for the emergence of working-class men as legitimate political subjects.

The papers agreed that active participation of workingmen was the sine qua non of any meaningful patriotic event. "For those that love this noblest and greatest of Nations," a 1908 *El Diablito Rojo* editorial advises, "rejoicing and pride gush from the pores of our souls when we see a public demonstration in which workers take the principal part and lend grandeur and character, honor and animation to a civic act."[50] Moreover, the paper openly attacked authorities whenever they attempted to marginalize working-class participation in patriotic celebrations. Another *El Diablito Rojo* cover, for example, shows Mother Mexico, backed by a host of national symbols (eagle, serpent, *nopal* cactus, and volcanoes), wagging her finger at the president himself, depicted as an abashed school boy. The following year, *El Diablito Rojo* ran the same illustration with a new poem that reminded the president that "festivals 'without the people' are nothing but fake tinsel and pointless songs" (see fig. 3.5).[51]

La Guacamaya was especially concerned that official efforts to manage patriotic events by flooding the capital's central district with police would discourage workers' participation.[52] After the 1907 Independence Day festivities, a contributor lamented the pathetic appearance of the "*quasi* beautiful Anáhuac [Mexico City], whose streets, invaded by hundreds of patriots fearfully launching into space the accustomed cry of *¡Viva México!* would soon be completely deserted as the police *rounded up* enthusiastic citizens under the usual excuse that they were 'scandalous drunks.' "[53] "Kicks were what they gave us," Pitacio explains to a friend in the street talk column, "and us being worthy [waltzing] Mexicans and not scandalous as the foreigners [estrangis] call us." To which his friend replies: "Look, Pitacio, it's better if we don't talk about it [. . .] if this is the way Independence Day is going to be, I'm going to throw myself

EL REGAÑO DE MAMA

Conmigo ya hiciste muchas
(A Diaz le dice la Patria
Entre abatida, llorosa,
Resentida y disgustada.)

Es preciso que te enmiendes
Porque no tomas la papa,
Si haces otra de las tuyas
Con la «Prensa Americana.»

¿Qué tienes que andar diciendo
Lo que harás hoy ó mañana
A gente que no le importan
Los asuntos de tu casa?

Lo que tú debes hacer
Es vivir con desconfianza,
Velar por mi California
Y escudarme con las armas

FIG. 3.5 José Guadalupe Posada/Author Unknown, "El regaño de mama," *El Diablito Rojo*, March 16, 1908. Courtesy of the Benson Latin American Collection, University of Texas Libraries, The University of Texas at Austin.

headfirst off my pallet onto the floor even if I crack open my thick skull [me rompa la maceta]."[54]

Other penny press editors took a similar tack, echoing the widely shared complaint that municipal authorities cared more about reassuring foreigners than embracing fellow Mexicans. *Don Cucufate*'s 1906 post–Independence Day issue, for example, noted that many folks had stayed home instead of attending the traditional ceremony but that "to offset the absence of the public, the city was *granted* a considerable increase in police, public and secret."[55] Those who attempted to celebrate the *Grito* despite the increased police presence often ended up in jail. As *Don Cucufate* explained it: "Since the people were prohibited from *acting* like *trumpets*, they dedicated themselves to playing clay *trumpets*; but this— the act of playing [their trumpets]—constituted an additional infraction, which earned many *trumpeters* a trip to the local police station, accused of disturbing the nocturnal silence and assaults on the auditory organs of passersby."[56] In order to highlight the absurdity of official attempts to ban harmless (albeit noisy and often indecent) patriotic exuberance, the explanation plays off the double meaning of *trompeta*, the Spanish word for a musical instrument and an idiomatic expression for a noisy drunk, and the connotations of its popular derivative "trompetillas," a catch-all term for a variety of "windy" noises, like farts and raspberries (jeering noises made with the tongue), generally considered crude and disrespectful.[57] The *albur* (wordplay) thus adds an earthy, even visceral tone to *Don Cucufate*'s disgust at the repression of traditional forms of popular merrymaking by Porfirian authorities—an overresponse that it found especially galling in the context of a patriotic celebration. In contrast, the editor notes that foreigners, after having carefully boarded up their shops, "circulated tranquilly through the streets and plazas without being bothered by anyone."[58]

As these examples suggest, even though penny press editors in general stressed the importance of popular participation in patriotic events, some editors were considerably more tolerant of traditional modes of popular celebration than others. For all its gushing over "demonstrations in which workers take the principal part," *El Diablito Rojo* supported official efforts to police patriotic events, even if that meant rounding up disorderly working-class men. "The worker is credulous, simple, generous, and patriotic," an editorial observed, "he goes wherever enthusiasm leads him or illusion deceives him."[59] This susceptibility to enthusiasms and illusions on the part of "the people" was especially apparent during a traditional patriotic festivity like the annual Independence Day celebration: "When the First Magistrate [president] appears in full military dress, the tricolor, trisected sash on his chest adorned with golden medals, waving the Mexican flag, [when he] glorifies the Patria, rings the liberty bell of Dolores, and gives the '*Grito* of Hidalgo,' symbol of heroism and victory, twenty thousand spectators tremble to the roar of the cannons, the myriads of multicolored lights, and the triumphal hymn of the tower, whose metallic tongues carry to the city's inhabitants huge waves of patriotic enthusiasm."[60]

Although admirable for its display of collective energy and nationalist pride, for *El Diablito Rojo* the orgasmic outburst of patriotic enthusiasm produced by the *Grito* had a serious downside, serving as it did to "excite popular passions that overflow into insults, intemperate curses [*mueras destempladas*], and other manifestations through which the mob [*plebe*] vents its inveterate hatred of the rich and powerful."[61] Thus, in *El Diablito Rojo*'s account of the 1909 Independence Day celebrations, "the people" are roused to fever pitch by a potent combination of official excitation (orchestrated by a hypermasculine patriarch and abetted by roaring cannons, flashing lights, and metallic tongues), their own patriotic zeal, and the rare opportunity to publicly articulate the hidden transcript of resentment against their oppressors. Then, in collective waves of postcoital exuberance, they "circulate throughout [the city] shouting like savages, throwing stones, [and then] spend the night in parks and public gardens, transforming those places into something like the bivouac of a savage horde."[62]

The erotic overtones evident in *El Diablito Rojo*'s description are no accident. In response to reoccurring revolutionary violence (beginning with the 1789 French Revolution), European social theorists Gustave Le Bon, Gabriel Tarde, and others developed influential theories about crowd psychology that represented crowds as irrational, suggestible, and easily aroused—traits closely linked in the criminological literature of the period (and in the male bourgeois imaginary in general) with dangerous female sexuality.[63] The "scientific politics" favored by the Porfirian *científicos*, including important government ministers like José Ives Limantour and Justo Sierra, ensured these theories wide distribution, especially among the more cosmopolitan members of the Mexican bourgeoisie. Moreover, the imprimatur of European social science provided Mexican elites with further motivation and justification for increased crowd control.[64] Fearful that popular disturbances might disrupt the 1910 centenary celebration, an event the Díaz administration hoped to use to showcase its modernization projects, especially for an international audience, some bourgeois commentators wanted authorities to suppress the *Grito* altogether. Despite its concerns about patriotic mobs, *El Diablito Rojo* wasn't quite ready to advocate such a drastic measure because "suppression [of the *Grito*] would be unpatriotic and inopportune."[65] Nevertheless, editors did advise that municipal officials continue to deploy their usual methods of social control: closing bars, putting policemen on the streets, enforcing severe penalties against "scandalous behavior," and augment-

FIG. 3.6 José Guadalupe Posada/Author Unknown, "¡15 de Septiembre!," *La Guacamaya*, September 20, 1906. Courtesy of the Benson Latin American Collection, University of Texas Libraries, The University of Texas at Austin.

ing security forces, along with other "more discreet and proven" tactics. Should these methods prove insufficient, they suggested holding the ceremony during the daytime, when the crowds would be easier to manage. *El Diablito Rojo*'s concerns about rowdy workers reveal a disjuncture between editorial expressions of working-class solidarity and unqualified defense of working-class culture and hint at divisions within the city's working classes between respectable and disreputable workers that mirrored elite attitudes toward the worthy and unworthy poor.

For *La Guacamaya*, in contrast, genuine patriotic expression was all about energetic, exuberant, disruptive, even "scandalous" public behavior—however much the collective enthusiasm of "the people" might trouble municipal authorities, foreign shopkeepers, or international capital. A 1906 post–Independence Day cover illustration by Posada, for example, shows a crowd of happy celebrants playing guitars and singing in front of the presidential palace as the liberty bell rings and fireworks explode overhead (see fig. 3.6). The poem below notes that "even though various

THE APOTHEOSIS OF THE WORKING MAN

—

FIG. 3.7 José Guadalupe Posada, "¡¡El Grito!!," *La Guacamaya*, October 4, 1906. Courtesy of the Benson Latin American Collection, University of Texas Libraries, The University of Texas at Austin.

gringos came out with the big news that on September 15 we would see a revolution; all the Mexican people in friendly reunion sing, enjoy, eat, and shout and watch the celebration."[66] In this instance, aside from the gentle poke at nervous gringos, neither the poem, with its "friendly reunion," nor the image, with its mixed crowd of Mexican men and women from all social classes, gives much cause for alarm.

The following week, however, *La Guacamaya* explicitly addressed some of the more contentious aspects of popular patriotic celebrations.[67] The cover illustration, also by Posada, interrupts two uniformed policemen in the act of confiscating the flags, bottles, and noisemakers of three men as they attempt to celebrate in the aftermath of "¡¡El Grito!!" (see fig. 3.7).[68] The three men are easily identified as working class by their floppy sombreros, work clothes (open shirt, serapes, white cotton trousers, etc.), and footwear (sandals, hobnail shoes, bare feet). At the first policeman's feet lies a pile of confiscated Mexican flags, liquor containers, and bugles. Ready to intervene on his behalf should the working-class celebrants attempt to resist stand three *rurales*, members of Díaz's "legendary" rural police force whose regular occupations included suppressing local insurrections, chasing bandits, and protecting foreign interests in the sometimes turbulent countryside.[69] The accompanying poem reads as follows:

En años pasados el pueblo podía
beber libremente, cantar y gritar,
marchar con banderas, tambores, cornetas
y toda la noche felices gozar,

Mas pasan los años y al paso que vamos
el quince [de septiembre] tendremos no más que rezar,
estar en la iglesia, marchar a casita
y al estar llorando, á Hidalgo implorar.

[In years past the people could
drink freely, sing and shout,
march with flags, drums, and horns
and enjoy themselves happily all night long,

But as the years pass and at the rate we're going
on the fifteenth [of September] we will be allowed only to pray,
to go to church, to run along home
and to cry and while crying, to Hidalgo implore.]

In this example, *La Guacamaya* openly defends public drunkenness and carousing as normal, even praiseworthy expressions of the working man's deeply felt love of country and his sincere appreciation of the hero-martyrs, like Hidalgo, who had sacrificed to bring the nation into being.

La Guacamaya's defense of scandalous celebration was a recurring theme. For example, in a 1903 post–Independence Day "Desde la estaca" column, Pitacio complains to Chema about the mayor's order to close the bars (*emborrachadurías*) at 2 p.m. and then describes in considerable detail how he and his "honey" (*jaña*) managed to smuggle liquor onto the

Zócalo to celebrate the *Grito*. In its aftermath, overcome with emotion and presumably tipsy as well, Pitacio clambers onto a bench to deliver a rambling speech in honor of Hidalgo—the "venerable elder with pains in his side" (*venerable anciano con Dolores en las Costillas*)—that ends with an attack on official efforts to curb patriotic enthusiasm:

> Well my fine friends this is the universery [anniversary] that we now celebrate, we celebrate the *Grito* of liberty, although only halfway, since this year it did not please the authorities that we should drink our libations [condiments] since that is only allowed in places the *rotos* gather like Chapultepec, the Clubs, the Casinos, setcetera, setcetera.[70]

> [Pos sí valedores ese es el universario [aniversario] que en este momento celebramos, celebramos el grito de la libertad onque á medias [medidas], pos en este año no le dió gana alutoridá [a la autoridad] de que bebieramos nuestro reconflais [reconflaites] pos eso solo esta permitido adonde se arrejuntan todos los rotos como en Chapultepec, en los Clús [Clubs], en los Casinos, cicetera cicetera.]

The *albur* "con Dolores en las Costillas" plays off the double meanings of *dolores* ("pains" or "sorrows" and the name of the town from which Hidalgo launched his revolt) and *costillas* ("ribs" and the second part of Hidalgo's surname, Hidalgo y Costilla) in order to convey both Pitacio's lack of civic education and his state of inebriation, the latter further evidenced by his telltale lisping of "*cicetara*" (et cetera). Neither flaw, however, detracts in the least from the sincerity of his patriotic sentiments. His complaints about the double standard at work in official efforts to repress popular festivities downtown while permitting middle-class celebrants in less central locations to drink freely imply that the deeply felt, if crudely expressed and alcoholically enflamed, patriotic sentiments of uneducated workers ought to carry more weight with "the authorities" than the frivolous pursuits of the better-educated (and better-spoken) bourgeoisie.

In the same vein, a 1904 post–Independence Day *La Guacamaya* editorial denounced police for confiscating and breaking the empty bottles of poor workers, thereby depriving them of their ten- to twelve-cent deposits, while at the same time ignoring an "agent of the public order in an advanced state of drunkenness who created a scandal . . . threatening with

FIG. 3.8 Artist/Author Unknown, "Preparativos para el Grito," *La Guacamaya*, September 5, 1907. Courtesy of the Benson Latin American Collection, University of Texas Libraries, The University of Texas at Austin.

pistol in hand his companions and anyone else who had the misfortune of passing by."[71] Editors added disingenuously that "we don't defend the hateful vice of drunkenness, since we can't ignore that doing so violates article 840 of our penal code, which clearly states that he that publicly defends a vice or crime, illegal or not, or makes excuses for them or for their authors, will be punished with felony arrest and a second class fine."[72]

Despite the tongue-in-cheek denial, *La Guacamaya* persisted in defending the common man's right to *correr el gallo* (cut loose), especially during Independence Day celebrations, by pointing out the depressing consequences of continued police repression.[73] A 1907 pre–Independence Day cover entitled "Preparativos para el grito" (preparations for the *Grito*), for instance, vividly captures the distress of a working-class patriot forced to celebrate Independence Day at home for fear of getting arrested should he join the downtown festivities (see fig. 3.8).[74] In the lower center of the image, the man kneels at the foot of a bust of Hidalgo, covering his eyes with his hands in sorrow and humiliation. On the left,

Mother Mexico, wearing a Phrygian cap and cradling a Mexican flag, sets a victor's laurel crown on Hidalgo's head; a framed picture of the twin volcanoes Popocatépetl and Iztaccíhuatl, symbols of *México profundo* (deep Mexico), hangs on the wall to the right. Elaborate floral *ofrendas* (offerings) have been carefully arranged at its base. Beneath the volcano picture on the right, his wife arranges the bedclothes while three children read at her feet. The book is entitled *Historia Patria*. In the far upper right-hand corner of the image is a large armoire; along with the bed it helps to distinguish the domestic space of the home from the public spaces outside. This poem explains the scene:

> —Tiende la cama, Narcisa,
> que no tenga ningún bicho,
> porque el quince de Septimbre [*sic*]
> en vez de irme á oír el GRITO,
> pienso meterme en la cama;
> no sea que me agarre un cuico,
> pues ya no se puede chata,
> demostrar el patriotismo.

❀

> [—Make the bed, Narcisa,
> and make sure it doesn't have fleas
> because the fifteenth of September
> instead of going to hear the *Grito*,
> I'm thinking about staying in bed;
> so that some cop doesn't grab me,
> because, sweetheart, one can't
> demonstrate patriotism anymore.]

The cover is striking for two reasons. First, this respectable working-class family has clearly gone to considerable trouble to "demonstrate patriotism" with a bust of Hidalgo, the heap of *ofrendas*, a volcano picture, and history lessons for the children. The man's lament is thus not that he is unable to celebrate Independence Day—the domestic "preparations" are beyond reproach—but that police repression makes it too risky for him to publicly celebrate the *Grito* with his compatriots in front of the presidential palace. In this instance, then, both artist and poet insist that public celebration en masse, rather than private celebration at home with the women and children, is the only meaningful way for real men to demonstrate their patriotism. Moreover, the man's concerns about arrest suggest that these public patriotic demonstrations involve more than a little drinking and carousing.

Domestic celebrations might suffice for bourgeois men, but working-class men and their advocates understood that the public performance of patriotism—preferably on the Zócalo, at the center of Mexican political life—was an essential component of their political subjectivity. To illustrate the point, the artist locates the kneeling paterfamilias in a position of powerlessness (at the same level as the children) vis-à-vis the dutiful wife whose moral rectitude is represented by her upright posture, selfless actions, and superior position in the right-hand (feminine) side of the image. She is able to do her patriotic duty; he cannot. So trapped at home in the feminine domestic space, the kneeling man has sunk into deep despair. Prevented from carrying out the performative requirements of working-class male subjectivity, he can only bemoan his political emasculation at the hands of a despised *cuico*, the slang term for a police agent or spy who betrays the confidence of his fellows.[75] Thus, while the moralistic *El Diablito Rojo* encouraged workers to model themselves on an idealized version of the sober, restrained bourgeois subject (an ideal seldom attained by the despised Porfirian bourgeoisie), *La Guacamaya* insisted on a distinctly working-class subjectivity grounded in the exuberant collective expression of patriotic sentiments and even "irrational" behaviors, including public drunkenness, raucous carousing, and the shouting of xenophobic slogans, like the traditional response to the presidential *Grito*: "¡Viva México! ¡Hijos de la Chingada!" (Long Live Mexico! Motherfuckers!)[76]

The second striking feature is the image's staging of the domestic scene. The well-dressed, literate family and the comfortable accommodations—represented by the fancy patriotic paraphernalia, solid wardrobe, and wrought-iron bedstead—bespeak a level of material comfort and cultural capital higher than most Mexico City workers enjoyed. The grieving man might well be working class, as the poem's references to bedbugs and his fear of arrest seem to imply, but he is hardly typical. His higher status suggests at least two possible interpretations. The most obvious interpretation is that all workers, from the poorest *pelado* to the relatively prosperous artisan, ran the risk of harassment and arrest at the hands of police. At the same time, the image suggests that *La Guacamaya* was especially concerned that "respectable" workers would stay home on Independence Day, turning over the public celebration to their less discriminating and less vulnerable (to the stigma of arrest) compatriots—a practice that would align respectable workers with the bourgeoisie and thus endanger the affective bonds of working-class solidarity.

Be that as it may, a 1908 "Desde la estaca" column made a similar case for men at the poorer end of the working-class spectrum. In the column, Pitacio happens upon a friend ranting on a street corner shortly after Independence Day and asks him if he's reciting a speech, to which his friend replies disgustedly:

> No brother, don't accuse me of such things because I'm not a speech giver, speeches don't suit me, and I'll do no more than take out my flag, give out a timid *grito* so I don't wake up some cop and take off for my place, where no one will harass me, so I can shout out with all the force of my loins [lungs]: Long live liberty! And the heroes who extracted it [called on it] to save the Patria.[77]

❦

> [No mano, no mi haga esas acomparaciones, porque yo no soy descursero ni me cuadran los descursos y saco mi bandera no más, doy un grito quedito pa que no se despierte el choco y me pinto pa mi taribel [caribal?], onde naiden me agorzoma [molesta] pa poder gritar con toda la juerza de mis lomos [pulmones] ¡Viva la libertad!¡Y los héroes que la estiraron [excitaron] por salvar á la Patria!]

In this example, Pitacio's far-from-respectable friend shares the concern of the grieving man in "Preparativos para el grito" that any public expression of patriotism might land him jail. And even though, as it turns out, he did go to the Zócalo to mark the occasion with his compatriots, the celebration was so constrained that the only place he feels that he can give full voice to his true feelings is at home behind closed doors. Pitacio responds with a similar tale, one that includes being accosted by a policeman. "Tell me about it," he says to his friend, "I was walking along with my woman [*mi garrote*] when a cop grabbed me, and as soon as he found out that I couldn't walk straight, he roughed me up some and, well, so I wouldn't end up in the new jail, I went to my place, because when it comes right down to it some of them [the police] are real thugs."[78] Thus, despite their relatively low status as street vendors and erratically employed *jornaleros* (day workers), Pitacio and his friend are no better off than their prosperous and presumably more vulnerable compatriot in "Preparativos para el grito." A respectable worker like the kneeling man might suffer more from the indignities of harassment (in terms of damage to his "good" name) and the stigma of arrest (which could threaten a steady job), but his less fortunate compatriots seem to have born the brunt of police violence. Regardless of considerable differences in their life circumstances and social status, all three men feel deprived of access to a public space in which to perform one of the essential rites of working-class political subjectivity *as part of a group of like-minded compatriots.* All three sense that "the authorities" have come up with yet another way to unman them by further eroding their tenuous citizenship claims and undermining their newfound class solidarity.

Conclusion

This discussion of working-class political subjectivity brings us full circle to chapter 1 and specifically to *La Guacamaya*'s "¡VIVA la LIBERTAD!"[79] Recall that the "¡VIVA la LIBERTAD!" illustration was divided into two frames: rowdy working-class celebrants (and interfering police) on the active left and sleeping bourgeois *catrines* (dandies) on the passive right. Recall too the accompanying poem, which explained that despite police harassment, "the enthusiastic people cheer those that gave us Liberty . . . [while] in contrast the *catrines*, the patriots (?) dedicate themselves to sleeping off their drunkenness." That initial analysis focused on the symbols, iconographic conventions, and spatial logics at work in the image in order to recover its political message. Examined later was the cult of national martyrs, including Hidalgo (who appears weeping in the portrait above the sleeping *catrines*), and their enshrinement as working-class heroes—more precisely, as hero-martyrs whose sacrifices on behalf of Mexico were truly appreciated and celebrated only by humble workers. This lengthy exploration of penny press attempts to remake working-class political subjectivity positions us to grasp the full import of an image like "¡VIVA la LIBERTAD!" and its representation of patriotic working-class men.

"¡VIVA la LIBERTAD!," which appeared just a week after "Preparativos para el grito," provides an optimistic rebuttal to that depressing scenario. Workers of all kinds, from barefoot paperboys to men in business suits and bowler hats, have turned out to celebrate Independence Day together after all—despite the visible threat of violence and arrest at the hands of truncheon-wielding policemen. Even though no evidence of alcohol appears in the image, the excitement of "the people" is palpable. Certainly none of the celebrants seems the least bit inclined to mumble a "timid *grito*" and go home, as Pitacio's friend threatened to do. On the contrary, a worker in striped overalls toots loudly on his "trumpet" and the scruffy paperboy (clutching yet another trumpet) shouts indignantly at the policeman who is trying to confiscate his flag.

At this point in the analysis, we can better appreciate the significance of enthusiastic workers celebrating en masse as a disorderly crowd while their apathetic bourgeois countrymen sleep off their drunkenness in some private dormitory, each frock-coated "gentleman" snoozing away on his own frilly bed with his back turned to his fellow. Bourgeois regulatory norms might require that men demonstrate "character"—an ill-defined combination of propriety, probity, and property—in their public lives in order to emerge as legitimate political subjects. But as *La Guacamaya* understood, most workers could lay claim to none of these traits, and those few with reputations to lose and a bit of property occupied a tenuous position on the shabby fringes of "decent" society. Taken as discrete individuals—the classic liberal measure of social "worth"—working-class men had little hope of living up to bourgeois standards. Taken en masse, however, they could put themselves forth as the true embodiment of *el pueblo*—which is how the poet identifies them in the image—a claim that the ruling class and the dominant bourgeoisie could no longer make in the face of their patent inability to deal with the nation's massive and persistent social inequalities.

Political theorist Ernesto Laclau's analysis of the political logic of populism sheds considerable light on the seemingly preposterous claims of any marginalized subgroup to represent all of "the people."[80] As Laclau explains it, the emergence of a "populist configuration" depends on three preconditions: an institutional system that is unable or unwilling to meet a growing number of social demands and thereby prompts "the formation of an internal antagonistic frontier separating the 'people' from power"; the linking together of these diverse unmet demands into an "equivalential chain," a linkage that opens up a space in the political arena for marginalized social groups (*plebs*) to voice those demands in the name of the people (*populus*); and "the unification of these demands . . . into a stable system of signification," a process which constitutes the "people" as a recognizable political actor and thus enables their ensuing "war of position" against the powers that be.[81]

We have seen that all these preconditions were present in late Porfirian Mexico City. The extensive list of unmet demands regularly articulated by the penny press on behalf of Mexican workers—adequate employment, equitable wages, decent working conditions, better public services, freedom from forced conscription, an end to police repression—displays all the hallmarks of Laclau's equivalential chain (a chain of distinct demands that are equivalent primarily in the sense that all remain unsatisfied). Moreover, the gradual forging of this chain into "a stable system of signification" during the first decade of the twentieth century threatened to crystallize the many fissures in Porfirian society into two opposed camps divided by "an internal antagonistic frontier," with the oppressed "people" on one side and the oppressive "regime" on the other. Indeed, the "¡VIVA la LIBERTAD!" cover with its two clearly delineated frames—abetted, as noted in chapter 1, by the antagonists facing each other in *La Guacamaya*'s masthead—does precisely that.

Recognizing the penny press "war of position" as an incipient populist configuration is important because it challenges previous interpretations of the role of urban workers in the 1910 Revolution. The Introduction noted an interpretive split between postrevolutionary historians, who picked through the historical record for traces of working-class radicalism in order to establish urban workers as legitimate revolutionaries, and revisionist historians, who argued that most workers were reluctant revolutionaries who joined the struggle only after exhausting all viable alternatives. Connecting Porfirian working-class politics with Laclau's interpretation of populism as a political logic that constructs "a global identity [the people] out of the equivalence of a plurality of social demands" allows us to shed some much-needed light on this dispute.[82]

According to Laclau, previous analysts (many historians among them) have been frustrated by the impossibility of categorizing populism's diverse historical manifestations. As a consequence, they have condemned it as vague and inconsistent, as the irrational counterpart to "a mature political logic governed by a high degree of precise institutional determination."[83] Laclau accepts the description but not the condemnation. Instead, he argues that populism's vagueness and inconsistency is a *logical* reflection of and response to a "vague and undetermined" social milieu. This means that populism, "rather than [being] a clumsy political and ideological operation, [is] a performative act endowed with a rationality of its own"; it works by "subverting and complicating the operations of the so-called 'more mature' ideologies."[84] As a political logic, populism "simplifies the political space, replacing a complex set of differences and determinations by a stark dichotomy whose two poles are necessarily imprecise," but that simplification nonetheless generates "relevant political meanings" and thus the possibility of collective political action—a result which hardly seems premature or immature despite its ideological imprecision.[85]

Seen in this light, we can make a strong case for the penny press formulation of working-class populism as an incipient revolutionary political act. As noted earlier, the satiric penny press and many urban workers espoused a loosely defined variant of classic Mexican liberalism that historians have identified as "popular liberalism." This terminology seems backward, at least for the early twentieth century. Certainly many Mexican workers identified strongly with the *puro* liberal tradition, especially with major icons like Father Hidalgo and Benito Juárez, but the innovative thrust of their appropriation of liberal ideology was to use its catchphrases and icons as "empty signifiers"—Laclau's preferred term for the slogans and symbols that come to "signify" the diverse unmet demands that make up the equivalential chain—around which to rally the "people" against their oppressors.[86] With the discrediting (but not disappearance) of conservatism after the disastrous French intervention and the execution of imperial puppet Maximilian, liberalism ruled the ideological roost. There were divisions within the fold, to be sure, but shared principles confounded efforts to differentiate clearly among the profusion of liberalisms. Given this "vague and undetermined" ideological field, the populist move was a logical and potentially revolutionary response, allowing as it did the formation of an oppositional strategy capable of reaching across ideological and sociological divisions in a way that *puro* liberalism, for example, never managed. The hybrid term "popular liberalism," in which the adjective "popular" modifies the noun "liberalism," suggests yet another variant of liberalism. A reversal of the noun-adjective relation to "liberal populism" would, I think, more accurately reflect the radical shift in political logics that occurs with the popular/populist appropriation of liberal discourse. Further, I would argue that liberal populism, with its stark dichotomies, equivalential chain of unmet demands, and proliferation of "empty signifiers," served as both precedent and model for the shifting political logics that would characterize the 1910 Revolution.

Nowhere is the difference between classic liberalism and liberal populism clearer than in their respective approaches to political subjectivity. Liberalism sees citizenship first and foremost as a set of *individual* rights and obligations enshrined in constitutions, specified in legal codes, and represented by solitary acts, like casting a ballot. In contrast, populism (like Civic Catholicism) stresses *collective* responsibilities and participation. Populism thus privileges the affective aspects of politics that join "the people" together in opposition to power, while liberalism insists on the primacy of rational-critical debate among individual interlocutors. This is so because populism's equivalential chain is made up of heterogeneous demands forged by a "radical investment" on the part of "the people" in the unifying symbol or slogan—Laclau's "empty signifier"— that binds those demands together. That radical investment, Laclau tells us, "belongs necessarily to the order of *affect*," with its bodily and psychological dimensions.[87]

The preceding chapters have already shown the affective dimension of liberal populism at work. As the Introduction noted, Mexican labor historians have stressed the powerful influence of European socialist ideas of social harmony, cooperation, and association on late-nineteenth-century Mexico City workers' organizations, directed for the most part by better-educated artisans—the same sector that likely produced most penny press editors and contributors. Chapter 1 discussed the ubiquity of religious language and imagery in Mexican public language, including its privileging of "associative life" over liberal notions of personal autonomy, which added resonance and prestige to penny press calls for worker solidarity. Chapters 1 and 2 then examined how penny press editors and collaborators constructed a working-class cult of hero-martyrs out of liberal icons like Father Hidalgo and Benito Juárez, which they used to revile (by way of comparison) contemporary politicians, like the hated *científicos* and sometimes even the president himself, in order to undermine the legitimacy of "the regime" in the eyes of "the people." This chapter has shown how the penny press sought to deepen these affective bonds by inserting working-class men into the national narrative as active participants in their own right—even as hero-martyrs in the case of Churubusco—in order to highlight their entitlement to full-fledged citizenship and to constitute workers as "the people." And just discussed were the revolutionary implications for Mexican politics of a potential populist configuration enabled by the forging of affective bonds between workers and the nation in opposition to an oppressive regime. Still pending, however, is an assessment of the impact of all this on working-class subjectivity—an impact Laclau acknowledges but doesn't examine in any detail (a sensible enough decision given the broad scope of his analysis).

This line of inquiry requires a shift in theoretical focus from populism's political logic to the implication of that logic for working-class subjects. The Introduction concluded with an analysis of Judith Butler's work on subjectivity and its implications for historical analysis. That analysis focused in particular on Butler's contention that regulatory norms embedded in "the domains of political and linguistic representation" determine the conditions under and through which subjects become "culturally intelligible" (make sense to themselves and to others). It also noted Butler's insistence on the centrality of gender to subjectivity, especially to political subjectivity and citizenship. Finally, it dealt with the tricky question of resistance—the ways in which subjects, despite their ongoing subjugation by the regulatory norms that enable their subjectivity, can act as agents to change the conditions of subjectivity through the deployment of "insurrectionary language" capable of disrupting and even reconfiguring the domains of political and linguistic representation.

The relevance of questions of cultural intelligibility, gendered citizenship, and insurrectionary language to the penny press project should be obvious enough at this point. Penny press editors and collaborators well understood that Porfirian workers lived at the repressed margins of respectable society, intelligible to the bourgeoisie mostly as an undifferentiated mass whose labor value was offset by unsavory cultural practices, poor work discipline, and disruptive political tendencies. Under these

circumstances, only a reconfiguration of the domains of political and linguistic representation could hope to realize workers' aspirations to full-
fledged citizenship; hence the singular importance of the penny press
as a public forum in and through which to contest the bourgeois conditions of subjectivity that legitimized their continued exclusion from public life. At the same time, this working-class contribution to the public
sphere, like its bourgeois counterpart, was decidedly masculine: its vision of citizenship inseparable from notions of working-class manhood
and the image of the grateful, self-sacrificing, enthusiastic, and (for some
editors) hard-drinking patriot, working and celebrating in solidarity with
like-minded subjects. And in order to challenge the bourgeois regulatory
norms that conditioned political subjectivity in Porfirian Mexico, penny
press editors and their fellow travelers developed an insurrectionary language that sought to contest those norms and to constitute *nostros los
pelados* as *nostros el pueblo*.

This linguistic "war of position" with the Porfirian regime produced
two significant changes in the conditions of subjectivity for working-
class men. The first change—the sense of the working-class male subject
as a collective actor, as one of "the people"—was fairly uncontroversial in
penny press circles, even if *El Diablito Rojo, La Palanca*, and other papers
adhered more closely to bourgeois standards. Uncontroversial or not, the
populist move was a radical departure from bourgeois notions of political subjectivity predicated on the "inalienable" rights and duties of individual subjects/citizens. The classic liberal formulations of such political
theorists as Thomas Hobbes and John Locke predicate popular sovereignty on the consent of the governed, sovereign individuals who agree
to surrender some portion of their personal autonomy in exchange for
protection from the uncertainties (and brutalities) inherent in a "state of
nature." In a populist configuration, however, popular sovereignty more
closely resembles Jean-Jacques Rousseau's notion of the "general will" of
the people taken in aggregate, but with "the people" set in opposition to
"power" in a divided political arena. Political subjects under populism
thus become culturally intelligible primarily as members of a group; the
resulting sense of collective identity binds their subjectivity to that of
their compatriots. As noted, the prominence of Civic Catholicism in the
public discourse of the period lent legitimacy, strength, and inspiration
to the notion of associative life. For the Mexico City penny press and its

loyal readers, collective identity was expressed as class consciousness, which in its emergent form included a heavily gendered notion of citizenship. Thus, working-class men became culturally intelligible political subjects in early twentieth-century Mexico City, first and foremost through the public performance of patriotic sentiment in concert with like-minded men.

The second change—the endorsement of less savory aspects of working-class culture, including drinking and carousing at patriotic events—was hotly contested. *El Diablito Rojo*, on one hand, endorsed police repression of popular celebrations, and *La Guacamaya*, on the other, suggested that "real men" didn't always behave respectably. Thus, for *La Guacamaya* at least, political subjectivity for male workers meant much more than just collective participation in patriotic celebrations; it also involved a distinctly working-class patriotic style that emphasized the affective bonds produced by shared cultural practices over the inevitable alienations of bourgeois individualism (as depicted, e.g., by the front-to-back *catrines* in "¡VIVA la LIBERTAD!"). This controversial linkage between a class-specific patriotic style and working-class political subjectivity further intensified the affective ties that bound workers to the nation by binding the workers to each other as "the people" (in opposition to the traitorous bourgeoisie) and thus in turn binding the nation to the workers as its true representatives. And that wasn't all. As the remaining chapters show, penny press controversies over working-class subjectivity and traditional cultural practices were hardly confined to politics.

CHAPTER 4

RUMBO PERDIDO

Transgressive Journeys into Manhood

Chapters 1 through 3 of this book deal with the charged issue of citizenship for working-class men; this chapter and the next turn to closely related but analytically distinct questions about working-class men as gendered subjects.[1] We have seen that political citizenship in late Porfirian Mexico City (as in most places) was profoundly gendered. At the same time, the concept aspires to be—at least in its liberal incarnations—a gender-neutral designation given to those who belong to a nation-state and who accept all the rights and responsibilities that citizenship entails. Once we move out of the political realm into everyday life, however, the pretense of neutrality drops away and the gendered subject comes fully into view. This chapter and the next, then, reconstruct penny press efforts to constitute working-class men *as men* in the dialectical interplay between work and leisure and in the fraught nature of their intimate relationships with women.

The Civilizing Process

In his classic analysis of "the civilizing process," sociologist Norbert Elias argues for a gradual but radical revolution in affect, manners, and bodily comportment that accompanied the rise of early modern and modern nation-states in the western European countries, colonies, and spheres of

influence.[2] For Elias, this revolution involved "the moderation of spontaneous emotions, the tempering of affects, the extension of mental space
beyond the moment into the past and future, the habit of connecting
events in terms of chains of cause and effect."[3] Although the civilizing
process began in the late medieval period as a marker of aristocratic re-
finement, it reached its apogee in the eighteenth and nineteenth centuries as the ascendant European bourgeoisie sought to set themselves
apart and above the less privileged members of the Third Estate.[4] The
bourgeois phase of this "civilizing process" was very much at work in fin-
de-siècle Mexico City, personified by President Porfirio Díaz's makeover
at the capable hands of his second wife, Carmen Romero Rubio.[5] The
well-educated, well-mannered daughter of a prominent Mexico City
family, "Doña Carmen" ensured that the president learned some English,
dressed in the latest European fashions (whether civilian or military),
carried himself like the distinguished leader of a modern nation, and appeared increasingly whiter in official portraits despite his well-known
mestizo origins. Mexico City gossips even credited her with teaching the
"crude" warrior from provincial Oaxaca not to walk into the full-length
mirrors in the presidential palace—an improbable story that reflects in
a startlingly literal way the role of the civilizing process in promoting
detached self-awareness, a psychic state that European bourgeois culture considered the foundation of proper human social development. But
not every disadvantaged mestizo who migrated to Mexico City from the
provinces was lucky enough to acquire a Doña Carmen to supervise his
education and manage his public image.

This chapter examines the ways in which early twentieth-century
Mexico City satiric penny press editors exploited the productive tension
between proper and improper behavior for working-class men. Their
project confounded the conventional image of the well-behaved male
citizen-subject by confronting middle-class notions of civic virtue with
popular resistance to bourgeois prescription, which they saw as a form
of class privilege rather than a marker of social superiority. In opposition
to long-standing negative stereotypes of working-class behavior, penny
press editors offered up positive (if sometimes patronizing) images of
hardworking proletarians whose genuine patriot expression was all about
energetic, exuberant, disruptive, even "scandalous" public behavior—
however much that enthusiasm might trouble municipal authorities, for-

eign shopkeepers, or international capital. Bourgeois regulatory norms required that men demonstrate "character"—an ill-defined combination of propriety, probity, and property associated with European culture and racial superiority—in their public lives in order to emerge as legitimate political subjects. Workers could lay claim to none of these traits, and those few with reputations to lose and a bit of property occupied a tenuous position on the shabby fringes of decent society. Taken as discrete individuals, the classic liberal measure of social worth, working-class men had little hope of living up to bourgeois standards. Taken en masse, however, penny press editors could put forth workers as the true embodiment of "el pueblo," a claim that the ruling class and the dominant bourgeoisie could no longer make in the face of their patent inability or unwillingness to deal with Mexico's "durable inequalities."[6] The result was a "satire of sentiments" that mocked bourgeois masculine sensibility as pretentious and hypocritical, on one hand, and celebrated its working-class counterpart as unaffected and honest, despite (and perhaps because of) its inconsistencies and absurdities, on the other.

Street talk columns, written in the tortured vernacular of the streets, were a regular feature of the early twentieth-century Mexico City penny press. Staged as a conversation between two less-than-respectable workers—almost always men, almost always out of work—these columns allowed penny press editors to comment (through their worker mouthpieces) on contemporary events and the vicissitudes of everyday life for Mexico City's working poor. In most instances, this involved one of the two men recounting the previous day's adventures as he wandered through the city searching for work, entertainment, food, drink, and women—in whatever order these attractions might appear. Embedded in these transgressive journeys through the capital's well-traveled *rumbos* were subtle and not so subtle critiques of bourgeois notions of proper masculine behavior, which most press editors considered self-serving, moralistic, and unmanly.[7] In contrast, they constructed loving portraits of Mexico City's working-class men in all their unapologetic, irreverent, cynical, sentimental, picaresque glory. These men, editors implied, were the true sons of Mexico, ready and willing (given half a chance and a bit of instruction) to tackle the demons of nationhood. The strategy at work was a straightforward symbolic inversion: workers (*nostros los pelados*) emerged as real men, their middle- and upper-class counterparts (*los rotos y los catrines*) as pretenders to manhood.[8] More complex is the way this strategic inversion complicates our understanding of working-class Mexican masculinities, especially the persistent caricature of working-class Mexican men as irredeemably macho.

Contemporary social scientists have done quite a bit of work on the "protest masculinities" adopted by marginalized men in response to their subordinate position vis-à-vis what sociologist R. W. Connell and others have called "hegemonic masculinity," the culturally dominant script for masculine behavior operative at any given historical time and geographical location.[9] In most of these studies, protest masculinities are characterized by an array of "toxic" behaviors, including substance abuse, violence directed against themselves and others (especially women), and various other antisocial activities. As in Octavio Paz's rewriting of late nineteenth-century Mexican criminological discourses on *pelado* culture, these marginalized men are often criminalized at the same time.[10] What both Paz's stereotype and most recent sociological literature ignore or downplay are the complexities of oppositional masculinities. Like their late nineteenth-century criminologist predecessors (and Porifirian elites), these scholars typically represent working-class men as members of an undifferentiated mass of improvident, apathetic, violence-prone nonsubjects, whose cultural unintelligibility (as discreet individuals), at least from the perspective of the *gente decente*, disqualifies them from full citizenship.[11]

In response to the crude generalizations of bourgeois social critics, penny press editors used street talk columns to develop memorable working-class characters whose irreverent attitudes and questionable behaviors looked more like inspired, *individualized* responses to unfortunate circumstance than self-defeating, *generalized* resentment of their social "superiors." As a means to this end, the narrative vignette (as a genre) provided context for the alleged antisocial activities of working-class Mexican men. If bourgeois social reformers could sometimes bring themselves to acknowledge that material deprivation and inadequate socialization might encourage or fail to discourage working-class criminality, penny press editors chose instead to focus on its production through discriminatory laws, regulations, and policing—practices that targeted the lower classes, especially men, while ignoring the shady dealings of more

EL PELADITO.—Oigame Don Tequis, ¿pos por qué se lleva á mi vale el Ardilla, siendo questa menos mamey que este roto?
EL ROTO.—No seas menso, por que el hilo siempre se revienta por lo más delgado.

FIG. 4.1 Artist/Author Unknown, "El peladito . . . ," *El Diablito Bromista*, July 14, 1907. Courtesy of the Benson Latin American Collection, University of Texas Libraries, The University of Texas at Austin.

privileged social sectors (see fig. 4.1).[12] By locating (rather than denying) working-class criminality in the everyday lives of their protagonists, they shifted the blame for crime from the collective failure of workers to live up to their civic responsibilities to the collective hypocrisy of the Porfirian bourgeoisie, which ignored the needs of ordinary Mexicans, preached what it refused to practice, and produced the criminality it pretended to abhor.

This chapter listens in on two street talk protagonists, Pitacio and Chema, from *La Guacamaya*'s long-running column "Desde la estaca" (from the stake), as they tell each other about the trials and tribulations of their everyday lives in Mexico City.[13] Through a close reading of three exemplary stories, it draws attention to the subtle interplay of linguistic games, narrative strategies, and ideological agendas that made street talk columns so popular with penny press readers—and make them so useful to the historian.

Before the stories themselves, let's quickly review how penny press editors used popular language to establish the social location of their protagonists and foster the class loyalties of their readers. As noted in chapter 3, street talk columns invite the reader to eavesdrop on a personal conversation between two working-class friends, usually but not always men, on a street in downtown Mexico City. Casual intimacy between the two protagonists is marked in several ways: the familiar form of address (*tú*, "you" singular); repeated terms of endearment (*hermano* and its variants: *mano*, *manito*, etc.); passing references to female partners and mutual friends; the sometimes explicit, sometimes covert, sexual banter typical of working-class male friendships in Mexico (and elsewhere); and appropriation of the inflections, rhythms, and vocabulary of popular speech through deliberate misspellings, improper word substitution, unconventional verb forms, fractured syntax, and use of slang and popular idioms, as well as big words that sound more "important" or more colloquial than their standard Spanish equivalents. These different linguistic strategies represent the closeness of the two men for the reader and construct an affective bond between interlocutors and reader that allows for open articulation of an otherwise "hidden transcript" of resistance to the Porfirian regime in particular and Mexican social relations in general.[14] Although the exact makeup of the penny press's diverse readership is impossible to determine—it was probably something of a mystery even to the editors—the evident popularity of the street talk columns, despite their elaborate linguistic games, suggests the formation of a distinct penny press "counterpublic" of those in on the joke, a counterpublic composed of everyone from well-educated artisans (the most likely audience) to illiterate street corner auditors.

Billiard-Playing Women and Vigilant Policemen

LA GUACAMAYA, "DESDE LA ESTACA," OCTOBER 13, 1902

Like nearly every other street talk column, the story of the billiard-playing women and the vigilant policeman involves a chance (but not infrequent) encounter between two friends, Pitacio and Chema in this case, somewhere along a shared *rumbo*, probably in central Mexico City (see fig. 4.2).[15] This column starts, as most do, with a salutation and a misunderstanding:

FIG. 4.2 José Guadalupe Posada/Author Unknown, "Desplumaderos Modernos," *La Guacamaya*, October 13, 1902. Courtesy of the Benson Latin American Collection, University of Texas Libraries, The University of Texas at Austin.

—¡Pitacio! ¡Pitacio! Oye manito ¿pos que ya te volvites sordo?

—Asuétlame, asuéltame no me agarres, ¿no miras que se me hace tarde?

—Pos adonde vas, ya pareces eleitrico, ni suenas la campana.

—Pos voy á la Academia antes que se me haga más tarde.

—Cómo, ¿pos que ya te golvites choco ó estás aprendiendo el inglés?

—No mano, no seas güey, voy á la academia de billar, que me han contado que hay allí unas jañas muy sazonas, que manejan el taco con mucha destreza, y juegan las bolas con mucha agilidá.

—¡Hay Pitacio! ni se te ocurra semejante cosa, pos allí no es más que un verdadero robadero, pos te voy á contar lo que asucede en esas casas de juego de nuevo cuño . . .

RUMBO PERDIDO

—

[—Pitacio! Pitacio! Listen to me my friend, are you going deaf?

—Let go, let go, don't grab me. Can't you see that you're making me late?

—Where are you going? You're acting electric [like an electric trolley car], and you're not even ringing the bell.

—I'm going to the Academy if you don't make me too late.

—What? Are you becoming a cop or learning English?

—No, man, don't be an idiot, I'm going to the Academy of Billiards, because they told me about some hot women there, who handle the cue with great dexterity and play the balls with great agility.

—Hold on, Pitacio! Don't even think about it, because it's truly a rip-off. Let me tell you about what happens in these fancy new gaming houses . . .]

After establishing that Pitacio is in a huge hurry and clearing up the confusion over which kind of academy he's attending, Chema, seemingly oblivious of his friend's desperate condition, begins to explain in some detail what Pitacio can expect at the Academy of Billiards, in addition to the much-anticipated *jaranas muy sazonas* (hot women)[16]:

llega uno allí y aluego, un jaño que está allí en la puerta le vitoquea á uno luego luego la fila . . . y si le ven á uno cara de maje hasta lo arrenpujan pa dentro, y luego que entra uno, se va uno incontrando como si estuviera en la prevensión de un cuartel con unas jaranas muy sazonas sentadas con su maüsser en la mano, (lease taco) esperando que les llegue lora pa lanzarse sobre las bolas y la mesa, pa decidir la suerte de cado uno de los jaranos que están haciendo el papel de . . . china, de china mano.

[you arrive there, and then a guy at the door looks you up and down, and then there's the line . . . and if they see you have an Indian-looking face, they push you inside, and then after you enter, you feel like you are in the entryway to a barracks with some hot women seated with Mausers in their hands (read: cues), waiting for the time to come when they launch themselves at the balls and the table, to decide the fate of each one of the guys who are playing the role of . . . suckers, of suckers my friend.]

The most important details of Chema's story, before the appearance of the *jaranas muy sazonas*, involve new modes of surveillance and crowd control—the scrutiny of doormen, standing in lines—and their intersection with old forms of discrimination against anyone with Indian features (*cara de maje*) who gets pushed rudely inside or just as likely escorted out of an upscale establishment like a billiards academy.[17] When the *jaranas* first appear in the story, it's not as sexy young women but as barracks guards with rifles at hand, ready to throw themselves into combat, to "decide the fate of each one of the guys who are playing the role of . . . china, de china mano"—"*china*" being in this instance a euphemism for *chingado*, someone who is about to be fucked over.

At this point, the harried Pitacio is intrigued but wants to know more about the *jañas*; so when Chema continues in a similar vein—"unos ojales mano, que parece un toro á media plaza" (huge eyes, brother, like those of a bull in the middle of the arena)—he interrupts, eager to get to the sexy bits. An attentive storyteller, Chema obliges:

> —Güeno, pos nos quedamos en la chaqueta, ques de seda muy fina y está muy desgogotada, pos poco falta pa que enseñen por los que lloran los chamacos, sus naguas también del mismo género, nomás que zanconas, que dejan ver unas piernas ¡ay! Mano . . . y luego que se acuestan sobre la mesa y alzan las patotas se ven unas cosas que ¡qué cosas! ¡huuyy mano!

> [—Well, we were talking about the jacket, which is of fine silk and very low cut, so that it barely covers the things that babies cry for, skirts of the same type, no more than slips, that show off their calves, oh brother! . . . and then when they lie across the billiard table and raise their big legs, you can see some things . . . what things! whew brother!]

In this climax to the story's central vignette, Chema finally delivers the goods with a low-cut jacket that "barely covers the things that babies cry for," short skirts by Porfirian standards "that show off their legs, oh brother!" and the thrilling moments when the young women lie across the billiard table, raise their big legs, and "you can see some things that . . . what things! whew brother!" But he quickly follows this invocation of desire—a decidedly "modern" desire linked to consumption and public spectacle—with the cautionary tale of *un jincho* (rube) from around Taji-maroa who got so caught up in the "eicibición de piernas y bolasos, que le dejan las bolsas vacías, mano, y que eran de cuero" (exhibition of legs and ball shots he was left with his purses empty, brother, and they were made of leather).[18] Even the "probes tortilleras" (poor tortilla sellers), Chema goes on, lost their *fierrada* (cash) betting on the game.

The sense of climax and release in this episode is heightened and satirized by Chema's *albur* (wordplay) on the Spanish word *chaqueta*, "jacket," a common euphemism for masturbation.[19] The *albur* acknowl-edges that Chema is "jerking" Pitacio around: prolonging his departure, while at the same time inflaming his desire to get to the academy and see the *jaranas muy sazononas* for himself. Pitacio's response—"prosigue pero no me hagas tan larga contesta" (keep it up but don't give me such a long answer)—suggests he knows exactly what Chema is doing but is too caught up in the story to leave. After Chema satisfies Pitacio's curiosity/desire, the anecdote about the *jincho* from Tajimaroa who gets his leather purses (a.k.a. scrotum) drained of money by the exhibition of legs and ball shots (*bolazos*) leaves little doubt as to the unproductive and fleeting pleasures to be had at the Academy. Having heard enough, a chastened, wiser (and vicariously satisfied) Pitacio supplies the story's moral:

> Peroye, yo no sé como se puede tolerar aquí en la Capital donde reina la moralidá y las güenas costumbres, se permita que[a?][c?]iencia y paciencia, lo asalten en las calles prencipales, tres ó cuatro jaranas de cu . . . tis sonrosado adicen los poétas y les dejen á uno las bolsas vacías.

> [Well listen, I don't know why such things are tolerated here in the Capital where morality and good customs reign, why it is permit-ted that one can be assaulted in the principal streets by three or four women with rosy ch . . . eeks (as the poets say), who leave one with empty pockets.]

Pitacio's disheartened response exposes the hypocrisy of Porfirian ef-forts to create a Mexico City, "where morality and good customs reign," presumably at the expense of working-class men like him and Chema, while permitting immoral "jaranas de cu . . . tis sonrosado" (with "cu . . . tis sonrosado" probably substituting for "cu . . . los sonrosados" or "rosy butts") to hustle gullible workers out of their hard-earned pay. Here the author adds a gendered dimension to his inversion of the conventional binary, lower-class criminal/upper-class citizen, in which sexy, unprincipled female billiard players stand in for Porfirian modernity's allurements and false promises, which fan the flames of working-class desire only to drain workers of their money and manhood. In the official imagination and bourgeois prescriptive literature, working-class men were potential criminals and working-class women potential prostitutes; in this vignette the class location of criminality and sexual transgression has been cleverly inverted to reflect the indisputable truth that existing social relations for workingmen "leave them with empty pockets" or, as the *albur* implies, "with their balls drained." The author, speaking through Chema, makes no attempt to deny the thrills to be had at the Academy of Billiards but clarifies the consequences for those in no position to profit from the game, except perhaps for a fleeting glimpse of "unas cosas ¡que cosas! ¡huuyy mano!!" Once Chema explains the game, Pitacio loses interest, adding that "no quero que mientras son tunas ó no son tunas me vayan á dejar sin mi fierrada esos plagiarios del siglo xx" (scoundrels or not, I don't want those twentieth-century frauds to leave me penniless).[20]

Pitacio's decision to cast off the chains of false consciousness provides a denouement of sorts, but the story doesn't end there. As the two men finish their chat and Chema contemplates going to see his *jaña* when she gets off work so he can get some money, they notice an approaching policeman, "el choco ese que era matarista y nos vaya á machucar ó que diga, nos vaya á llevar a la sucrusal del tabique" (the cop who was a murderous trolley car driver and who's going to beat us or something like that, who's going to take us off to the precinct house). Afraid of being harassed, beaten, or arrested for loitering, they head for a local shop "á hechar una copa de pugidos de machucado con lágrimas de matarista y gotas de eleitricidá" (to toss down a cup of moans from a beating with tears of a murderous trolley driver and drops of electricity). Building on the longer story that preceded it, this final vignette reminds the reader of the true nature of Porfirian efforts to make the capital a place "donde reina la moralidá y las güenas costumbres": an ongoing assault on the everyday practices of lower-class men whose habit of hanging around on street corners ran counter to official initiatives to clean up the central city by removing its unappealing (to elites and foreigners) and potentially dangerous *pelado* population. The offhand comment that the policeman was a former *matarista* (killer)—the popular term for trolley car drivers (*motoristas*) whose callous disregard for pedestrian safety was a recurring theme in the penny press—emphasizes the connection between these two seemingly distinct modernization initiatives (trained gendarmes and streetcars) and their negative impact on the everyday lives of the working classes.

An Obligatory Bath and the Death of Maximilian
LA GUACAMAYA, "DESDE LA ESTACA," JULY 2, 1903

The previous "Desde la estaca" story juxtaposed the "tolerated illegalities" of privileged Porfirians and discriminatory policing directed at the everyday practices of the working classes.[21] The following story of obligatory baths and patriotic exuberance provides a humorous context for working-class criminal behavior that exposes official concerns as overwrought moral panics though which authorities produce criminality out of simple, often deliberate misunderstandings.[22] In official Porfirian reports (typically accompanied by statistics), trial transcripts, and mass media accounts, a range of bureaucratic, legal, and journalistic "experts" identified, categorized, and dissected the criminal acts committed by Mexico City residents. The context in which a given crime took place mattered to the extent that it supplied motive as well as mitigating and aggravating circumstances, the kinds of things authorities or the tabloid public might weigh as they passed judgment on alleged criminals. But these well-publicized cases garnered this attention to context precisely because of the notoriety of the crime or the criminal—in other words because the cases were *extra*ordinary. In contrast, the everyday crimes of the working poor, although overrepresented by volume in official crime statistics, were of little interest to anyone but the criminals involved and the poorly trained gendarmes who struggled to keep things together in a rapidly expanding metropolis. Interesting or not, working-class crimes, compiled as statistics, "proved" the fundamental criminality of the capital's lower classes. For these cases, despite their statistical importance, official and mass media sources provided no context at all. This situation the "Desde la estaca" author sets out to rectify.

EL BAÑO OBLIGATORIO

Prendedores chapeados
de oro con el estrabo
de la persona 25 cts.

Fotografía Daguerre

Migran desde 50 cts. docena. Visita desde 1.50. Im-
postal desde 4. Amplificaciónes tamaño natural 4.95.

Hay que tener gian cuidado
con algunos jardineros
pues se hallan, según párece,
con el Gobierno de ácuerdo.

Pasa uno por la Alameda
y lo dejan como nuevo
y de este baño no escapan
ni los *rotos*, ni los *cueros.*

FIG. 4.3 Artist/Author Unknown, "El baño obligatorio," *La Guacamaya*, April 26, 1906. Courtesy of the Benson Latin American Collection, University of Texas Libraries, The University of Texas at Austin.

In this vignette, the salutary confusion that initiates the chance meeting between Pitacio and Chema raises the issue of obligatory baths, a misguided attempt on the part of municipal authorities to clean up the city's lower classes by forcing them to bathe despite the difficulty and expense this usually entailed in a city with a paucity of clean water and grossly unequal distribution of resources (see fig. 4.3).[23] Pitacio initiates the encounter with a mangled popular idiom—"¡Agua le á mi Dios!" (Water him for me, God!) instead of the ubiquitous "¡Ayúdame Dios mio!" (Help me, my God!)—and a sacrilegious invocation of the feast of St. John the Baptist (June 24), a traditional day for ritual bathing that also marks the coming of the rainy season in central Mexico.[24] A few exchanges into the dialogue, an irritated Chema interrupts Pitacio's convoluted joking about St. John, sheep, and sheepskin coats to remind him that "al que no se baña ese día lo bañan . . . pos oye manito, tú no te has bañado y ora te voy a bañar" (he who doesn't bathe himself today gets bathed . . . so listen, brother, you haven't bathed and now I'm going to bathe you). At this point Pitacio explains why he hasn't bathed and doesn't intend to: "Gueno, me pones algo en las de burro pa que no me mojes las orejas, porque como lotro día mi vieja tiró un juerte cañonazo, me reventó un güido y el doitor mia proibido que me moje las orejuelas" (Well, you'll have to put something in my ears so you don't get them wet, because the other day my old lady set off a strong cannon blast, broke my ear drum and the doctor forbade me to get my ears wet).[25]

As it turns out, a couple of days earlier Pitacio's "vieja [como es] muy patriota, siacordó que era el aniversario de cuando restiraron á don Marsimiliano y á los traidores don Miramón y Mejía en el 'Cerro de las Esquilas'" (Pitacio's old lady, being very patriotic, remembered that it was the anniversary of when they shot Don Maximilian and the traitors Don Miramón and Don Mejía on the "Hill of the Sheepshearers").[26] After tempting Pitacio with a plate of beans (*alverjones*), she convinces him to get out the old shotguns (*trabucos*) so they can celebrate the event: "y que aluego nos rolamos, pero á la medio hora empieza mi vieja á disparar y al rato hay viene la casera, los chocos, el Inspeitor y toda la guarnación" (and then off we go, but at the half hour my old lady begins to shoot and after a while here come the landlord, the cops, the Inspector, and the whole garrison). When Chema asks him why, Pitacio explains:

> Pos nada, manario, estaban tan juertes los cañonazos, que todos creiban que era pronunciamiento; y cuando estaba más juerte la refrriega [*sic*], que me atina uno de los ojales, que me adeja ciego, y que me revienta el güido, y en estado lamentable me llevaron á la Inspeición; allí me curó el doitor y me proibió que me mojara las orejas.[27]

[That's obvious, my friend, the cannon blasts were so strong that everyone believed that it was an uprising, and when the recoil was strongest, it hit one of my eyes, which left me blind, and burst my eardrum, and in that sorry state they took me to the Station House. There a doctor cured me and forbade me to get my ears wet].

On the surface, the vignette details a simple misunderstanding between Pitacio and his *vieja*, on one hand, and the authorities, on the other. But the misunderstanding nevertheless generates two ostensibly criminal acts: refusing to bathe on obligatory bath day and shooting off guns in the city. In this instance and presumably many others, the context for the two crimes makes all the difference, since Pitacio and his *vieja* were in fact celebrating a patriotic holiday rather than thieving or fighting—the two public disorder crimes most often associated with the urban poor. There's no doubt that their ill-considered reenactment of Maximilian's execution was a serious public disturbance and that authorities might be a bit upset to discover that Pitacio kept guns at home (leftover perhaps from earlier mobilizations on behalf of the liberal cause and the great Benito Juárez), but patriotic excess could hardly be considered a moral failing even by conventional bourgeois standards. And Pitacio's refusal to comply with obligatory bathing looks more like a personal sacrifice on behalf of *la patria* than a congenital lack of hygiene. Here, as in the previous story, the author's point is not to deny that working-class men (sometimes women) committed criminal acts but to demonstrate the sometimes laudatory, almost always trivial, nature of their crimes, which were in any case more a product of simple misunderstandings or aggressive policing than the mutinous rumblings of the "dangerous classes." The explanation satisfies Chema at least, and he offers to buy Pitacio a drink—"yo con mojarte el hocico estoy contento" (me, I'm content to wet your snout)—instead of forcing him to bathe.

The principal message about the authorities' misrepresentation of working-class criminal acts is obvious enough—and not particularly threatening to the status quo either. Less obvious is the "hidden transcript" embedded in the initial exchange between Pitacio and Chema over obligatory baths, the feast day of St. John the Baptist, the lamb (*borrego*), and the sheepskin coat (*zalea*):

—¡Agua le á mi Dios! Y á San Juan que baje el dedo.

—Oye mano ¿qué te asucede que vienes dando esos gritotes tan desaforados?

—Pos qué mia de asuceder, oy es el día de San Juan y quero que baje el dedo.

—Pos pa mí que baje toda la mano, miace el mismo efeito que la baje ó que la suba; si me adijeras que lo iban á trasquilar, sería otra cosa.

—Oye manicio, dialtiro lo tanteas borrego.

—Pos te adigo eso, porque si no lo has vitoquiado bien, yo sí; ¿no miras que San Juan no será borrego, pero tiene su zalea?

—Hay nomás, valedor, sin meterse con la corte celestial.

—Oye Pitacio, no seas tan res . . . si te adigo de la zalea; yo no me meto con la santidad de San Juan, nomás con su zalea; sino ques un santo que me da alazo porque no consiente porquerías pos al que no se baña ese día lo bañan.

❦

[—Water him for me, my God! And by St. John lower your finger.

—Listen brother, what's up with you that you're going around shouting like a madman?

—Well, what should be up with me, today is the feast day of St. John and I want you to lower your finger.

—Well then, I'll lower my whole hand, it's all the same to me if I raise it or lower it; if you told me you were going to shear it off, that would be another thing.

—Listen brother, now you're really squeezing the lamb.

—Well, I'm telling you this because in case you haven't been paying attention, I have. Don't you see that even if St. John isn't a lamb, he does wear a sheepskin.

—That's enough, my friend, no more mixing it up with the celestial court.

—Listen Pitacio, don't be such a sheep . . . if I tell you about the sheepskin; I'm not getting mixed up in the holiness of St. John, just with his sheepskin; besides, he's a saint that I venerate because he doesn't tolerate swinish behavior, and he who doesn't bathe himself today, gets bathed.]

The hardly coincidental connection between the feast day of St. John the Baptist, who preached spiritual purification through baptism, and obligatory baths to wash away the unhygienic sins of Mexico City's poor suggests a certain sense of humor or condescension (probably both) on the part of municipal authorities. Chema appears to have bought into the idea of forcing the unwashed masses to bathe, at least enough to threaten Pitacio with an unwanted bath.[28]

For Pitacio, however, the problem has little to do with bathing per se and everything to do with authoritarian public health campaigns. This attitude explains his apparently hysterical insistence that Chema lower the finger, which is most likely pointed in his direction. In traditional Catholic iconography, St. John points at Jesus after his baptism and announces "behold the lamb of God," thus revealing to the multitude the purified Christ, cleansed of sin in preparation for his public ministry. As the scene opens, Chema points at Pitacio, not as someone who has been cleansed but as someone in need of a bath. Pitacio understandably resents (perhaps fears) the public attention and reacts with righteous indignation fueled by a strong sense of betrayal.[29]

Traditional iconography also depicts St. John holding a lamb and wearing an animal skin. Both images appear in the dialogue, with Pitacio introducing the image of the lamb (*borrego*) and Chema, the sheepskin (*zalea*). On the surface, the exchange seems little more than an excuse to play word games at the saint's expense, but Pitacio's evident seriousness hints at something more. In addition to its basic meaning, *borrego* is often used in Mexico to describe both an ignorant man who submits without protest to the will of others and a false rumor with a hidden purpose.[30] Thus Pitacio is not just playing with words; he's also accusing Chema of being a "lamb," of being perversely complicit in authoritarian decrees whose real purpose is to oppress the working classes in the name of hygiene—a classic case of "false consciousness," in which an oppressed person takes on the attitude of the oppressor. Chema responds to the accusation by changing the subject from complicit lambs, which suggest a permanent character flaw, to removable sheepskins, a temporary condition that can be put on or taken off as the wearer sees fit. This indicates to his friend that he has chosen to support this particular decree of his own free will, presumably because he sees its purpose as beneficial or inconsequential, despite the dubious source, rather than because he's deluded by official propaganda.

At the risk of finding sexual innuendo where none is intended (which would be rare in the street talk columns), it's hard to imagine that the author and his readers would fail to notice the connection between Chema's removable sheepskin and the traditional lambskin condom (*piel de borrego*), which is supposed to protect its wearer and his sexual partner from the unwanted complications of intercourse, whether reproductive or pathogenic.[31] In a metaphorical sense, then, Chema conjures up a pro-phylactic sheepskin to protect himself from Pitacio's accusation that his cooperation with the obligatory bath decree necessarily entails an embrace of corrupt bourgeois values and the rejection of his working-class loyalties. "Don't you see," he tells his friend, "that even if St. John isn't a lamb, he does wear a sheepskin."

To extend the sexual innuendo still further, the two textual references to shears, with regard to the possible severing of Chema's hand and Maximilian's execution site, taken in conjunction with a bible story that results in St. John's beheading at the behest of Salome, hint at the unsettling subject of castration—a worker losing his hand, a saint his head, a nation its ruler—a possibility that reinforces Pitacio's concern that Chema's cooperation with the authorities has somehow unmanned him. Prodded by symbolic castration fears or not, Chema's defensive tone is unmistakable, and the implication that working-class men were compelled to justify even relatively innocuous compliance with official demands reveals a much more serious problem for authorities than Pitacio's overzealous patriotism. This is hardly the precipice of insurrection, but it does suggest that many Mexico City workers actively resented and resisted Porfirian modernization in all its guises—and encouraged their fellows to do the same.

The story's curious final twist helps explain Pitacio's suspicions and Chema's defensiveness. As the two men finish up their conversation, Pitacio questions Chema about his suddenly prosperous appearance: "Pero oye, Chema, antes de todo, no me ha dicho con que número te sacates la lotería, pos que te veo hecho todo un roto ¿ya te nombraron menistro?" (Hey listen, Chema, you still haven't told me which lottery number you picked, since I can see that you've become a real *roto*. Have they appointed you a minister or what?) In response, Chema explains that his *jaña* had "pinched a briefcase" (*se trincó una papelera*) from the house of a *roto* where she worked and passed it to him along with some money (*jando*). Although it's not clear from Chema's account that the money was stolen—petty theft is a bit out of character—the use of *jando*, jailhouse slang for "money" or "loot," and his admission that he "took off, brother" (*me peló mano*) suggests a criminal act. Regardless, as he's rushing to the bank to stash the money, Chema runs into a buddy, Antonio García, who convinces him that the money would be safer if he spent it on clothes, adding that "por tres locos, te pongo hecho todo un catrín" (for three bucks, I can turn you into a total dandy). Although hardly the most responsible choice, this isn't quite as crazy as it sounds, since Mexico City workers routinely pawned clothes and jewelry to even out their erratic incomes. Thus Chema's decision to spend the money on clothes and accessories, rather than demonstrate a lack of foresight and self-control, might well have provided a financial resource more dependable and flexible than money in the bank.[32] The decision makes sense in other ways as well—especially in light of the city's unwritten but regularly enforced sumptuary "laws." As Chema explains:

> yo pensé, si me canteo y me llevan al chero siquiera iré como gente decente . . . cuando miren que va llegando mi real y distinguida personalida, la guarida batirá marcha, mandarán hechar cuetes y ellos me recibirán con los brazos abiertos, creyéndome un alto personaje, como adicen los rotos, por eso ves que me merqué todo el aparejo que llevo encima.

✻

> [I figured, if I give myself away and get taken to jail at least I'll go as a respectable person . . . when they see the arrival of my royal and distinguished personality, the guards will start playing a march, set off fireworks, and receive me with open arms, believing that I am a person of rank, as the *rotos* say, that's why you see me wearing all this stuff.]

Although Chema and his *jaña* have probably broken the law by stealing from her *roto* employer—a fortune to them but likely of little consequence to her boss—the point of this final anecdote is to expose another of the pernicious inequities of the Mexican criminal justice system: its differential treatment of prisoners. In other words, Chema's crime, if indeed he committed one, is an individual failing stemming from a lack of education and opportunity that pales in comparison to the systemic abuses suffered by members of the urban underclass once they come to the attention of municipal authorities.

Don Juan and the Ghost

With the exception of Pitacio's quick dinner with his *vieja* in the preceding tale, the first two "Desde la estaca" stories dealt with everyday life in Mexico City's public spaces. In those stories, social exchanges in public spaces presented challenges and opportunities for working-class men— challenges and opportunities they understood and responded to in explicitly gendered ways. Most involved class-related affronts to their masculine dignity, which they met with a provocative mix of symbolic inversion, self-deprecating humor, subtle satire, and outright mockery. In contrast, the following story of a ghostly visitation centers on the inner sanctum of the nuclear family: the home. This time the author directs his inversion, humor, satire, and mockery at the masculine pretensions of his protagonist rather than at the classic villains of Porfirian society—corrupt politicians, the decadent bourgeoisie, coercive urban administrators, hypocritical clergy, pushy policeman. By the story's end, however, the critical lens has shifted predictably back to discriminatory policing, persistent social inequalities, and the unmet promises of Porfirian modernization.

This encounter begins with Pitacio singing the enigmatic refrain of a popular song: "¡Upa! y ¡apa! / dicen los de Cuernavaca, / que el animal ques del agua / nomas la pechuga saca." (¡Upa and apa! / say folks from Cuernavaca / the animal that comes from water / shows no more than its breast.)[33] When Pitacio explains to a curious Chema that his stomach is "making like a trampoline," his friend asks "pos que te sacates la lotería ó ha dado á luz, como adicen los rotos, tu jaña algún chamaco con cuatro cabezas?" (well, have you won the lottery or has your *jaña* given light, as the *rotos* say, to a baby with four heads?).[34] "Ni soca manario" (Don't worry about it, brother), Pitacio replies, "sino que Peláez el gordo, mia felecitado por la reaparición de 'La Guacamaya,' pos ya sabes manito, que diay saco los parraleños" (it's just that Peláez the Fatty has congratulated me on the reappearance of *La Guacamaya*, which as you know is how I make my living).[35]

Although no surprise to a regular reader, the occasional reminder that Pitacio happens to be the *La Guacamaya* editor's *pelado* alter ego works to reinforce the paper's ties to a presumably working-class audience, many of whose members had inner *pelados* of their own. In this instance, it also makes the revelations to follow, which focus on personal rather than societal inadequacies, all the more poignant, coming as they do from the generally self-assured and frequently self-righteous Pitacio. These revelations begin with his admission that

> quiora que estaba sin chamba, los chilpayates, lloraban de jaspia y mi jaña me quería coronar, como si fuera rey de bastos, pus no sabes que lo pior es estar sin fierrada, pos hasta mis amigos me deconocían y tan luego como me visentiaban se pelaban, como si miubiera dado la peste bubónica.

> [when I was out of work, my little kids cried from hunger and my woman wanted to crown me, as if I were the King of Wands, but you don't know the worst part of being without cash; it's that even my friends disowned me, and as soon as they saw me coming, they took off, as if I had bubonic plague.]

Pitacio's pitiful lament exposes his guilt and shame over his failure as the family breadwinner and his subsequent loss of prestige in the eyes of his *jaña*—hence the ironic reference to the King of Wands from the tarot deck, a potent symbol of romance, resolve, entrepreneurship, and masculine responsibility. Worst of all, he tells Chema, is the social shunning he suffers at the hands of friends and neighbors. On a practical level, social ostracism represents the loss of a crucial safety net for a sporadically employed worker like Pitacio or Chema. On a symbolic level, it deprives Pitacio of the public validation he needs to maintain his sense of masculine self-worth. In other words, while his *jaña*'s opinion matters a great deal, his greatest concern is his public reputation as a dependable and honorable *man*. Despite Chema's reassurances—"siempre he sido tu cuate" (I've always been your buddy)—he is clearly devastated.

In an effort to distract his distraught friend, Chema tries a touch of sacrilegious teasing—"No me acuentas los de los espantos de la Amargura, como quedamos hoy hace ocho y ques lo que mas minporta" (Don't tell me about the horrors of Our Lady of Sorrows, since today we're at eight, and that's the most important thing)—in order to reawaken Pitacio's wounded masculine pride by reminding him of the seven sorrows stoically endured by the Holy Mother with the death of Jesus. The ploy apparently works, and Pitacio begins what seems to be an unrelated story about a recent ghostly visitation:

> pos has de tener que, muy reciente la chumbanba esa de los espíritus, y con todo lo que adijeron los periólicos esos grandotes, que me pongo muy retiasustado, y que en la noche, como lo liabía metido al bofeteo, que me pongo á calibar sobre los espeitros y que de repente, ¡¡¡uuyy!!! Mano que se me va parando el bulto de mi mujer por delante.[36]

❧

> [well let me tell you, what with the recent gathering of spirits and all that's been said about it in the big newspapers, I'm really frightened, and at night, as I was pretty beaten down, I started thinking about ghosts, and suddenly, whew! Brother, standing there right in front of me is the figure of my woman.]

Aroused, Chema asks "haber, haber, como estuvo eso" (tell me, tell me, what was that like). Never one to resist a sexual innuendo, Pitacio responds by warning Chema not to interrupt "porque si no miaces mas larga la contesta" (or you'll make my answer even longer).[37] Stage set, Pitacio continues his story:

> —Pos como tiba diciendo, se me para el bulto de mi mujer por delante, me toca un pié, es decir, el único que me quedaba, y que voy alzando la fila y que voy mirando el espeitro flaco y escuálido de mi jaña en traje de Eva, antes que se mocara la manzana, y que le adigo: aparta piedra fingida, suelta suéltame la pata, ó te levanto una acta de comisaría, y luego se pone aserme jestos y le adigo: no creas que me causan terror vuestros semblantes esquivos, vuesta cara compungida, jamás ni muerta ni viva, humilarás mi valor. Tenías que aberme visto parodiando á ese siñor que se arapaba muy revalentón y que se llamó D. Juan Tiñoso, pero yo con la cabeza metida debajo de la mula ques la que me sirve cialmuada, y aluego me adice mi jarana, no Pitacio, no tiasustes, que no soy de lotro mundo, pos soy su querida badana, que le vengo á dicir, que no se quen; pero mian jalado los pelos . . . de la cabeza, y como me puesto tan erritada, vengo á que me arapes mi ración de armada pa ver si me pongo trobita y miagüito, por que no puedo dormir,

saco entonces la cabeza, me quedo vitoquiándola y le adigo, alma mía de tí queres tan güena, y yo que tiabía confundido con ese fraile fantasmón que tray á todos mis parcias vueltos locos, ¿queres tu ración de armada? pus toma, y que le voy arapando la botella que tenía junto á mi cantoncito, y que le mete muy recantiado, y quial ratón ya estaba tirada en medio de la pieza con patas en forma de aguja de grújula güeno, y que al día siguiente, voy dispertando con unas ojerotas como las que se pintan las hermosas tiples de jacalón, pos toda la noche estube vitoquiando, espeitros y mas espeitros.

[—well as I was telling you, standing there in front of me is my woman, she touches my foot, the only one I had left [outside the covers], and I'm peeking out and I'm seeing the skinny, squalid ghost of my *jaña*, naked as Eve, the way she looks before she clears her throat, and I say to it: "depart false stone, let go, let go of my paw, or I'll get a court order," and then it begins to mock me and I tell it: "Don't think that you can scare me with your fearsome looks, with your remorseless face, never in death or in life will you humiliate my valor." You should have seen me imitating that gentleman with the swagger, the one called Don Juan Tiñoso, even though my head was stuck under the pad that I was using for a pillow. Then my *jarana* says to me: "No Pitacio, don't be afraid, I'm not from the other world, I'm your beloved lambkins [literally, sheepskin], and I've come to say that I don't know who, but someone has pulled the hair . . . on my head, and since they got me so upset, I've come for my ship's ration, to see if you'll give me a small slice [of food] and a tiny sip of water, because I can't sleep." Then I take out my head [from under the pad], and I'm there looking at her, and I tell her: "my soul of you who are so good, I had you confused with that ghostly monk who's driving all my buddies crazy. Do you want your ration? Go ahead and take it, and I'm passing over the bottle that I had right next to me, which you'll find pretty worked over, and that rat over there that's thrown in the middle of the room with its paws splayed like the needles of a compass." So the next day, I'm waking up with huge eyes like the ones the pretty music hall sopranos paint on themselves, since all night long I was seeing ghosts and more ghosts.]

RUMBO PERDIDO

—

Some elements of this tragicomedy of imagined haunting and mistaken identity are fairly straightforward, especially the fact that Pitacio and his *jaña* are desperately, if temporarily, poor. Details like the worked-over water bottle and the rictus-stricken rat are evidence enough. But Pitacio also confesses that he's using a "mula," the pad used by cargo carriers to cushion heavy loads, instead of a pillow, a detail that connects him to one of the most grueling and least appreciated occupations of the urban working class. Likewise, his "skinny, squalid" *jaña*'s pitiful request for her "ración de armada," a notoriously skimpy ship's ration, provides a further clue to their impoverished circumstances. To add insult to injury, Pitacio's descent into poverty has both immiserated *and* unmanned him. The punch line about waking up with "huge eyes like the ones the pretty music hall sopranos paint on themselves" is one telltale sign of emasculation. But the contrast between the male ghosts that Pitacio fears and the female ghost he actually confronts is even more revealing.

Like most off-the-cuff references in "Desde la estaca," this one has a backstory. Don Juan Tiñoso [literally, Don Juan the Mangy] refers, in Pitacio's malapropic way, to Don Juan Tenorio, the infamous seducer of women and defier of social convention, well known in Mexico through the perennially popular stage play of the same name by Spanish playwright José Zorrilla.[38] In the opening scenes of Zorrilla's play, Don Juan is caught up in a competition with a fellow nobleman, Don Luis, over who can seduce the most women and kill the most men (in duels to restore their lost honor). Having come out on top, he ups the ante, betting that he can seduce two "unattainable" women—a novice about to take her vows to become a nun and a betrothed woman—over the course of the twenty-four hours. At the time of their latest bet, both men are engaged to different women, but when Don Juan's future father-in-law, Don Gonzalo, overhears the conversation, he breaks off the marriage and sequesters his daughter in a convent. Never one to back down from a challenge, the supremely arrogant Don Juan quickly seduces his rival's fiancée (through trickery) and kidnaps his former bride-to-be from her convent (which in the legal codes of the time would have been considered *rapto*, rape). Outraged by these affronts to their masculine honor, Don Luis and Don Gonzalo confront Don Juan, who has meanwhile fallen in love with his former betrothed, Doña Inés, and made a vow to reform. When the repentant seducer begs the forgiveness of the aggrieved men, they accuse him of cowardice. Unable to withstand the insult to his manhood, Don Juan kills them both, resumes his rakish ways, and goes into exile to avoid punishment, thereby causing the death of his heartbroken beloved. On his return five years later, a disinherited Don Juan encounters the stone statues of his victims in a cemetery built on the ruins of his former house by his angry father. When they appear to move in response to his disruptive presence he defiantly announces: "No, no me causan pavor / vuestros semblantes esquivos; / jamás, ni muertos ni vivos, / humillaréis mi valor." (No, you don't scare me / with your fearsome visages; / never, dead or alive, / will you humiliate my valor.) These are the lines that Pitacio repeats nearly word for word at the spectral appearance of his naked *jaña*, along with a version of Don Juan's terrified response—"¡Aparta, piedra fingida! / Suelta, suéltame esa mano" (Depart, false stone! / Let go, let go of this hand)—after the ghostly statute of his former father-in-law tries to drag him off to hell in a later scene.[39]

According to his reconstruction of the previous night's events, a malnourished, agitated Pitacio, attempting in vain to get some much-needed sleep, conjures up three traditional male archetypes—the family patriarch (Don Gonzalo), the monk (*fraile fantasmón*), and the rake (Don Juan). The first two figures reflect the principal "hegemonic masculinities" of the Mexican colonial era, which revolved around two distinct, sometimes oppositional axes: aristocratic notions of masculine honor and spiritual ideals of masculine renunciation.[40] In this context, Don Juan's devil-may-care approach to life represents a privileged form of "protest masculinity," which shares with stereotypical twentieth-century working-class machismo a predilection for instant gratification, misogyny, violence, and a deliberate rejection of social and moral convention. Troubled by the ghosts of respectable men, an honorable patriarch and a reproachful monk, Pitacio attempts to channel the cavalier bravado of the resistant Don Juan—although he's forced to acknowledge to Chema that his efforts were only a "parody" and his head was tucked under his pillow the whole time.

Despite the masculine focus of Pitacio's night fears, the specter that actually appears at the foot of his bed is not a traditional patriarch come to admonish his manly failings but the "skinny, squalid specter of [his] *jaña*, naked as Eve." This unexpected feminine apparition exposes the inadequacy of colonial-era masculine scripts for an ordinary working-class man who has neither the resources nor the inclination to sequester his *mujer* to prevent her seduction, especially when he can't even feed and clothe her or the *chilpayates* (children). The haunting of Pitacio points to much more than outmoded masculine scripts. As sociologist Avery Gordon explains:

> haunting is one way in which abusive systems of power make themselves known and their impacts felt in everyday life. . . . Haunting is not the same as being exploited, traumatized, or oppressed, although it usually involves those experiences or is produced by them. What's distinctive about haunting is that it is an animated state in which a repressed or unresolved social violence is making itself known, sometimes very directly, sometimes more obliquely . . . haunting [is] precisely the domain of turmoil and trouble, that moment (of however long duration) when things are not in their assigned places, when the cracks and rigging are exposed, when the people who are meant to be invisible show up without any signs of leaving, when disturbed feelings cannot be put away, when something else, something different from before, seems like it must be done.[41]

Although it has little to say about the satirical aspects of Pitacio's story (which we'll get to in a moment), Gordon's explanation of haunting captures its representational logic as "an animated state in which a repressed or unresolved social violence is making itself known . . . when the people who are meant to be invisible show up without any signs of leaving." In this case, contrary to Pitacio's fears and expectations, his ghostly visitor turns out to be his own flesh-and-blood *jaña*, reduced to begging for a "ship's ration" of food and water from her self-absorbed, self-pitying husband. Previously invisible but jolted awake by someone tugging at her hair, she intrudes on Pitacio's anxious musings about his inability to "man up" to his responsibilities to make very real, if modest, demands on his resources and his conscience. And her suggestive phrasing—"le vengo á dicir, que no se quen; pero mian jalado los pelos . . . de la cabeza" (I've come to tell you, that someone, I don't know who, but they pulled the hair . . . on my head)—implies that the unnamed perpetrator might well be Pitacio, whose inability to provide for his family has figuratively "yanked her chain," or perhaps the fundamental unfairness of a social system that routinely fails its most vulnerable members.[42]

Along with noting the connection between haunting and social violence, Gordon takes care to distinguish it from exploitation, trauma, and repression by insisting that haunting represents an instance "when disturbed feelings cannot be put away, when something else, something different from before, seems like it must be done." This sense of something-to-be-done (to end the haunting) certainly fits the authorial agenda in this particular column as well as the editorial spirit of the satirical penny press, with its relentless insistence on a fair shake for the laboring classes. Just what that something-to-be-done might actually be, especially about systemic social violence, is hard to tell. Pitacio's pathetic offer of a nearly empty water bottle and a dead rat might temporarily placate his thirsty, hungry *jaña* but does nothing to address the larger social problems generated by endemic political corruption, economic instability, and social inequality—the true sources of their plight.

Short of social revolution—a "something-to-be-done" penny press editors never openly endorsed—the best response was laughter, a classic "weapon of the weak" that works to expose and mock the very things the social order prefers to keep out of sight and out of mind. Those things included the hidden-in-plain-sight structural causes for the masculine insecurities of out-of-work men and the social violence visited on poor women, the main subjects of this particular essay.[43] As Pitacio sings at the beginning of the vignette, "el animal ques del agua / nomas la pechuga saca" (the animal that comes from water / shows no more than its breast), a refrain which anticipates with metaphorical grace the "natural" limitations on social mobility for Mexico City workers, who could never seem to raise themselves out of the sea of poverty for more than a moment or two. In this context, it should come as no surprise that the vignette ends when Pitacio and Chema spot an approaching policeman and head off to a nearby bar to "hecharnos la salud de los espeitros" (toast the health of the specters). In Jacques Derrida's commentary on the specters that haunt the work of Karl Marx, he argues that: "the conjuration [of the ghost] is anxiety from the moment it calls upon death to invent the quick and to enliven the new, to summon the presence of what is not yet there. This anxiety in the face of the ghost is properly revolutionary." If this is so, perhaps Pitacio's conjuration signifies a truly revolutionary spirit.[44]

Some Final Thoughts on Protest Masculinities
and the Civilizing Process

A close reading of the preceding "Desde la estaca" vignettes demonstrates the inextricable links between social critique and masculine subjectivity (the ways men see themselves and are seen by others as *men*) in the satirical penny press. Contrary to much of the literature on "protest masculinities," which focuses on its misogynistic, dysfunctional, and antisocial aspects, the gendered response to social critique that emerges in these stories is sympathetic, reflexive, and nuanced. In the final vignette, for example, Pitacio's *jaña* responds to his fatuous bluster à la Don Juan with a gentle "no tiasustes, que no soy de lotro mundo, pos soy su querida badana" (don't be frightened, I'm not from the other world, I'm just your beloved lambkins). To which he responds not with violence or insults but a well-intentioned, if grammatically awkward, "alma mía de tí queres tan güena" (my soul of you who are so good). In the second vignette, it is Pitacio's patriotic *vieja* who initiates the patriotic salvo that earns them both a trip to the police station and Chema's *jaña* who passes over the (probably) stolen money—acts of female agency that suggest egalitarian complicity rather than male domination. As a matter of fact, the only women who come under criticism in these three columns are the first vignette's billiard-playing women, who use feminine wiles to cheat working-class men out of their hard-earned *fierrada*, and these women are either *rotas* or middle-class *chicas modernas* (modern girls) rather than the female companions of working-class men. So although the antics of Pitacio and Chema represent a form of "protest masculinity" presumably drawn from the real-life experiences of working-class men in early twentieth-century Mexico City, they are hardly the woman-hating, self-destructive behaviors of damaged men that elite critics and mainstream sociological literature lead us to expect.[45] For the "Desde la estaca" author and his readers, working-class masculinity might well be in crisis, but it was also a rich source of humor, especially when it crossed over into unsustainable macho posturing.

Penny press efforts to reimagine working-class manhood through a satire of both working-class and bourgeois sentiments brings us back to the ideological foundation of bourgeois political, economic, social, and cultural hegemony—the civilizing process. As noted earlier, for Norbert

Elias the civilizing process involves "the moderation of spontaneous emotions, the tempering of affects, the extension of mental space beyond the moment into the past and future, the habit of connecting events in terms of chains of cause and effect."[46] All of these so-called civilized traits—self-restraint, equanimity, patience, foresight—require a kind of self-awareness or reflexivity that bourgeois elites (like their aristocratic predecessors) have considered the special provenance of the educated upper classes, traits that might (but usually didn't) trickle down to the unwashed masses. For the most part, social commentators of all stripes have accepted this trickle-down account of civilized behavior despite its blatant class bias and transparent ideological agenda.

Portraying the Porfirian bourgeoisie as cruel, corrupt, lazy, and unpatriotic and then inverting the terms of the debate by exposing the tolerated illegalities of the middle classes and downplaying the "crimes" of the lower classes might have generated some sympathy and perhaps even a quick fix or two from a reform-minded public official, but it failed to get at the ideological foundations of bourgeois hegemony those terms upheld. The "Desde la estaca" vignettes, however, sought to undermine those foundations by revealing—through a satire of bourgeois sentiments— that the class pretentions behind the civilizing process were unwarranted and even absurd. At first glance, Pitacio and Chema might come across as the poorly educated, ill-mannered, misogynistic, live-for-the-moment *pelados* caricatured in Porfirian-era official discourse and social commentary, but a closer look suggests otherwise. While neither man could hope (or would want) to display the effortless self-mastery and careful calculus of the bourgeois masculine ideal, their practical (and comical) mix of self-awareness, flexibility, and enthusiasm provides a much more supple and realistic model of reflexive behavior than the rigid, unrealistic, ideologically driven claims of their "betters." In this instance, then, satire works to validate the sentiments of working-class men, however confused and ridiculous those sentiments might be. Their capacity for creative adaptation to changing circumstances makes them considerably more modern, too—at least if we accept the recent claims of social theorists like Anthony Giddens.

Giddens and others have noted that the concept of modernity—most often associated with the rise of industrial societies, market economies, nation-states, and mass democracy—is also intimately bound up with notions of self-identity. On this view, traditional societies provide individuals with well-understood social roles or "identities," while modern societies require that we figure things out for ourselves. "What to do? How to act? Who to be?" Giddens insists, ". . . are focal questions for everyone living in circumstances of late modernity—and ones which, on some level or another, all of us answer, either discursively or through day-to-day social behaviour."[47] The answers to these focal questions emerge as we make sense of ourselves and our lives by developing and reworking our life stories. As Giddens explains it: "A person's identity is not to be found in behaviour, nor—important though this is—in the reactions of others, but in the capacity *to keep a particular narrative going*. The individual's biography, if she is to maintain regular interaction with others in the day-to-day world, cannot be wholly fictive. It must continually integrate events which occur in the external world, and sort them into the ongoing 'story' about the self."[48]

The hallmark of the modern self, then, resides in its ability to develop and sustain a narrative that enables it to manage the inevitable "risks" that accompany rapid social change. As Giddens carefully notes, a successful narrative "cannot be wholly fictive" since it "must continually integrate events which occur in the external world, and sort them into the ongoing 'story' about the self." Freighted with ideological baggage about personal integrity, self-control, and social status, conventional turn-of-the-century bourgeois narratives of the self lacked the requisite flexibility to respond effectively to external events. The hallmark of the ideal bourgeois man was his "constancy." In contrast, the "Desde la estaca" vignettes are marked by the improvisatory nature of the life narratives they relate—in other words by the continual sorting of external events into the ongoing stories of its protagonists. While it would be foolish to assume that a typical Mexico City worker shared both the linguistic virtuosity and literary craft of *La Guacamaya*'s editor, working-class men did provide the inspiration for a new way of being in the world that would trickle *up* to the Mexican bourgeoisie in the "revolutionary" decades that followed, when the middle-class civilizing process engaged with working-class practical sensibilities to produce the modern self. And as chapter 5 shows, revolutionary ideas about "modern love"—glimpsed in the preceding "Desde de la estaca" vignettes—had a similar and similarly surprising trajectory.

CHAPTER 5

DON JUAN AND THE TROUBLED BIRTH
OF MODERN LOVE

Todo el mundo cree tener la auténtica doctrina sobre él—sobre
Don Juan, el problema más recóndito, más abstruso, más agudo
de nuestro tiempo. Y es que, con pocas excepciones, los hombres
pueden dividirse en tres clases: los que creen ser Don Juanes, los
que creen haberlo sido y los que creen haberlo podido ser, pero no
quisieron. Estos últimos son los que propenden, con benemérita
intención, a atacar a Don Juan y tal vez a decretar su cesantía.

JOSÉ ORTEGA Y GASSET

The final anecdote in the preceding chapter hints at the ubiquity of the
Don Juan figure in Mexican popular culture.[1] Spanish playwright José
Zorrilla's soon-to-be world-famous play *Don Juan Tenorio* premiered in
Madrid on March 28, 1844, and at the Teatro Nacional in Mexico City
just a few months later.[2] Since its Mexican premiere, professional and
amateur theater companies in cities, towns, and villages throughout the
country have regularly staged the play, most often as the dramatic centerpiece of annual public celebrations for the Day of the Dead (November
1–2).[3] It was certainly popular in Porfirian Mexico City, with regular the-
atrical performances and countless offhand references to Don Juan in the
newspapers, social commentary, novels, poems, and songs of the time. If
that weren't enough, film historians consider pioneer cinematographer

Salvador Toscano Barragán's 1899 adaptation of *Don Juan Tenorio* to be Mexico's first nondocumentary film.

Several of these sources targeted working-class audiences. For example, a popular Day of the Dead broadside (see fig. 5.1), produced by Antonio Vanegas Arroyo and illustrated by Manuel Manilla, proclaimed:

Aquí está don Juan Tenorio
De valor siempre notorio;
Pues aunque hoy es calavera
No lo babosea cualquiera.
Y es capas [capaz], si se le obliga
De meterse en la barriga
A medio género humano
Para hacerse el mundo miga.⁴

[Here lies Don Juan Tenorio
Of valor forever renowned;
For although today a skeleton
None dare spit on his grave.
For he is capable, if he's obliged
To stab in the belly
Half the human race
To make the world his crumb.]

Another widely distributed Vanegas Arroyo broadside for Day of the Dead, this one illustrated in the more fluid style of José Guadalupe Posada, strikes the familiar chord (see fig. 5.2). Here a skeletal Don Juan, with plumed hat, cape, tights, raised sword, and clenched fist, taunts his opponents (and the reader): "I am Don Juan Tenorio and make no mistake / I will make mincemeat of your *calaveras*."⁵ Although in the poem (as in the play), Don Juan's bravado eventually succumbs to the gentle pressure of Doña Inés's undying love, his aggressive assertions of masculine honor—highlighted by a visit to hell to take on the devil himself—provide the dramatic centerpiece of the text and the subject for Posada's striking image.

Penny press editors, too, made frequent reference to Don Juan and the infamous *tenorios de barrio*, neighborhood lotharios who seduced and abandoned vulnerable young women.⁶ With this kind of exposure, it

FIG. 5.1 Manuel Manilla/Author Unknown, "La calavera de Don Juan Tenorio," Mexico City: Antonio Vanegas Arroyo, n.d. Courtesy of the Library of Congress Prints and Photographs Division (www.loc.gov/pictures/item/99615907/).

FIG. 5.2 José Guadalupe Posada/Author Unknown, "Yo soy Don Juan Tenorio y sin Quimeras," Mexico City: Antonio Vanegas Arroyo, n.d. Jean Charlot Collection, University of Hawaiʻi at Mānoa Library (inventory no. JCC:JGP:C2).

seems safe to assume that all but the most isolated Mexicans knew the Don Juan story well, had seen it performed several times, however poorly, and could even recite the most dramatic lines from memory, as Pitacio does in the story of Don Juan and the Ghost. The point is that when Mexican men and women, whatever their station in life, thought about manhood, they couldn't help hearing the defiant taunts of Zorrilla's legendary antihero.

In *Nightmares of the Lettered City*, Juan Pablo Dabove argues that the bandit, more precisely the bandit trope, functioned for nineteenth-century Latin America's *letrado* elite as the constitutive outside to the "modern" nation-states they struggled to forge for more than a century after independence. That is to say, the bandit "marks what needs to be excluded, subordinated, or suppressed" for the nation-state to come into being. At the same time, Dabove observes: "it also marks what escapes the material and symbolic control of the elite. It is what exceeds its paradigms. This excess denaturalizes the hegemonic identity [of the modern nation-state] and its mechanisms of representation, since it also shows the fissures that tear it."[7]

This chapter suggests that a similar dynamic characterized another symbolic struggle not unrelated to the birth pangs of nation building: one between a hegemonic identity and its constitutive outside. In this case, however, the hegemonic identity was modern manhood, in particular its approach to gender relations, and the constitutive outside was not a bandit but another kind of criminal, the notorious Don Juan Tenorio, serial seducer of women and serial killer of men, most often in *affaires d'honneur*.

The connection is not as farfetched as it might appear at first glance, even with regard to the manhood of decidedly nonelite men. While their "betters" likely considered working-class male attitudes toward women as barbaric as any bandit's, the satiric penny press depicted working-class men in early twentieth-century Mexico City as actively engaged in rethinking—modernizing if you will—their affective relations with the women in their lives. All the same, editors and contributors recognized that their worker-protagonists were hardly in a position to pretend to mastery of self and society after the fashion of the manly nation builders who sought to banish bandits to the hinterlands of national history. So while, they sought to imagine and represent workingmen's struggles to overcome atavistic impulses—associated in this case with the prickly arrogance of a fictional aristocrat (a telling reversal of the bandit trope)—for the sake of "modern love," they also recognized that workers lacked the authority to plaster over the "fissures" in the facade of modern manhood. Rather than cover up these glaring contradictions, penny press editors and contributors embraced them with a sense of humor, compassion, and self-awareness that mostly escaped their bourgeois counterparts.[8]

This chapter looks at how the penny press challenged accepted views on working-class masculinity by satirizing traditional notions of manhood predicated on male domination of women and hinting at the possibility of modern "companionate" relations between working-class men and the women in their lives. The first section reviews historical critiques of irresponsible masculine behavior, a problem linked directly to *donjuanismo* (identified later in the twentieth century as "machismo") for Mexican men of all classes. The second section examines the connections between *costumbrista* literature, which helped establish a sense of national culture (including "typical" gender relations) in the years following independence from Spain, and "foundational fictions," popular nineteenth-century novels featuring heterosexual romances between lovers from disparate social classes, romances that served as a metaphor for national consolidation during the same period. The third section looks at penny press *romances callejeros* (street romances), a late romantic *costumbrista* poetic genre that exploited the tragicomic tension between normative and transgressive notions of proper gender relations. While most *romance callejero* poets imagined working-class gender relations as an ongoing battle between the sexes, the fourth section analyzes the unconventional romances of penny press contributor Canuto Godines, which feature strong female protagonists who force their male counterparts to treat them as true companions rather than household help, sheltered innocents, or sequestered symbols of masculine honor. The conclusion explores the implications of the penny press representations of working-class gender relations as transitioning from traditional relationships characterized by patriarchal domination to modern partnerships grounded in mutual respect.

The Specter of Don Juan

On one level, the enduring popularity of *Don Juan Tenorio*, the play and the man, produced a shared trope or symbol that transcended (and continues to transcend) the profound disparities of political power, economic class, social status, and cultural attainment that have plagued Mexican society at least since the sixteenth-century conquest. At the same time, however, Don Juan and the *donjuanismo* that he allegedly inspires in men represent a serious social problem that some commentators have seen as the foundation of dysfunctional gender relations in Mexico and elsewhere. For example, in a 1951 collection of essays with the suggestive title *Don Juan delincuente* (Don Juan, Delinquent), Mexican criminologist Carlos Franco Sodi argued that

> Queremos o no Don Juan está constantemente entre nosotros. Su tenaz presencia resulta un profundo problema para el médico y el pedagogo, el sociólogo, el jurista y el literato. Su perdurar a través de los siglos y en los pueblos todos, es la inquietante afirmación de que la humanidad de ayer, de hoy y de mañana lleva consigo, ignorado e irresoluto, el problema de los sexos y es también—su misma presencia fanfarrona—, un alarde y una viviente comprobación de su victoria sobre teólogos y moralistas, sobre profesores alarmados con sus cínicas hazañas y sobre juristas que, indignados, han pretendido amedrentrarlo con el bíblico anatema del Código Penal.[9]

> [Whether we like it or not Don Juan is always with us. His tenacious presence produces a huge problem for the doctor and the pedagogue, the sociologist, the jurist, and the man of letters. His persistence across the centuries and among all peoples, is the disquieting affirmation that the humanity of yesterday, today, and tomorrow carries with it, ignored and unresolved, the problem of the sexes and he is also— his very boastful presence—arrogant and living proof of his victory over theologians and moralists, over professors alarmed at his cynical deeds and over jurists who, indignant, have attempted to frighten him with the biblical curse of the Penal Code.]

Coming from the author of the modern Mexican Code of Criminal Procedure, a man about to become the nation's attorney general (1952–56), the accusation that the misdeeds of this "hateful rapist" represented the "perfect manifestation of manliness" to most Mexicans gives some sense of the depth of official concerns about the perennial problem of male irresponsibility toward women in particular and toward the social bonds that ensure good citizenship in general—a problem that would soon come to be identified in popular and official circles as machismo. Crucial to Franco Sodi's understanding of the problem was his insistence that *donjuanismo* was holding back social and moral progress by encouraging sadistic, antisocial behavior in men and masochistic tolerance of male philandering and violence in women. In other words, for a social reformer like the future attorney general, the construction of "modern" gender relations, based on mutual respect between the sexes, required that men and women give up their perverse obsession with the "elegant and always amiable" Don Juan. "Either we erase the Criminal Code," Franco Sodi advised, "or we send Don Juan to the gallows."[10]

Franco Sodi was hardly the first social commentator to denounce the pernicious effects of *donjuanismo* on Mexican social relations or allege that men and women alike were susceptible to Don Juan's dubious charms. In a September 1908 commentary, the *El Diablito Rojo* editor—more moralistic than most of his colleagues—noted disapprovingly that

> El pueblo mexicano tiene en grado máximo el espiritú donjuanesco de la raza hispano-azteca. Amar y reñir—como los gallos—es la característica del nacional legítimo. Sin que esto quiera decir que no sea trabajador y artista, patriótico y valiente . . . ¿Y qué decir de una 'chorchita' de jóvenes de ambos sexos, decentes de ropa, pero con audacia de calaveras? Con honrosísimas excepciones, allí todos son Tenorios.[11]

> [The Mexican people have the donjuanesque spirit of the Hispano-Aztec race to the nth degree. To love and to squabble—like roosters—is a truly national trait. This is not to deny that they are also hardworking and artistic, patriotic and brave. . . . But what to say about a "pack" of young people of both sexes, dressed decently enough, but with the audacity of *calaveras*? With a few very honorable exceptions, all are Tenorios.]

While acknowledging the virtues of the Hispano-Aztec race, *El Diablito Rojo* nonetheless despairs over the "maña erótica nacional" (national erotic custom) of verbally harassing women on the street. "In the Aztec capital—the center of culture—the donjuanesque mania is out of hand," he groused. "Here the dandy 'flatters' and the poor man 'gropes.' Each makes love after his own fashion, but both in the same ridiculously flirtatious way."[12] To make matters worse, despite suffering from endless verbal assaults on the part of Mexican men—which the author casts here as the product of an atavistic "Hispano-Aztec" culture—Mexican women seemed more inclined to play along than take offense. In a mock scenario constructed for readers, a young servant girl out on an errand responds to a proposition like this:

> —¿Que húbole? ¿Sí, o no?
> Ella baja la picaresca faz, muerde la punta del delantal, hace un hoyito en la tierra con el talón desnudo, y muerta de risa lanza un
> —¡No!
> que es un "¡si!" más clara que un sí sobreagudo de la Patti.[13]

🌼

> [—What do you think? Yes or no?
> She lowers her mischievous face, bites the corner of her apron, digs a small hole in the ground with a bare toe [literally "claw"], and dying with laughter lets out a
> —No!
> which is a "sí!" clearer than a high C from la Patti.]

Only when Mexican women of all classes insist on the "respect due their sex" and the authorities start punishing offenders, he concludes, will the problem disappear.

In follow-up editorial for Day of the Dead, *El Diablito Rojo* revisits the theme. This time he shifts focus from the everyday cultural practice of *donjuanismo* to the troublesome figure of Don Juan himself.[14] As he sees it, the problem is that everyone knows Don Juan: "Who hasn't seen him? Who isn't acquainted with him? Who doesn't remember him?" Moreover, everyone loves him despite, perhaps even because of, his damnable flaws. Don Juan's annual resurrection on Day of the Dead, the editorial observes: "is greeted with joy, with enthusiasm, with satisfaction. He's a skeleton, a rake, but he has three virtues: he's extremely rich, he's brave, and he's our friend."[15] All this adulation for a despicable criminal, "a gallows fruit . . . [who] kills thirty-four men and seduces seventy-three women, taking 'a day to love them / another to have them / another to leave them / two to replace them / and an hour to forget them.'"[16] Don Juan's popularity, *El Diablito Rojo* argued, might be absurd, but it was nonetheless an unavoidable fact of Mexican life. In a comment prefiguring Franco

Sodi by forty years, he ends his tirade against the annual celebration of masculine misbehavior with world-weary resignation: "Well, long live the Tenorios; but let no one later invoke the [criminal] codes. That's just the way it is."[17]

Although *El Diablito Rojo* had nothing good to say about Don Juan, colleagues and competitors sometimes disagreed about his ongoing impact on masculine behavior. Just a year later, an *El Diablito Rojo* contributor lamented that the gallantry of the "legendary Tenorio" and the innocence of the virtuous Doña Inés had been replaced in contemporary Mexican society by the hypocrisy and crass self-interest of "los Calixtos, las Melibeas y las Celestinas."[18] "These days gentlemen don't romance and seduce ladies, they deceive them," he complained. "Tenorio didn't steal their love, he took advantage of it. Then, Doña Inés was an immaculate maiden in a convent, idealistic and pure. Now, the Inéses are other men's women."[19] For this social critic at least, *Don Juan's* popularity was more a matter of mourning the death of chivalry than testimony to its antihero's influence on contemporary mores: "the crowds go to see *Don Juan Tenorio*. On Day of the Dead. Because 'Tenorio' is dead."[20] Whatever their take on Don Juan, critics and fans alike have cast him as the embodiment of traditional masculine values (however dysfunctional), in particular a heightened sense of personal honor and a willingness to defend it at all costs.

The Romance of Popular Culture

In contrast to the recurrent concerns voiced by social commentators like Franco Sodi and *El Diablito Rojo*, most penny press responses to Don Juan and *donjuanismo* evoked a playful nostalgia tinged with irony, satire, and parody rather than an endorsement of hypermasculine misbehavior. This nostalgic mode is especially apparent in another penny press feature, the *romance callejero*, or "street romance," a short vignette written in assonant verse and set amid Mexico City's vibrant street culture.[21] A typical *romance callejero* chronicled in mock epic fashion the trials and tribulations of ordinary people: their leisure activities, love affairs, quarrels, betrayals, and violent (occasionally fatal) outbursts.

Despite the cavalier tone, quotidian subject matter, and humble venue, the *romance callejero* had a distinguished literary pedigree. In his extensive work on the emergence of popular nationalism in the mid-nineteenth century, Ricardo Pérez Monfort argues that the introduction of *costumbrismo*—a Spanish romantic-era genre grounded in local "customs"—provided Mexican writers the perfect vehicle for constructing an imagined national community freed from the shackles of Spanish cultural dominance.[22] The cosmopolitan character of elite society offered little that was unique to Mexico; so *costumbristas* turned instead to the heterogeneous popular culture of the country's less privileged classes, which they put forth as the essence, for better or worse, of *lo mexicano* (Mexicanness). As Pérez Monfort explains: "'The Mexican people,' as the protagonist of novels and stories, presented itself in multiple ways. Language, costumes, customs, games, traditions, and fiestas played a central role. . . . And although it was this people that the [writer] presumed to mold, critique, or moralize; it was also in revealing its qualities and creativity that the narrator affirmed his nationalism and contributed to the creation of a 'Mexican stereotype.'"[23]

Literary excursions into popular culture have a long tradition in Spanish letters, one stretching at least as far back as the publication of the anonymous sixteenth-century picaresque novella *La vida de Lazarillo de Tormes y de sus fortunas y adversidades* (The Life of Lazarillo de Tormes and His Fortunes and Adversities).[24] Like the picaresque novelists, Mexico's mid-nineteenth-century *costumbristas* and early twentieth-century *romance callejero* poets trafficked in such popular stereotypes as the ubiquitous *china poblana* and the *chinaco* that "purported to synthesize the physical and psychological characteristics of a social sector or cultural type."[25] Similar too was a tendency to overrepresent social sectors and cultural types from the colorful margins of decent society. In the Mexican case this included groups, like *pelados* and *léperos*, that *gente decente* (decent folk) considered debased, deviant, and prone to criminal behavior. In their dubious company, readers ventured into "forbidden places . . . *pulquerías*, cantinas, brothels, dives and all the places that made up the underworld."[26]

Despite these shared generic conventions, two major differences distinguished nineteenth-century Mexican *costumbrismo* from earlier picaresque celebratory condemnations of popular culture. One was its eager embrace of the "customs" of the common folk as the symbolic core of *lo mexicano*, the signifier of the essential difference that set the new nation and its people apart from the metropole and the rest of Spanish America. Pérez Monfort notes that *costumbristas* often depicted the Mexican people as in dire need of redemption—a condition they typically blamed on imperial abuse and neglect—but they nonetheless admitted even the much-maligned *pelados* as citizens of the sovereign nation constituted in their name. In other words, *costumbrismo* was a gesture of literary inclusion despite its occasional forays into social critique, while picaresque novels sought principally to shock and entertain readers with lurid accounts of life among society's outcasts.

Another major difference was the "strong flavor of nostalgia for a not so distant past" evident in most *costumbrista* writing, especially in later works like the penny press *romance callejero*. Distressed by the radical transformations in urban life noticeable as early as midcentury, especially in the capital, *costumbristas* wrote "against the grain" to evoke "México de los recuerdos" (Mexico in memories), where lower-class transgressions took on a folkloric patina that belied any serious dangers to the social order.[27] A central figure in this poetic endeavor was liberal *letrado* icon Guillermo Prieto (1818–97), whose much-admired *costumbrista* poetry, collected and published in 1883 under the title *Musa Callejera* (Street Muse), supplied *romance callejero* poets with a receptive audience, literary models, a bohemian tone, and a range of popular types.[28] By the late Porfiriato, however, *letrados* like novelist Federico Gamboa had dropped romantic-era nostalgia for the gritty, if still overwrought, naturalism of Émile Zola and other contemporary Continental writers. For Gamboa and many of his contemporaries, Mexican popular culture had lost its picturesque nation-defining allure. Their readers could still experience the vicarious thrills of a literary journey into the urban underworld, but in Mexican naturalist fiction the no longer quaint "customs" of its denizens threatened to erode the still vulnerable foundations of Porfirian progress.

In contrast, *romance callejero* poets stayed true to the mid-nineteenth century romantic aesthetic found in a writer like Prieto, just as in their political commentaries they went on espousing *puro* liberalism long after it had fallen out of favor among the ruling classes. To counter naturalists' literary assault on popular custom, *romance callejero* poets distilled the *costumbrista* nostalgia to its folkloric essence, dispensing with moralistic digressions and playing up local color. And if their "native" protagonists sometimes resorted to public violence to settle disputes or restore lost honor, working-class troublemaking never left the confines of the local *vecindad*, or barrio. A social problem perhaps but nothing the neighborhood police couldn't handle (however badly); nothing to concern the up-standing residents of the capital's new class-segregated neighborhoods; nothing to threaten national development.

Important as *romance callejero* may have been to the penny press's uphill battle to promote working-class culture and downplay lower-class delinquency, its principal message to readers was altogether different. In *Foundational Fictions*, Doris Sommer examines the interplay of romantic love and patriotism in the nineteenth-century canonical novels that came to embody the patriotic aspirations of most Latin American nations. Despite profound national differences, Sommer argues, these novels represented "a common project to build [nations] through reconciliations and amalgamations of national constituencies cast as lovers destined to desire each other." To this transcendent end and "whether the plots end happily or not, the romances are invariably about desire in young chaste heroes for equally young and chaste heroines, the nation's hope for productive unions."[29]

At first glance, the high-minded national allegories identified in *Foundational Fictions* have little connection to the humble *romance callejero* other than common roots in the nineteenth-century romantic *costumbrista* tradition.[30] Superficial differences aside, however, the notion that romantic love was the cornerstone of national consolidation is also implicit in the *romance callejero*, although in a less deliberate way that leads back to Don Juan as the constitutive outside to modern manhood and national consolidation. According to Sommer, foundational fictions were allegorical novels singled out by public officials, educators, and bourgeois readers as especially edifying for young future citizens because of the different ways they reconciled, through love, courtship, and marriage, the social divisions that had made forging the postindependence nation-state such a Sisyphean task.

Not all romantic-era national allegories, however, met official expectations. Take, for instance, a popular romance published in 1885 by another liberal *letrado* icon, Vicente Riva Palacio, with the title "El amor del chinaco" (The *Chinaco*'s Love) and reprinted in 1904 by *El Diablito Bromista* under the heading "Romances nacionales." The poem tells the tragicomic tale of a *chinaco*, Encarnación Torreblanca, who has fallen in love with the beautiful daughter of a prominent local rancher.[31] Encarnación is "valiant and fortunate," and the young lady "purer than an old woman," but her elderly father sets four conditions for their marriage: "That [Encarnación] not take too much pride in his bravery, prove constant in love, agree to *give up his friends*, and be unafraid to work."[32] To which the despondent young man responds: "It makes me so *angry* I'll surely fail; what he asks is even more impossible than [the demands of] an old woman at her rosary."[33]

There can be no doubt about the allegorical elements at work in Riva Palacio's poem. The first line gives us the hero's name, Encarnación Torreblanca, the "ivory tower incarnation" of chivalrous manhood, and three lines later we learn that this Mexican knight-errant is also "the mirror of the *chinacos*," the renowned horsemen who fought so valiantly against the usurper Maximilian (many of them under General Riva Palacio himself). Unstated in the poem but taken for granted by most contemporary readers was the assumption that as a *chinaco* Encarnación would have been mestizo (mixed race) and from a humble background, circumstances that account for the father's concerns about his future son-in-law's prospects. Following Sommer's criteria, the mismatched couple is ideally suited to an allegory about the joining together of antagonistic social classes through romantic love and marriage—just what we might expect from a prominent liberal ideologue like Riva Palacio. We are left instead with the petulant hero's refusal to sacrifice his independence, his manhood, and *his friends*, all essential elements of his social identity as a *chinaco*, to take on the responsibilities and hard work of a respectable marriage, to say nothing of nation building. Riva Palacio acknowledges Encarnación's matchless skill as a horseman, his heroism in battle, and his success with "las muchachas del barrio" (neighborhood girls), but these martial virtues are ill suited to the more daunting if less glamorous challenges of mature adulthood and responsible citizenship. The sly parting twist gives the poem much of its charm, both because it surprises the reader who expects a more conventional love story with a happy ending and because it rings true—in the real world good *chinacos* were unlikely to make good husbands and fathers. Thus the purpose of Riva Palacio's national allegory is not to spin fantasies about romantic love and marriage as a cure-all for the country's deep social divisions but to point out that deeply ingrained attachments to "traditional" masculine identities rendered such a solution "even more impossible than [the demands of] an old woman at her rosary." Although "El amor del chinaco" predates the penny press romances callejeros by at least fifteen years, takes place in a small rural town rather than the national capital, and features a dashing horseman rather than a humble laborer, the underlying message isn't all that different: the male protagonists of the romances callejeros are as ill prepared for modern manhood as any *chinaco*.

Romance in the Streets

The best *romance callejero* poets excelled at local color—at capturing in vernacular language the sights, sounds, tastes, and smells of the Mexico City streets, not as they actually were but as they might appear to a recent migrant from the countryside, a bemused foreign visitor, or in the writer's childhood memories. In some cases conveying local color rather than contributing to the national allegory was the principal objective. For example, the anonymous poet (or poets) for several *El Diablito Bromista* romances offered up bohemian-inflected vignettes about popular fiestas, local characters, and overheard snippets of conversation that had little or nothing to do with romantic relationships or national dilemmas.[34] "El baile de la Petra" (Petra's Dance) starts off with fifty-eight couples "pressing hard up against each other to the sounds of the dance," introduces the hostess and the band, proceeds to a detailed description of the available alcohol ("six buckets of pulque from Tlamapa, along with ten bottles of *to love you without hope*, and a vat of punch laced with cheap whisky and water"), recounts the antics of the drunk harpist, repeats a long series of humorous toasts in honor of Petra, and finishes back on the dance floor with the fifty couples who are still sober enough to continue.[35] In a similar vein, "El santo de la casera" (The Household Saint), chronicles the movable feast of Doña Challo, which begins at the Plaza de San Lucas, a few blocks south of the Zócalo, travels about five miles southeast by street car to Ixtacalco, then back to the pleasure gardens at Tívoli de San Cosme, several blocks west of the Alameda. As befits the festive spirit of this urban adventure, the dramatic highpoint is an exquisitely detailed description of the birthday banquet.[36] Yet another romance chronicles the adventures (including food and alcohol) of a group of friends who journey downtown to the Callejón de la Nana to celebrate independence by *corriendo gallo* (literally, running the rooster), singing and playing their way through the city streets as roving minstrels in anticipation of the annual *Grito*.[37] Although colorful urban characters, usually including a narrator/guide, have important roles to play in this subgenre of the *romance callejero*, the main protagonist is the city and the popular culture it inspires.

More typical were romances that allowed the reader to experience the urban milieu through stories about local types. One particularly gruesome vignette, "El muerto recusitado" (The Resuscitated Dead Man) records the final hours of a street vendor: "a poor devil without a home or family . . . one of those gypsies of lost Bohemia who always wake up hung over and with their guts tied in knots." As the poem begins, the poor man suffers an epileptic fit that lands him in the morgue and then under the knife of the attending surgeon, who decides to cut him open for the edification of a group of medical students. Toward the end of the poem (and halfway through the autopsy), the victim revives and complains to the doctor: "Don't chop me down while I'm still green, the field will dry up." When the startled surgeon asks why he didn't say something earlier, the fatally wounded man replies: "because the job was so fine, the boss such a gentleman [*charro*], that I didn't even have to take off my boots."[38]

Another tongue-in-cheek romance about a classic urban type—this time a *garbancera*, "a pretty Indian maid . . . dark with soft skin and scarlet cheeks, very black and provocative eyes"—eavesdrops on a conversation in a local open-air food market between the girl and an older market woman that ranges from the high price of tomatoes to the *garbancera's* intimate relations with her employer's handsome son. In response to the maid's confession of illicit love, her confidante admits to having had a similar affair in her youth with a "licenciado cuenta chiles" (miserly lawyer), congratulates the girl on having snagged a considerate young man, and advises that she "never fail to serve him his dinner, or whatever he takes, in bed."[39] As both vignettes demonstrate, traffic in stereotypes can work to reinforce traditional social relations by suppressing the dark side of dramatic social inequalities. This suppression enables the story's humor and makes otherwise shocking events—the surgeon's cavalier decision to autopsy the epileptic street vendor, the domestic servants' acceptance of sexual exploitation—seem like natural occurrences rather than causes for alarm or indignation. At the same time, however, this apparent dismissal of social inequalities also works to disguise serious social critique in ways that might escape the notice of an inattentive or incurious reader.

In the preceding vignettes, for instance, the final ironic twist—a generic convention intended to shock the reader into awareness of the fundamental strangeness of the situation at hand—derives from the protagonists' cheerful acceptance of their appalling lot in life and its destructive effects on their relationships. So while the stories themselves contain no overt social criticism, the authors set up their readers to experience the strangeness of its absence, especially in a venue devoted to working-class issues.

In other instances, authors embedded tangible clues that might alert a savvy reader to the "hidden" meaning beneath the innocuous surface of the text. For example, in "Hay te van de canto" (Now You're Taking It Too Far), the reader listens in on two street musicians, a female singer and a male organ grinder, as they bicker over turf, respective musical abilities, and personal failings. The singer is identified as

> . . . una grulla
> De aquellas de la Merced,
> Que usan su tacón de hueso
> Y su fachoso tupé,
> Con las pilas de pomade,
> Si no de cerdo, de res,
> Y sus enaguas planchadas
> Que hacen un ruido de tren
> Más grande que Temamatlá.[40]

> [. . . a crane
> One of those from Merced,
> Who wears high heels
> And a ridiculous hairpiece,
> With piles of pomade,
> If not made from pigs, then from cows,
> And her starched petticoats
> Which make more noise
> Than the Temamatlá train wreck.]

And the organ grinder comes from the same underworld milieu as his interlocutor:

un coime de alquiler
De esos de cara cortada
Que versan mucho y bien
Y disparan su fierrada
En amarte con placer.[41]

[a gambler for hire
A typical scarface
Who is a great talker
And blows his dough
On giving you a good time.]

Given the personality types involved, the sarcastic bantering that makes up the bulk of the romance seems little more than the latest salvo in an endless war between the sexes: wronged woman rebukes irresponsible man, annoyed man derides nagging woman. The clue to the vignette's meaning lies in the opening lines sung by the *grulla*:

Macetita embalmasada
Con hojitas de laurel,
Qué bonitos son los bueyes
Cuando empiezan á querer;
Con palabras y canciones
Engañan á la mujer,
Y ya que la ven perdida
La van haciendo furriel.[42]

[Sweet flowerpot infused
With little leaves of laurel,
How pretty bullocks are
When they begin to love;
With words and songs
They deceive the woman,
And when they see her lost
They treat her like dirt.]

The verse is a slightly mangled version of a popular folksong, and the sentiment expressed in these opening lines, with their not so subtle reference to the singer's sweet "maceta embalsamada" (literally, her perfumed flowerpot, figuratively her vagina), seems to support the resentments voiced by the singer later in the poem. However, a more complete version of the song, included in a 1905 Vanegas Arroyo broadside, has a surprise ending of its own:

Macetita embalsamada
Con hojitos de laurel,
Que bonitos son los hombres
Cuando empiezan á querer
Con cartitas y regalos
Consiguen á una mujer,
Y luego que la han perdido
La empiezan á aborrecer.

Un señor me dió un pañuelo
Como prenda de palabra
Para casarme con él
Y de engañarme trataba,
Pero se pegó buen chasco
Porque no soy tan dejada;
La basura yo la tiro
Porque me tiene mareada.

Macetita de mi vida,
De flores muy perfumada
¡Qué bonito es el amor
De la mujer que es honrada!
Yo tengo una macetita
En la que sembré un clavel
Para darselo á mi novio
Cuando me sepa querer.

El que sepa amar
Que compre una macetita
Y siembre luego en ella

Del amor una matita,
Que nunca se muestre ingrata
Ni aborrezca á las mujeres
Que al hombre que sabe amar,
La mujer siempre lo quiere.[43]

[Sweet flowerpot infused
With little leaves of laurel,
How pretty men are
When they begin to love
With sweet letters and gifts
They snare a woman
And then when they have ruined her
They begin to abhor her.

A gentleman gave me a kerchief
As a token of his pledge
That he would marry me
And then he tried to trick me.
But I frustrated his plans
Because I'm not that desperate;
Trash, I throw it out
Because it makes me nauseous.

My beloved flowerpot
Infused with the scent of flowers
How pretty is the love
Of a woman who has respect!
I have a sweet flowerpot
In which I will plant a carnation
To give to my betrothed
When he learns to love me.

The man who knows how to love
Who buys a sweet flowerpot
And plants in it
With love a sweet sprig

Who never shows ingratitude
Nor abhors womankind
The man who knows how to love
The woman always cares for.]

The complete lyrics, like the first verse that begins the romance, reflect long-standing female grievances about male duplicity, especially the false promises—letters, gifts, tokens, pledges—of *los tenorios*. Hence the street singer's deliberate substitution of *bueyes*, or "bullocks" (castrated bulls), for *hombres* in the romance. In the second verse of the longer song, the narrator/singer shows no hesitation in throwing her *novio* out like "trash" when he tries to take advantage of her. The deliberate use of the subjunctive tense in subsequent verses suggests that she has lingering doubts about ever finding a good man ("que *sepa* querer") even though the penultimate line of the poem, cast in the indicative mode, asserts that a woman will always care for a man who really knows how to love ("que *sabe* querer"), an emotion defined earlier in terms of gratitude, respect, companionship, and nurturance (the subject of the final section of this chapter).[44] So while the romance presents the dialogue between street singer and organ grinder as a somewhat equal exchange, the introductory song shifts the balance in the singer's favor by reinforcing the notion that deceitful men are the principal culprits in the degradation of women.

Despite the picaresque flavor of the *romances callejeros* and the enduring popularity of Don Juan, *tenorios de barrio* were most often cast as either banal villains or laughable buffoons. Cast as villains, they manage to seduce only the most vulnerable, naive, or greedy of women; as buffoons they serve as the target of women's scorn, as happens in the song "Macetita embalsamada." In "El Rapto de Dorotea" (The Abduction of Dorotea), the villain Julian—identified as "de los tenorios modernos" (a modern *tenorio*)—seduces the foolish Dorotea whose new job as a factory worker has given her delusions of grandeur and prompted her to throw off her *novio*, a poor organ grinder named Cenobio.[45] According to the catty neighbor who narrates the romance, Julian seduces the naive young girl with love songs, offers to marry her, abducts her, and then gets her pregnant—a fact that the disgraced young woman tries to cover up by feigning stomach problems when it comes time to give birth. "Lo más claro es suponer," the neighbor observes. "Que la enferma es Dorotea / Está muy flaca, muy fea / Y ya no quiere . . . co . . . mer" (all one can suppose is / that the sick woman is Dorotea / she's very skinny, very ugly / and no longer wants to . . . eat). In the Spanish text, the ellipsis produces a deliberate slippage between *co . . . mer* (to eat) and *co . . . ger* (to fuck), which suggests that the young woman's inability to control her appetites for food, gifts, romance, and sexual pleasure is more to blame for her humiliation than Julian's seductive powers.

Confronted with a strong-willed young woman, the *tenorio* in "La güera del cantero" (The Stonemason's Blonde) has considerably less success. The romance opens with an elaborate forty-line spiel that begins thus:

> Adios, pedazo de cielo
> Adornado de estrellitas,
> Encantadora del barrio,
> Pedacito de mi vida;
> ¿Dónde vas tan de manana
> Y tan repechi tan linda?
> ¿No quiere que la acompañe
> Aunque sea por la orillita? [46]

❦

> [Greetings, slice of heaven
> Adorned with little stars,
> Enchantress of the neighborhood,
> Light of my life;
> Where are you going so early in the morning
> So shapely and so pretty?
> Would you like me to accompany you
> Even if it's just along the sidewalk?]

When the *tenorio* shows no sign of letting up, the young woman interrupts with "Pos oigasté, yo no puedo / Aunque usté me regocije" (listen you, I can't / even if I liked you). When this brush-off fails to discourage further advances, she calls him a coward and threatens to tell her boyfriend, the stonemason, whom she characterizes as a *real* man willing to "beat the dust from death itself." To which her harasser responds, "Dígale usté á su cantero / Que lo quiero en pulquería / Y lo he de vestir de charro / Con paciencia y con saliva" (tell your stonemason / that I want to see him in the *pulquería* / and I'll be dressed as a *charro* / with patience and saliva). The expression *paciencia y saliva*—from the adage "con paciencia y saliva se la metió el elefante a la hormiga" (with patience and saliva the elephant fucked the ant)—is intended as a threat but it's unclear whether the *tenorio* is referring to his plans for the young woman or the stonemason or both. Regardless, the stonemason's girlfriend dismisses it with a curt "Adios, mugre, hasta la vista" (good-bye, scum, see you later), and the *tenorio* retreats to a nearby *pulquería* to repair his wounded pride. Although the seduction succeeds in one romance and fails in the other, neither *tenorio* comes across as admirable or noteworthy since success or failure depended entirely on the character of the women rather than their prowess as men: Julian is able to seduce the fatuous Dorotea, but the self-styled *charro* is easily routed by a confident young woman.

Much more threatening to most *romance callejero* poets than the seductive capabilities of *tenorios de barrio* was the damage inflicted on sensitive, hardworking men by heartless, ambitious women. In their poems bad women generally come to a bad end, sometimes through their own devices. In "Romance callejero," the feckless Secundina abuses the generosity of her boyfriend Melaquides, a hotel manager, until he can no longer afford to buy her fancy clothes, at which point she dumps him for what turns out to be a string of equally gullible men.[47] Eventually, however, her nemesis appears, a "jicarero bárbaro" (barbaric pulque seller) who beats her "Hasta que ya no pudiendo / Soportar tu amancebato / Le sambutió una chaveta / En el perol de los garbanzos" (until no longer able / to put up with his devotion / she stuck a knife / in his bean pot).

Although Secundina deals directly and violently with the consequences of her behavior, most duplicitous women incited violence in their male victims. The jilted man in "Así me gusta agarrarlos" (That's How I Like to Grab Them) hides behind a tree until his former girlfriend and her new boyfriend appear. Having caught them in the act, he sinks a knife into his rival "con todo y mango" (up to the hilt), and the romance concludes with one man in the cemetery (Dolores), the other in jail (Hotel Wulfrano), and the woman "sigue por las noches dándose vuelo en el barrio" (goes back to walking the barrio streets at night).[48]

The dramatic possibilities inherent in female betrayal narratives inspired more elaborate romances, and love triangles with male competitors vying for the attentions of a beautiful but deceitful woman proved especially popular. The three-part serial "La Verbena de los Angeles" (The Los Angeles Fair) opens with two young lovers, Chano Pipa and Juana Brincos, all dressed up and headed to the Metropolitan Cathedral on the Zócalo to enjoy the annual fair for the Assumption of the Virgin Mary.[49] The poet lets the reader know that "Los ojos se iban tras ella: / él caminaba soberbio, / como diciendo á los bobos / '¡Uy! Majes, miren que cuero'" (Eyes followed after her: / he walked haughtily, / as if saying to the fools / Hey! losers, this is my woman). By the second installment Chano and Juana have arrived at the fair, where they encounter Petronilo el "Ojos Negros" ("Black Eyes"), who gives Juana a look that causes her to turn "more yellow than death itself."[50] When Pipa asks "¿Por qué tiemblas, pichoncita?" (Why do you tremble, little dove?), the brooding Petronilo offers his services as doctor: "Y los males de esta jaña / que se hallan dentro del pecho / aliviaré yo en el auto / con un gran medicamento" (And the evils that this woman / carries in her breast / I will cure right away / with a great medicine). Juana begs Pipa to take her away, but before he can react Petronilo informs him harshly that Juana

> tiene el alma más cochina
> que el muladar más infecto.
> Las caricias que á usté le hace
> á mi tambien me las ha hecho;
> y como usté ha saboreado
> sus más requiriosos besos,
> besos que saben á dulce
> pero destilan veneno.

> [has the most swinish soul
> in the most putrid of sties.
> the caress that she shares with you
> she has also shared with me;
> just as you have savored
> her most intimate kisses
> kisses that taste sweet
> but ooze poison.]

A stunned Pipa demands that Petronilo prove the accusations, and the second episode abruptly ends. A week later, in the romance's conclusion, the wronged man launches into one final harangue against the "black hearted" young woman before he "sinks his blade into the flesh of the unfortunate Brincos until he wets his fingers."[51] Having brought the tragedy to its bloody end, the poet can't resist the impulse to moralize: "Jaranas, no seais taimadas, / sed fieles á vuestro cuero . . . / ¡Que no os vaya á suceder / lo que á la jaña del cuento! (Women, don't be deceitful / stay faithful to your men / Otherwise things might turn out for you / as they do for the woman in the story).

The facetious moral, along with the suggestive names of the protagonists, give the romance an allegorical tone. The haughty Chon Pipa brings to mind the common phrase *pasarlo pipa* (to have a good time), making him the Mexican equivalent of a good-time Charlie; the fickle Juana Brincos "jumps" from man to man, and the phrase "quitar los brincos a alguien" (to take someone down a peg) deftly summarizes her unhappy fate; the implacable Petronilo el "Ojos Negros" likely gets his nickname from a popular Mexico City *danza* of the era, "Los ojos mexicanos," which notes the superficial virtues of blue and green eyes before concluding that only "los ojos negros son todo corazón" (only black eyes are pure of heart).[52] The allegory here might center on romantic love, but this is no foundational fiction with a promise of reconciliation and hope. In this tale, "Ojos Negros," the only person capable of true love, is driven to murder, and the violence of his blow (like the stabbing "con todo y mango" in the previous poem) is so forceful that his hands end up covered in the victim's blood.[53] If the poet intended this romance about working-class gender relations gone awry as a national allegory, then the prognosis for Mexico would have been dire indeed.

Sense and Sensibility

Canuto Godines (a.k.a. Mimi)—the subtlest of the *romance callejero* poets and the only one who consistently signed his work—had a more sanguine take on neighborhood Don Juans, duplicitous women, and the war between the sexes.[54] While Godines shared his colleagues' disdain for *tenorios*, his preference for strong female characters rendered sexual predators less threatening to women, other men, and society at large than was the case with most romance poets. For instance, in the romance about the stonemason's blonde, the reader never learns the determined young woman's name, and she succeeds in routing her harasser only after she invokes her tough boyfriend. The young women in Godines's romances don't require male assistance to fend off unacceptable suitors. At the beginning of "No Judas mejor Matraca" (Better a Matraca than a Judas), the reader meets "Lola La Quiriosa" (Lola the Coquette):

> Que sin duda así la llaman
> Porque le gusta vestirse
> La verdad, con mucha gracia,
> Y además que tiene un cuerpo,
> Unos ojos y una cara
> Y un modito de sonreirse
> Que cualquiera se ataranta.[55]

✻

> [Who no doubt gets that name
> Because she likes to dress
> To tell the truth, with a lot of style,
> And besides she has a body,
> Eyes and face
> And a way of smiling
> That would dazzle anyone.]

The description suggests that Lola is "asking for trouble," and she finds it in a smooth-talking leather tanner named Modesto, known as Pica Poco (it doesn't hurt much). Modesto courts Lola with sweet promises and knick-knacks (*cachibaches*) then waits until her mother goes off to mass to invite the young woman out on an unchaperoned date that starts with quite a bit of drinking and ends "in front of a squalid house," where an old lady "trembling with pleasure" waits to escort her in. No fool, Lola refuses to enter, berates Modesto for his dishonorable intentions, and when he attempts to force her to comply, she beats him bloody with the old woman's cane and goes off to rejoin her mother. The poet ends with a moral directed to male readers: "Se acuerda de Modestito, / Y al acordarse así exclama: / Señores, sí ustedes quieren / "¡No judas, mejor matraca!" (Remember little Modesto / and when you do, exclaim, / gentlemen, if you please, / "better a matraca than a Judas!").

Another Godines romance with a tough female lead, "Pero de qué . . . ?" (But what then?), relates the thwarted seduction of Magdelena, "who is neither rich nor pretty" but has a small inheritance from her grandmother.[56] The local *tenorio* Julian, "who if he wasn't exactly a worker still tried to look like one," attempts to woo her with love songs: "¡Ay! Magdalena tú eres / Para mí, la rosa blanca / Cuyo aroma me enardece / Cuyo perfume me embriaga." (Oh! Magdalena, you are / for me, the white rose / whose scent inflames me, / whose perfume intoxicates me.) Once he thinks she's hooked, he starts pressuring her to sell off the inheritance, allegedly so that they can afford to marry. Although flattered at first by Julian's attentiveness, Magdalena soon catches on, scolding her ardent suitor: "¡qué desgracia! / Que venda yo el estanquillo, / Que venda yo mis alhajas / Y con todo mi dinero / Que nos casemos ¡¡qué plancha!! / ¿Pero de qué? . . . si me quieres / Trabaja, chico, trabaja." (What a disgrace! / That I should sell the kiosk / that I should sell my jewelry / and with all my money / that we should marry: How foolish!! / But what then? . . . if you love me, / work, boy, work.)[57]

A third example, "Para que la cuña apriete" (For the wedge to stick), provides an interesting twist that hints at the larger social context in which Godines set his stories.[58] In this variation, the local *tenorio* is a guitar-playing gadabout named Gerundio, known as Fra Diablo (Brother Devil), and the object of his attention is a beautiful *garbancera* named Rosario, "la Chollo (the Godsend)."[59] As was the case with Lola in the earlier romance, Rosario likes to put on makeup and dress "coquettishly" when she goes out, taking on the appearance and manners of an elegant young woman rather than a *garbancera* and "the niece of uncle Chema Chinampero de Ixtacalco," both references to her humble, probably Indian parentage.[60] Smitten by her beauty and style, Gerundio follows her around, trying to catch her eye with furtive glances and shy smiles. When he finally gets up the nerve (or so it seems) to speak with her, he pretends to be a bit tongue-tied: "Porque no soy de esos hombres / Cuyo lema es el engaño / Y á fuerza de urdir mentiras / Y á fuerza de usar alhagos [*sic*] / Seducen á las mujeres" (Because I'm not one of those guys / whose motto is deceit / and who by contriving lies / and by using flattery / seduce women). Although Rosario has indeed noticed his efforts to attract her attention and has even responded with subtle signals of her own, she has also taken the precaution of checking up on her admirer, who turns out to have at least two mistresses and four children. "I know your history," she tells Gerundio, "I know who you are because I've done some investigating; so don't waste your time and don't follow me again." Although a few lines later the stunned Fra Diablo recovers his composure and goes back to plotting more seductions, the triumphant young woman has already left to visit friends in Mixcalco.

These three romances are remarkable in several respects. As noted earlier, Godines's female characters are entirely self-sufficient, with no hint of male interference or support in either their daily lives or their interactions with *tenorios*. And even though all three women are initially attracted to their prospective seducers, once they discover the men's true motives, they dump them quickly and without remorse, like the singer in "Macetita embalsamada" who throws her *novio* out like "trash" after he tries to take advantage of her. Even more striking is that the poet identifies two of the women, Lola and Rosario, as coquettes and comments at length on their clothes, shoes, makeup, and poise. Lola even goes out drinking alone with her *tenorio*, thus putting herself at considerable risk for abduction, rape, and life as a prostitute. Yet neither woman seems the least bit chagrined. All three women recognize the social stigma that comes with lost honor, and that awareness shapes their refusal to continue in the relationships once courtship starts to slide into seduction. But not one chides herself for past mistakes, promises to reform, or seeks out male protection.

Godines also tweaks the ubiquitous female betrayal narrative in ways that either vindicate the woman's behavior or expose the double standard behind social stigmas. One of his earliest romances, the seven-part "Juventina" for *El Diablito Bromista*, introduces a young couple, Juventina and Pancho, who are deeply in love but frustrated because they lack the means to marry.[61] Pancho promises that if Juventina agrees to become his wife: "I'll work like a black man, and in less time than a cock takes to crow, I'll take you out of service and you'll have everything you need," but as a meat hauler (*cargador*) at the slaughterhouse, he has little chance of following through. To make matters worse, Juventina's ailing mother tells her that she has only a year to live. "What do you want me to do," she asks him, "become a domestic servant (*meterme de gata*)?" Meanwhile, her mother has hatched a plot with an old bald lawyer to dragoon Pancho into the military so that he won't ruin her daughter's life. When Juventina tells Pancho about the plan, he becomes despondent and starts drinking (and pressuring her to drink with him). Just as Pancho convinces Juventina to run away with him, her mother enters the bar followed by the lawyer and a policeman. In the ensuing row, the old man gets hit on the head and falls to the ground, "thick blood spurting"; the police drag Pancho to jail, and the two women escape. When the scandal dies down, the two women go to church, Juventina to pray for Pancho, her mother "to offer her rosary to the Virgin for the unintentional miracle that freed her daughter from that meat hauler." Many years later, the epilogue tells us, the poet observes a detachment of soldiers marching down Reforma, "among them a young man, robust, strong, likable, beaming with noble pride . . . none other than Pancho, who still hadn't forgotten his brown-eyed, blonde-haired *novia* with bare feet and dressed in rags." Moments later, a fancy carriage passes by carrying three passengers: a beautiful, stylish young lady; a wrinkled, bald old man; and a white-haired old woman—Juventina, the lawyer, and her mother. "That completes the picture," the poet concludes, "and I leave the comments to your conscience, dear reader."

The story employs one of the standard tropes of female betrayal—a beautiful young woman who abandons a poor young man to improve her economic and social status by marrying a rich older man. In this instance, however, it's Juventina's mother who plots against Pancho. Although in the final scene Juventina seems pleased with the way things have turned out, she is loyal and loving to Pancho up until the arrest that results in his forced military service. And her crafty mother is never duplicitous: she doesn't think Pancho worthy of her daughter and she does her best to get rid of him, but her machinations are hardly a secret even to the young lovers. Even poor Pancho appears to have thrived in the army.

In *Why Love Hurts*, sociologist Eva Illouz argues that aspirations to a modern lifestyle transform the "marriage market" by introducing sex appeal as an *independent* variable that confers status, especially on young women, who can use it to better their social position.[62] While most societies consider sexy young women to be desirable commodities, the advent of urban consumer culture—evident here in Godines's elaborate descriptions of female fashion—made it much easier for a poor woman to look like a lady and use her sexiness to improve her social position through marriage at the same time that other changes in the urban landscape—including the mestizo provincial Porfirio Diaz's own marriage into a respectable Mexico City family—made it easier for men to retain their status even when they married "down."[63] So even though Juventina's social advancement is arranged by a traditional broker, her ambitious mother, the poet portrays her and others like her as capable of crossing class boundaries with relative ease and marrying into a modern lifestyle grounded in consumption—the essential component of personal identity.

Young men fare less well in Godines's romances. Pancho thrives under military discipline, but his churlish behavior in the bar, first with Juventina and later with his persecutors, suggests that her mother might have been right about his character. Even the far from innocent female lead in "¡Que pobre!" (How poor!), who leaves her *amasio* (lover) for a rich older man so that she can take care of her dying grandfather, comes across as infinitely more sensible than the self-pitying butcher she left behind, whose drunken antics have made him the *calavera de barrio* (neighborhood wastrel).[64] In "¡Adultera!" (Adulteress!), the poet relates an episode in the life of another unscrupulous woman, Lucrecia, the embodiment of a popular song: "Para chicharrón Texcoco / Para cajetas Celaya, / Para mujeres de pleito / Y hermosas, Guadalajara!" (For pork cracklings Texcoco / for caramels Celaya, / for women who are troublesome / and beautiful, Guadalajara!).[65] Lucrecia's current lover is Prudencio, one of those tough guys:

> Que porque traen su navaja,
> Pantalón muy ajustado,
> En el cuello una bufanda,
> El sombrero arremangado
> Y en el hombro una frazada
> Y escupen por el comillo
> Y fuman puros de á cuarta
> Parece que son la fiebre
> Que á todo el mundo le espantan.

[Who because they carry a switchblade,
And wear skintight pants,
A bandana round their neck,
A wide-brimmed hat
A serape over their shoulder
Spit out of the side of their mouth
And smoke thin cigars
Seem like the fever
That frightens all the world.]

When we first meet Prudencio, it is obvious that he's furious with Lucrecia over something she's done. That something turns out to be adultery; "your promises were lies," he tells her, "and now I'm here suffering because of your contempt, ungrateful one!" Confronted by her irate boyfriend, the young woman calmly retorts, "lo que se debe se paga" (you're paid what you're owed), and explains that when he abandoned her for another women, "el hambre subío a tal grado" (she got so hungry), that she went looking for man, picked up a stranger, got drunk, spent the night with him, and in the morning "no sé como pero amanecí con plata" (I don't how but I woke up with money). The shocked Prudencio responds with "¡Adultera! y así lo dices Lucrecia con tanta calma" (Adulteress! And you say it that way Lucrecia, so calmly); she answers back, "Pues si yo soy la culpable . . . (Well, if I'm the guilty one . . .). Although Prudencio finally confesses that he was the strange man in disguise—so Lucrecia hasn't committed adultery after all—and she lets him have the last word, the reader is left suspecting that the poised young woman knew about the ruse all along. Regardless, her apparent adultery ridicules the double standard in Mexican gender relations that tolerates male philandering while condemning women who "betray" their partners. And she's not afraid to make the point to her tough boyfriend's face.

Female toughness could even cross over into violence—against men. The first half of "De mala raza!!!" (Of a bad race!!!) is an ode to male toughness narrated by a crusty shoemaker, who blusters

Dicen que me han de matar
Pero sin decirme cuando
Pues vayan á la . . . ya saben [. . .]
Y á mi no me espantan vivos

Ni muertos del camposanto,
Ni soy de los que se arrugen
A la hora de los trancazos.[66]

✻

[They say I have to die someday
But won't tell me when
Well they can go to . . . they know where [. . .]
As for me I'm not afraid of any man alive
Or dead in the graveyard,
I'm not one of those who worry
When it comes time for blows.]

The first dramatic highpoint comes when two *valentones de fama* (notorious tough guys) square off with knives over the love of a beautiful prostitute, Lola la "pisa flores" (flower stomper). The fight ends when one of the rivals falls to the floor with two stab wounds. Not content with the outcome, Lola takes out a razor, tells the fallen man "this is how it's done," and slashes his opponent just below the heart. Her victim falls to the ground dying in a pool of blood at which point another prostitute pulls out a hairpin and attacks Lola—a fight several policemen fail to quell. In the romances of Godines, then, women turn out to be tougher, more resilient, more determined, and more sensible (with the obvious exception of Lola) than their male counterparts. In allegorical terms, the problem with the national romance isn't Mexican women.

In stark contrast to these strong young women, Godines paints even sympathetic men as weak-willed, self-pitying, quick to accept defeat, and too touchy to make rational decisions. Take for example poor Andrés in "Vaya un consejo!" (Here's some advice!). As the story begins Andrés and his childhood sweetheart Concha are making plans to marry: "Que seré yo tu marido / Y tú mi reina, mi cielo, / Y viviendo los dos juntos / Viviremos muy contentos" (I'll be your husband / and you my queen, my heaven, / and living, both of us together, / we will live very happily). Concha shares his sentiments, and they agree to talk with their parents the following day. But when Andrés arrives home, the caretaker informs him that his beloved mother is dying. The desperate young man runs to her house only to find her already dead. He kisses her forehead respectfully, puts things in order, leaves the body with neighbors, and goes off to his job as a butcher in the local market, hoping to get an advance from his boss to pay for a decent burial. To compound his bad luck, an inspector from the Consejo Superior de Salubridad (High Council on Public Health) decides to shut down the butcher shop that day, and his apologetic boss has to turn down his request for a loan. Despondent, Andrés, "without thinking that the outcome would be disastrous," goes into a nearby cantina and starts drinking. Hours later, he remembers his mother's body alone on her bed and stumbles into the street only to fall down, split his head open, and get taken off to jail. Meanwhile, the concerned neighbors, including his *novia*, have taken up a collection to bury the old woman. When the tardy Andrés arrives at the cemetery, no one will talk to him, not even Concha. Although the poet's final words blame Consejo bureaucrats for ruining the young man's future, from the perspective of his neighbors and fiancée the real problem is a fundamental weakness of character—a flaw his hard work, devotion to his mother, and fidelity to Concha can't overcome. Andrés isn't a *tenorio* or a tough guy, but he isn't much of man either, and that immaturity costs him his future happiness.[67]

The bohemian flavor of Godines's romances is part of their charm, giving them a lighthearted, live-and-let-live feel that takes some of the sting out of his damning critique of Mexican manhood. And he's not too proud to mock his own male hypocrisy, as happens in "Pero . . . que zapatos!" (But . . . what shoes!).[68] The poet starts off by explaining to his friend Antonio, to whom he has dedicated the romance, about his obsession with beautiful women and then launches into an anecdote about an afternoon spent in a *pulquería* near Mixcalco.[69] As he enjoys a glass of good pulque (*de légitimo tlamapa*) and a cheap cigar (*torpedero . . . humilde*), he suddenly spots a young woman, ravishingly beautiful from her coiffure (*peinado*) to her stockings, "unas medidas más coquetas / Que ganas daban . . . ¡vamos! / Que ganas daban de veras / De tocarlas con los labios" (stockings so sexy / that they made me want to . . . wow! / they really made me want / to touch them with my lips). But when his admiring gaze descends to the woman's feet: "¡Que terrible desengaño! / Eran sus pies muy pequeños / Pero tan viejo el calzado / Que exclamé con amargura: / Que zapatos! . . . ¡que zapatos!" (What a terrible disappointment! / Her feet were tiny, / but her shoes so old / that I exclaimed with bitterness: / What shoes!...what shoes!). After he repeats the story out loud for a friend who has just come in, the young woman takes notice.

Descansó por un momento
Y viéndome de zoslayo
Me dijo así: ¿no le gusto?
Ni usted porque está chorreando
Y si tiene cinco gruyos
Pues ¡compreme los zapatos!

[She paused for a moment
And looking at me out of the corner of her eye
Told me this: You don't like me?
Don't just be spouting off
If you've got five bucks
Then buy me the shoes!]

Chagrined, the poet checks his pockets, comes up empty, turns to his friend, and says, "She's right: who cares!" As the vignette makes clear, the author's alter ego is neither a feminist nor a gentleman, but as in all Godines's romances, the self-confident young woman dispatches her admirer/harasser with ease.

Godines's penchant for juxtaposing strong women and weak men offers few opportunities to imagine what a good relationship might look like. But two of his romances hint at a workable solution to the war between the sexes—and both involve men reluctantly abandoning their traditional prerogatives. "El Aguila de Oro" (The Golden Eagle) begins with the poet's alter ego excusing himself to his partner Concha for coming home drunk the previous night.[70] "It will be as you wish," he tells her, "because you know I won't contradict you. But hear me out. If I came home drunk last night, I'm going to explain why, and you can decide for yourself."[71] Having tried to soften her up a bit, he proceeds to tell her what happened—a long story involving a friend, Pancracio, who invites him for a drink at a very elegant tavern (El Aguila de Oro) in Tacuba, where they get extremely drunk and have a great time. "What an idiot!" she replies, "you prefer to spend your money drinking, but what do I eat? You're always telling me you love me, you love me, until you make yourself deaf."[72]

When he tries several times to get a word in, she ends the conversation with

Trabajar ya no te gusta,
Pretextos pones á todo
Y mientras yo, me refresco
Y gracias á lo que ahorro,
Tenemos cuartucho
Por no poder pagar otro,
Y ya te lo dije en antes
Que de esta manera pronto,
Tú irás para la . . . China [chingada]
Y yo á vender tostado de horno.[73]

❧

[You don't like to work anymore,
You have excuses for everything
And meanwhile, I get some rest
And thanks to what I save,
We have a shabby room
Because it's all we can afford,
And as I told you before
If you keep this up,
You can go to . . . China [go fuck yourself]
And I'll go sell cornmeal biscuits.]

Fortunately for the poet, his friend Pancracio shows up and convinces Concha that the excellence of the pulque, "de lo mejor es el colmo" (it's the best of the best), really was to blame. To prove it, he suggests that they take her along to "put an end to disputes and calm their stomachs." Concha happily agrees and a little while later they're running through the streets of Tacuba "like three crazy people," toasting the Aguila de Oro and its owner Don Julio Vázquez (to whom the romance is dedicated). Although an unsuspecting reader might be shocked at Concha's eagerness to join in the fun after berating her partner for his improvidence, the romance's final twist reveals that what was bothering Concha all along was drudging her life away while her partner enjoyed a night on the town with his male friends.

A second romance, "¡Qué viva la Independencia!" (Long Live Independence!), provides an even more explicit endorsement of companionate relationships.[74] The strong woman in this poem is Loreto: "Lo mejor de todo el barrio / Por su gracia, y su franqueza / Su patriotismo y su garbo" (The best in the whole barrio / thanks to her grace and her openness / her patriotism and her elegance). Although Loreto has learned from her beloved but recently deceased grandmother how to "live off her work," she is thinking about marrying her *flaco* (boyfriend), "Jesús el carnicero, / Inteligente muchacho / Versador con todo el mundo / Y como amigo el más franco" (Jesús the butcher / an intelligent lad / on good terms with everyone / and the most trustworthy of friends). On the eve of Independence Day (September 15), three male friends drop by Loreto's room to see if she wants to celebrate with them. They're drinking tequila, toasting Hidalgo and the other Independence heroes, and preparing to go to the Zócalo for the annual *Grito* when a furious Jesús shows up, a knife in one hand and his coat wrapped around the other. Turning to Loreto, he demands to know "¿donde / Te marchas con esos vagos; / Rotos mierderos que comen / De lo que dejo en mi plato / Y no traen en su bosillo / Para fumar ni un cigarro?" (Where / are you off to with these bums; / shitty good-for-nothings who eat / the scraps off my plate / and who don't have in their pocket / even a cigar to smoke?). "I'm going to the Grito," Loreto replies, "to have a wild time (*dar vuelo al hilacho*), to walk around with my friends, and then to sleep." "And what if I forbid it?" Jesús threatens. To which Loreto responds, "Pues eso sale sobrando / Porque no eres mi marido / Para evitarme lo que hago" (Well, that would be going too far / because you're not my husband / to be telling me what I can or can't do). Jesús escalates his threat with "Y á los dos nos lleva el diablo; / Pero quieras que no quieras / Has de hacer lo que te mando" (And the devil take us both / but whether you want to or not / you have to do what I say). When Loreto refuses, he brandishes his knife. At this point one of the other men intervenes, chiding Jesús that Independence Day is a time to celebrate and reminding him that they all have knives. The angry lover pauses for a moment, contemplates his *novia*, and announces

pues bien, al ¡*Grito*!
Así lo quieres, pues vamos;
Pero antes déme el que tenga

De sus botellas un fajo
Y perdonen mis ofensas
Soy un loco! . . . estoy muy briago!!

[well okay, to the *Grito*!
That's how you want it, so let's go
But first give me a swallow
Of whatever is in those bottles
And forgive my offenses
I'm a crazy man! . . . really messed up!!]

Crisis averted and lesson learned, the happy group heads off for the Zócalo. Later, as the crowd celebrates the *Grito*, Jesús gathers Loreto in a warm embrace, and they head off into the streets with their companions singing and shouting "Long Live Independence! Long Live the Mexicans!" As with Concha in the previous romance, Loreto is annoyed not because the men are planning to spend the night carousing but because Jesús tries to exclude her from the fun. After he relents, their relationship—or so the poet leads us to believe—becomes stronger because he's willing to change his mind and include her in the adventure, to treat her as he would his male companions rather than as a subservient woman, to respect her "independence."

Like most *romance callejero* poets, Godines preferred local idiosyncrasies to national allegories. Perhaps inspired by independence celebrations, he seems to have crossed over in this instance. The most obvious allegorical element is the romantic reconciliation at the poem's finale, which occurs just as the crowd erupts into cheers after the *Grito*: "Al escuchar tanto ruido, / Al ver tan soberbio cuadro, / Le dio Jesús á Loreto / Un estrechísimo abrazo" (On hearing such a roar, / on seeing such a proud sight / Jesús gave Loreto / the tightest of embraces). As in classic foundational fiction, the reader is presented here with a beautiful heterosexual couple whose emotional and physical bond promises to produce healthy, well-brought-up children—the foundation of a great nation. To reinforce the patriotic imagery, Godines layers on religious symbols, albeit with an incestuous twist. In this allegory, the redeemed Jesús is the "savior" of the nation of Mexico, and his soon-to-be wife Loreto, who takes her name from Our Lady of Loreto, a manifestation of the Virgin Mary, represents the holy mother. Loreto is also the location of the Italian pilgrimage site for the Holy House in Nazareth where Jesus was raised, an allegorical reference that links the Loreto in the story to both motherhood and domesticity.[75] Just as nineteenth-century *costumbristas* used popular culture to construct national identity, Godines uses a working-class couple to embody—in themselves and their children—the future of Mexico.

Despite the similarity to classic national allegories, "¡Qué viva la Independencia!" is a foundational fiction with a difference. Godines's romance makes no attempt to bridge social chasms of race, ethnicity, class, education, and the like through marriage and mestizo children. Instead it locates the working-class couple—presumably mestizo already—at the center of the nation-building enterprise. Once the perennial gender gap has been bridged through respectful and companionate marriage, he seems to say, the crucial step to national consolidation will have been taken, and other troublesome social divisions will either disappear or cease to matter.

Some Thoughts on Modernity and Companionate Marriage

Penny press editors could get quite sentimental and quite unrealistic about the transformative potential of solid working-class marriages. However, in the *romances callejeros*, wholesome sentiments and aspirations are leavened with a humorous appreciation of human failings, a tactic that works to breathe life and possibility into ideal forms. Only the most naive of readers would assume that Concha and the poet or Loreto and Jesús or Pitacio and his *vieja*, who celebrate the death of Maximilian together (see ch. 4), will live *happily* ever after. But the authors hint that a shared capacity for gratitude, respect, companionship, and nurturance—the virtues expressed in "Macetita embalsamada"—will strengthen their relationships, shape their identities, and make them better citizens. Moreover, these virtues mark the relationship as modern, defined in direct opposition to the traditional values represented by symbolic figures like Don Juan Tenorio and Doña Inés, whose troubled love can be resolved only in death.

The aptly titled "Romance modernista," for example, recounts the story of the beautiful, chaste, sensible, industrious Ramona, who helps support her elderly father, a blind beggar.[76] Having reached maturity, she approaches an equally responsible, equally poor young man from the neighborhood, Fernando, and asks him his "intentions." Although he has long admired Ramona, Fernando is dumbfounded by the question, since it is the first sign he has had of any interest on her part, but he quickly recovers by offering his hand in marriage.

> Escucha linda Ramona,
> Si tu te casas conmigo,
> Te juro que has de ser otra,
> Más no te ofrezco riquezas,
> Automóviles ni joyas,
> Porque no soy millonario,
> Pero tendrás caricias de sobra,
> Y si Dios nos da herederos,
> Alegrarán nuestra choza;
> Además, si hay araños,
> Ni te metes á celosa,
> Haremos una alcancía;
> Si eres mujer económica,
> Juntamos algunos fierros
> Y ponemos una fonda,
> Un estanquillo, ó taberna
> Según se presten las cosas.

> [Listen, beautiful Ramona,
> If you marry me,
> I swear that things will be different,
> I can't offer you riches,
> Automobiles or jewels,
> Because I'm not a millionaire,
> But you will have many things,
> You will never lack shoes,
> House, clothes and soup,
> We'll go on walks,
> You'll have caresses aplenty,

And if God grants us children,
They will gladden our hut;
Besides that, if there are no scuffles,
And if you stay steady,
We will get a money box;
If you're an economical woman,
We'll put together our coins
And open a small restaurant,
A kiosk, or a tavern,
Depending on how things fall out.]

As expected, after years of hard work, the couple realize their modest dreams: children, their own restaurant (which they name Don Cucufate, after the penny press in which the romance appears), and a respectable middle-class lifestyle, which allows Fernando to dress like a *diputado* (congressman).

"Romance modernista" lacks the bohemian charm of most penny press romances and perhaps for that reason makes the point about the virtues of companionate marriage with more clarity and force. And as the title indicates, the author considers this kind of romantic partnership quintessentially modern. The connection between loving marriages and modernity is not as surprising as it might seem at first glance. The editors' introduction to *Love and Globalization* notes that recent scholarship has identified a "trend away from 'traditional' notions of family that emphasize the role of social obligation in the reproduction of kinship systems and toward globalizing models of family that are increasingly based on a 'love' that is chosen, deeply felt, 'authentic,' and profoundly personal . . . that increasingly privileges a notion of people using love both as an ideal for which to strive and as the means through which they constitute their families."[77]

For one of the editors, anthropologist Jennifer Hirsch, this shift happened in rural Mexican towns in the mid-1980s, as young working-class women and men began to see *confianza*—which they defined as "the development and maintenance of emotional and sexual intimacy"—as central to a successful marriage. In contrast, "couples who married in the 1950s and 1960s talked about marriage as a bond of obligation, held together by an ideal of respect and the mutual fulfillment of gendered responsibilities. . . .

— ¡Onde va Doña Manuela?
— Voy á la plaza Perfirio.
— Y usté nomás me camela.
— Es que l'amo con delirio.

— No seasté tan hablador.
— Y usté no sea tan bribona.

— (Que suave está el valedor.)
— (La jaña está muy sazona.)

— ¿Te vas conmigo amor mío?
— Si Perfirio hasta el infierno.
— Pos ora si que me río
De lo crudo del invierno.

FIG. 5.3 José Guadalupe Posada/Author Unknown, "¿Onde va Doña Manuela?," *El Chile Piquín*, January 12, 1904. Courtesy of the Benson Latin American Collection, University of Texas Libraries, The University of Texas at Austin.

Love, if it existed, was the result of living well together, but it was not necessarily the goal."[78] While there's no reason to doubt the sincerity of Hirsch's informants, evidence from the early twentieth-century penny press suggests that their insistence on a dramatic recent shift in attitudes toward marriage might be a bit ahistorical and far too neat. Certainly, the transition from traditional to modern understandings of love, intimacy, romance, and matrimony was under way several decades earlier in Mexico, at least for the urban working classes.

That leaves sex. As we've seen, *romance callejero* poets had a penchant for sexual innuendo, mostly in the form of suggestive ellipses and *albures* (word games) intended to promote snickers rather than suggest intimacy. Despite their reticence, however, we do get an occasional glimpse into the role of sexual pleasure in sustaining intimate relationships. Take, for example, the 1905 cover of *El Chile Piquin* (see fig. 5.3).[79] The central image by José Guadalupe Posada depicts a plump working-class woman of indeterminate age and missing her front teeth talking to a scrawny working-class man with a scruffy moustache. The woman is on her way to market with apron and shawl and with a basket over one arm; the man looks like a *jornalero* (day laborer) with sandals, rolled-up pants, straw hat, and a pack of some sort on his back. She faces the reader, but her eyes are directed at the man, her right index finger pointing in his direction; he has his back slightly turned and listens attentively to what she's telling him. The accompanying text relates their conversation.

—¿Onde va Doña Manuela?
　—Voy á la plaza Perfirio.
　—Y usté nomás me camela,
　—Es que l'amo con delirio.

—No seasté tan hablador,
　—Y usté no sea tan bribona.
　—(Que suave está el valedor.)
　—(La jaña está muy sazona.)

—¿Te vas conmigo amor mío?
　—Si Perfirio hasta el infierno.
　—Pos ora si que me río
　—de lo crudo del invierno.

[—Where are you going, Doña Manuela?
　—I'm going to the plaza, Perfirio.
　—You're just flirting with me,
　—It's that I'm crazy about you.

—Don't be such a flatterer.
　—And you, don't be such a tease.
　—(How smooth this guy is.)
　—(How ripe this honey seems.)

—Are you going with me, my love?
　—Yes, Perfirio even into hell.

—Well now, I really am going to laugh

—at the harshness of winter.]

Perfirio might be a flatterer, but he's no *tenorio*: the exchange with Doña Manuela is perfectly balanced, compliment for compliment, innuendo for innuendo. The humor derives from the cognitive dissonance created by their frank expressions of mutual desire—especially the parenthetical "thoughts" that reveal the authenticity of that desire—and their decidedly unsexy demeanor. Moreover, Perfirio's final comment, about laughing at the harshness of winter with Doña Manuela to keep him warm, grounds the intimate tone of the exchange in the promise of bodily contact. If modern love is indeed tied to "the development and maintenance of emotional and sexual intimacy," these two are headed in the right direction—even if neither looks the part. In fact, their ugliness serves both to heighten the comic effect of their mutual seduction and to mark them as *ordinary* working people, a representational strategy typical of penny press satire.

Absent from this affectionately satiric scene is the specter of Don Juan Tenorio in either of his penny press guises: the seductive *tenorio de barrio* preying on weak-willed women or the hypermasculine tough guy eager to pull out a knife at the slightest affront to his manhood. Doña Manuela might see Perfirio as a suave *valedor* (literally, a valiant guy), but she doesn't seem the least bit worried about his temper or intentions. So perhaps the *El Diablito Rojo* contributor who insisted that Mexicans went to see *Don Juan Tenorio* on Day of the Dead because "Tenorio is dead" was right after all.

A 1903 *La Guacamaya* street talk column includes this exchange between two *cotorras* (chatterboxes), one of whom has just attended the annual performance of *Don Juan Tenorio* with her *viejo* (old man):

—pos mi Viejo lestubo danda á la chamba todo el día y hasta en la noche me llevó á ver Don Juan Tiñoso, y por cierto que estubo muy rete chulo sobre todo aquello cuando el incomododor D. Gonzales, solo en su cochesito, y le adice á Don Juan: Aquí me tienes don Juan ora que vienen conmigo los que en vida jueron majes pa respirar por lombligo.

—¡Huy! Mialma pos llamero se lo sabuiste de memoria.[80]

[—well my Old Man was working all day at his job but later that night he took me to see Don Juan Tiñoso, and it was really cute especially when the discombobulator Don Gonzales, alone in his little carriage, says to Don Juan: "Here I am Don Juan and now all those who were suckers in life have to go with me to breathe through the navel."

—Wow! My dear, now you really know it by heart.]

The joke revolves around the *cotorra*'s scrambled version of the Co-mendador's speech. Replacing *tenorio* with *tiñoso* (mangy) is a running gag that works as an editorial comment on Don Juan's reputation for manly elegance. Mishearing *comendador* (commander of a military order of knights) as *incomododor* suggests that he's someone who makes others uncomfortable—precisely his role in this scene—while it mocks his patri-archal authority. And the divine punishment that forces *majes* (gullible men who are cuckolded by their wives) to breathe through the navel for all eternity casts Don Juan as a cuckold, a role reversal that would indeed have humiliated the honor-obsessed aristocrat. These sly jibes at Don Juan's manhood, which emerge from an evening at the theater with her "old man," give some sense of how working-class audiences might have engaged—and might continue to engage—the pervasive spirit of *donjua-nismo*: not as a model for masculine behavior or gender relations but as an amusing foil against which to measure themselves as modern subjects.

LAS TRAMPAS MODERNAS

> Hay trampas que el hombre evita
> pero estas modernas, no . . .
> COPLAS DE DON SIMÓN

This book took far too long to write.[1] Like all tardy authors, I have a litany of irrelevant excuses for the delay. One of those excuses involved a move from a small town in Ohio to a small town in Colorado. While the professional and personal reasons behind the move are indeed irrelevant, the move itself produced unexpected insights into the ongoing sentimental education of working-class Mexican men. For instance, my neighborhood park now hosts an informal gathering of working-class Mexican immigrant men, ages anywhere from early twenties to late sixties, who hang out most seasonable afternoons, talking and joking with each other in a slang-inflected Spanish reminiscent of Pitacio and Chema: plenty of *"güeys,"* although more *"brodes"* than *"manarios,"* evidence nonetheless that they share their Porfirian counterparts' enthusiasm for playing around with English words.

My contemporary guide to this latest incarnation of working-class male sociability and socialization comes in the form of a five-hour afternoon radio show on *La Tricolor Denver 96.5 FM*, El Show de Erazno y la Chokolata—"el show más chido por las tardes" [the coolest show in the afternoons]—which is broadcast everyday all over the western and south-ern United States.[2] Although not especially political, the show resembles the early twentieth-century Mexico City penny press in most other ways: its principal mode is satire; it boasts a mix of topical and regular features; it is primarily directed at a working-class Mexicans; it is intensely chauvinistic about Mexico and being Mexican but cynical about the country's political class; its "editorial" perspective is mostly male even when channeled through female personas (although women do have a prominent voice); it alternately mocks and celebrates working-class Mexican culture; and it provides practical and psychological tips for coping with the trials and tribulations of modern life. Despite its billings as a family variety show, "Saturday Night Live de la tarde" [Saturday Night Live in the afternoon], Erazno y la Chokolata focuses much of its attention on adult gender relations, especially male insecurities about women and female complaints about men.

In *El fracaso de amor*, Ana Lidia García Peña argues that in nineteenth-century Mexico City "domestic conflicts between women and men were characterized by hatred, violence, and abandonment . . . in a century plagued by modernizing initiatives."[3] At one level, Erazno y la Chokolata would suggest that nothing much has changed despite over two centuries of modernizing initiatives, many of them aimed directly at reducing domestic conflict by fixing dysfunctional masculine behavior. Indeed, one of the show's principal protagonists, "El Doggie"—fictional sportscaster and host of "La hora del Doggie"—espouses the worst traits of working-class Mexican machismo and spends most of his airtime egging on male disciples (they refer to him as *maestro*) and antagonizing the angry women who call in to berate him for his blatant misogyny (which he alternately embraces and denies).[4] The other prominent male characters—Erazno (a wannabe wrestler), Chente (a caricature of former Mexican president Vicente Fox), and Los Super Amigos (parodies of Mexican mariachi greats Vicente Fernández and Antonio Aguilar)—are little better.[5] With all of these characters, humor typically comes in the form of *albures*, "a rhythmic game of words and gestures that combine humor with insult, which occurs principally in spaces of masculine interaction," in this instance a male-dominated broadcast booth. As sociologist Ivonne Szasz explains:

> The albur is generated in social contexts of the extreme repression of sexuality and serves as a means to communicate norms related to gen-

der and masculinity. As a language that begins in puberty in a society that denies sexual knowledge and curiosity in women and children, forbidden knowledge is transformed into a form of power, the power that adults exercise over children, husbands over their wives. . . . Young men display an impressive gamut of information about sexual anatomy and make a show of their handling of masculine language and masculine ability to break the rules. Mastery in the domain of language substitutes for mastery in deeds, knowledge implies experience, and constitutes proof of adulthood and virility.[6]

While Szasz's explanation of Mexican male humor certainly rings true for the male personalities on Erazno y la Chokolata—their female interlocutors regularly comment on their "juvenile" attitude toward sex—it fails to capture the complex layers of satire at the heart of the show's popular appeal, and quite possibly the complexities of working-class masculinity as well. Take for example, these two blog responses to a La hora del Doggie episode, posted on YouTube as "Llamada de radio escucha enojada por La hora de Doggy" [Call from a radio listener angered by Doggie's Hour], in which Doggie harangues a female listener who has called in to complain about irresponsible young boys who impregnate their girlfriends[7]:

> Male listener: Maestro doggy. Usted es un oasis en el desierto. una luz en la oscuridad, que bueno que ha llegado para dar el mensaje a todos aquellos que todavia permanecen ciegos, yo era uno de ellos pero ya salí del pantano y ahora me considero un hombre libre. [Maestro doggy: You, sir, are an oasis in the desert. a light in the darkness, how fortunate that you've come to give the message to all those who remain in darkness, I was one of them but have since left the swamp and now consider myself a free man.]

> Female listener: Pinche doggy pendejo no sabia ni ke decir el weee. [Doggy is a fucking idiot, the guy had no clue what to say.]

Although most posts for this popular episode came from Doggie's admiring male *alumnos* (students), the female listener's dismissive response in support of a female caller reveals a give and take approach to gender relations that complicates this "space of masculine interaction" in unexpected ways.

Masculine space is complicated even more by Erazno y la Chokola-ta's distinctive feature: all the major personalities (except the requisite talk show sidekick Garbanzo) are conceived and performed by the same man, Oswaldo Díaz. Díaz's multiple personalities include not only the male characters mentioned above but also the program's female cohost, La Chokolata (a.k.a. "Choko"), whose hyperfeminine persona and pro-female stance provides a steady in-your-face counterpoint to the macho posturing of the men.[8] Although all but the most naive listeners are in on the joke, everyone involved—radio personalities, guests, publicists, callers—stays in character, including on the program website and in public appearances, which are usually done by Erazno wearing a wrestler's mask that hides his creator's face.[9] Thus, while the show does indeed re-create a social world predicated on radical (and contentious) gender difference of the "men are from Mars, women are from Venus" variety, the female perspective is well represented through drag performance, female callers, and female guests. Topics certainly include nineteenth-century divorce case favorites like "hatred, violence, and abandonment," and frequently devolve into shouting matches between angry women and belligerent men (especially Doggie), but the overall effect is surprisingly good humored and gender inclusive, which no doubt accounts for the show's considerable popularity with both sexes.

Representing gender relations as always already troubled isn't necessarily a bad thing or reactionary thinking. In *The Queer Art of Failure*, cultural critic Judith Halberstam notes the limitations of "acceptable forms of feminism that are oriented to positivity, reform, and accommodation rather than negativity, rejection, and transformation," arguing that "there are definite advantages to failing. Relieved of the obligation to keep smiling through chemotherapy or bankruptcy, the negative thinker can use the experience of failure to confront the gross inequalities of everyday life in the United States."[10] The presence of a queer character in Erazno y La Chokolata, coupled with the anxious iteration of gender norms in light of their obvious and repeated failure in listeners' everyday lives, thus works to satirize masculine pretentions to self-mastery and domination of women. This is especially evident in the regularly featured game show, "Hembras contra Machos" [Females versus Males], which involves the principal characters and call-in listeners in a competition to determine whether women are smarter, kinder, tougher, more honest, more faithful, more loving, and so on, than men (or vice versa).[11]

Even more telling is the daily "Chokolatazo," an on-air surprise phone call from Choko at the behest of a listener who wants to "probar la fidelidad de la pareja" [test the faithfulness of her or his partner].[12] During the call, Choko pretends to represent a candy company offering to send a promotional box of heart-shaped chocolates to a person the recipient of the call would like to recognize in a special way, typically not the one who requested the Chokolatazo. This daily real-life soap opera with wounded lovers of both sexes confronting their betrayers "on the air" is particularly poignant for a transnational migrant community divided by a heavily policed political border that enforces prolonged separations and creates ample opportunities for deception—and indeed most calls are to lovers on the other side of the border or in other cities. Although the immediate appeal of El Chokolatazo is audience sympathy (voiced by Choko) and perverse satisfaction (voiced by the male characters), the confrontation that follows the failed fidelity test reveals as much about "the gross inequalities of everyday life in the United States," amplified by harsh immigration policies and the Global North/Global South divide, as it does the character flaws of the offending or offended partner.

Separated from the early twentieth-century Mexico City penny press by more than a century, over fifteen hundred miles (from Mexico City to Los Angeles), a political border, and a different medium (radio), Erazno y la Chokolata nonetheless shares its predecessor's strategy of cloaking social critique in layers of satire. And, as with the penny press, the show's social satire includes a self-mocking approach to gender relations that stands in for reflexivity—the essential marker of modern selfhood predicated on the continuous revision of knowledge in light of new information—even though both sources generally seek to promote reflection in their readers/listeners rather than model it in their fictional protagonists. In other words, the reader/listener is pushed to reflect on and adapt to the "modern" world by the stubborn cluelessness of the protagonists, who are too tradition bound to break free of the social norms that condemn them to endless cycles of betrayal, abuse, and dissatisfaction. An added benefit: as distinct voices of a single performer, the show's different personalities channel the stereotypical masculine and feminine "scripts" around and through which listeners seek to make sense of their lives.[13] A useful preview or rehearsal of the reception they might expect should they chose to go public with their problems and concerns.

The opportunity for listeners to reconcile these disparate voices comes in the final hour of the program when Choko teams up with celebrity doctor Elvia Contreras to provide listeners with practical, often quite explicit advice about all aspects of their sexual health. This matter-of-fact advice from the matronly *doctorcita* (dear doctor), often in direct response to call-in listeners, is accompanied by predictable reactions from the regulars, with Choko offering empathy and support while the men vacillate between mockery of troubled callers and deference towards their unflappable guest expert. If Szasz is correct in her observation that Mexican "society denies sexual knowledge and curiosity in women and children" and that "forbidden knowledge [expressed by men in the form of *albures*] is transformed into a form of power, the power that adults exercise over children, husbands over their wives," then Erazno y La Chokolata's final hour represents an radical revolution in the locus of sexual knowledge as an expert woman, abetted by a queer moderator, calmly dismisses the uninformed opinions of the men, thus undoing the power of the male-controlled *albur* and its pretensions to "mastery in the domain of language." Moreover, this strategic reversal is persuasive precisely because it first allows the male characters to voice sexist opinions, make snide comments, mock callers, and express shock at unconventional behavior (responses listeners might expect to hear in their daily lives), before they eventually cede ground to the *doctorcita*'s expertise—in effect scripting a mature professional woman as the calm, rationale spokesperson for modern ideas about sex and juvenile men as hysterical, uninformed apologists for an embattled tradition of male domination.[14]

While the Mexico City penny press could boast nothing quite like the final hour of Erazno y La Chokolata, both media evince a strong commitment to an alternative disciplinary strategy for their mostly working-class readers/listeners. The contemporary United States, like late Porfirian Mexico City, is no stranger to top-down social reform agendas that seek to impose, often through discriminatory policing (and harsh immigration policies), normative notions of proper behavior on allegedly recalcitrant minority populations that don't live up to middle-class standards. This is true for mainstream media as well as government agencies.

For example, when the *doctorcita* appears as a sex educator on Spanish-language television programs, the hosts nod appreciatively at her comments rather than channel the rancorous voices of macho men and "diva" women. The information may be the same, but the effect is much different, since it presumes an educated middle-class audience predisposed to accept and act on expert advice, after the fashion of the bourgeois prescriptive literature of late Porfirian Mexico City directed at the *gente decente*. In contrast, the satirical approach of the penny press and Erazno y La Chokolata derives its popular flavor (and perhaps its efficacy as well) from a willingness to engage with and give voice to popular resistance to high modernist social reform projects, in both instances a top-down sentimental education of "unexpected citizens" marked as marginal by class, race, ethnicity, and national origin.[15]

Producing a traceable genealogy that links the early twentieth-century Mexico City penny press to an early twenty-first-century U.S. radio program is far beyond the scope of this book. But the continuities between the two projects are many and striking: the strategic use of social satire, a variety show format that includes reader/listener contributions, an obsession with gender relations and changing notions of manhood, the injection of the improper voices of "unexpected citizens" into the public sphere, an embrace of alternative disciplinary projects, the role of editors/performers as intermediaries between the uncouth working classes and the *gente decente*, and so on. Rather than propose a general theory of social satire along the lines of Mikhail Bahktin's carnival, I would argue that these continuities reflect a distinctly Mexican genre—a satire of sentiments—shaped by specific convergences of historical and cultural forces and haunted by the specter of durable inequalities in Mexico (and the United States). I would argue further that analysis of this satire of sentiments can shed useful light on the complex, often contradictory history of working-class masculinities in Mexico and across the Mexican diaspora—unexpected insights that trouble conventional wisdom about the irredeemable misogyny of Mexican popular culture, the bourgeois origins of the "civilizing process," and working-class men as the spiritual progenitors and paradigmatic practitioners of macho. That then is what I have tried to do in this book.

NOTES

INTRODUCTION

1. Guerrero, *Génesis del crimen*, 119. Original: "Sus instintos morales se extinguían en las noches oscuras de la miseria y en la contigüidad del frío; la dignidad se gastaba en solicitudes infructuosas de trabajo; el porvenir se convertía en expectativas de cárcel; y sus sufrimientos y desesperación en una vagancia forzosa, que muchas veces terminaba en el pulque o el tequila." For more on Guerrero's pioneering sociological study, see Rodríguez Kuri, "Julio Guerrero," 43–56, and Buffington, *Criminal and Citizen*, 54–59.

2. "La resurrección de Lázaro," *La Guacamaya*, March 17, 1904. The image is signed by printmaker José Guadalupe Posada, who illustrated a large number of penny press covers. He left most of them unsigned, which suggests that he considered this particular image somehow special. The poem was probably written by one of the editors, Rafael R. y Rodríguez or Fernando P. Torroella.

3. A 1902 front-page editorial, e.g., assures readers that "Never will we affirm only that the worker is depraved, drunk, wasteful, lazy, ungrateful, inconstant, etc., but that every effect has one or another causes." Original: "Jamás asentaremos nosostros solamente que el obrero, es vicioso, ebrio, desperdiciado, flojo, ingrato, inconstante, etc., sino que todo efecto tiene una á varias causas." "El obrero," *La Guacamaya*, September 1, 1902. Italics in original.

4. "A los obreros," *La Guacamaya*, March 17, 1904. The letter is from Celaya, dated February 13, 1904, and signed "a worker."

5. "¡Viva la Independencia! ¡Viva la Libertad! ¡Viva el Derecho!," *El Diablito Rojo*, September 17, 1900. Pulque is a mildly alcoholic beverage made from fermented maguey cactus juice, which most upper- and middle-class Mexicans of the period

associated with the mestizo (mixed race) and Indian lower classes and their alleged propensity for indolence, alcoholism, and violence.

6. The Spanish word "macho" has a confused etymology, but most scholars agree that its current usage is Mexican in origin and dates from the 1930s or 1940s. Given the surprisingly late entry of "macho" into the lexicon as the preferred term for hypermasculinity, it is interesting to note the following entry in Ramos i Duarte's 1895 *Diccionario de mejicanismos*: "Machorra (Mej.), sf. Marimacho. La palabra *machorra* no quiere decir *marimacho* ó mujer que tiene maneras i acciones de hombre, sino la hembra estéril, infecunda, *agenis* (del gr. *a*, sin, *genis*, raza), atocia" [the word *machorra* does not mean *marimacho* or a woman with the mannerisms and actions of a man, but a woman who is sterile, infertile, unable to give birth]. Duarte provides no separate entries for marimacho or macho, but his definition of "machorra" suggests that the current use of "macho" in reference to men might derive from these two terms for nonnormative women (as its constitutive other). For useful overviews of the history of the word "macho," see Monsiváis, *Escenas de pudor*, 103–17, and Gutmann, *Meanings of Macho*, 221–32.

7. Paz, "The Sons of La Malinche," in *The Labyrinth of Solitude*, 65–88. For more on Paz's influential views on Mexican masculinities, see Gutiérrez, "Conclusion: Mexican Masculinities," 262–65. Whatever influence Guerrero's work may have had on Paz was probably via Ramos, *El perfil*, an influential 1934 psychoanalytical study of Mexican national character. Although the concept is implied in Guerrero's earlier study, Ramos is generally credited with the argument for a Mexican national inferiority complex, which he blamed on a pernicious mix of historical, cultural, and environmental factors (as had Guerrero three decades earlier).

8. Gutmann, *Meanings of Macho*.

9. Liberal opposition newspaper, *El Hijo del Ahuizote*, coined the title "El Indispensable Caudillo" in a parody of an official decree extending the presidential term indefinitely or "for as long as God wills it." *El Hijo del Ahuizote*, October 2, 1892. Quoted in Cosío Villegas, *Historia moderna*, 321.

10. Secretaría de Economía, *Estadísticas*, 9. During the same period the Federal District grew from 327,500 to 720,750 (7). In 1900 approximately half the population of the Federal District had been born somewhere else (12). For Mexico City, the percentage of "outsiders" was even higher.

11. On these shifts in social geography, see Lear, *Workers, Neighbors*, 15–48. On the transgression of urban spaces, see Piccato, "Urbanistas," 113–48; *City of Suspects*, 34–49; and Aréchiga Córdoba, "Lucha de clases en la ciudad," 19–50. On working-class consciousness and the satiric penny press, see Díaz, "Satiric Penny Press," 497–525.

12. The statistics are from Lear, *Workers, Neighbors*, 49–85.

13. Illades, *Hacia la República*, 185–86.

14. For an overview of wages, working conditions, and political organizing for printers during the Porfiriato, see Tapia Ortega, *Grito*.

15. On the financial difficulties and poor working conditions of Porfirian journalists, see Toussaint Alcaraz, *Escenario*, 57–60; Lepidus, "Mexican Journalism," 62–63; and Piccato, *Tyranny*, 73–83.

16. Rabasa, *Cuarto Poder*, 60.

17. Scholars as diverse as Jürgen Habermas, Raymond Williams, and Benedict Anderson have stressed the vital role played by newspapers in the development of modern societies. Habermas argues that the circulation of newspapers helped form a late eighteenth-century bourgeois public sphere in which ideas about social organization and social justice could be freely debated (at least among the rising bourgeoisie); Williams notes their crucial contribution to bourgeois class consciousness and revolutionary politics; and Anderson views them as essential to the construction of the "imagined community" that binds together the modern nation-state. Habermas, *Structural Transformation*; Williams, *Long Revolution*; and Anderson, *Imagined Communities*.

18. *La Guacamaya*: "Periódico hablador y de buen humor, revalsador y decidor de verdades, no papero ni farolero, azote de los burgueses y defensor de la CLASE OBRERA"; *El Diablito Rojo*: "Del pueblo y para el pueblo"; *El Diablito Bromista*: "Órgano de la clase obrera, azote del mal burgués y coco del mal gobierno."

19. These figures probably exaggerate sales a bit—which is not to say that the papers weren't widely distributed at least in Mexico City. For more on the thriving Mexico City newspaper business, see Smith, "Contentious Voices," and Toussaint Alcaraz, *Escenario*.

20. Ambulatory newspaper vendors helped ensure widespread distribution of all kinds of newspapers, including the penny press. See, e.g., Gutiérrez and Gantús, "Los pequeños," 81–116. The prominent penny press poet Canuto Godines (discussed at length in ch. 5) even wrote a *romance callejero* (street romance) about a paperboy, harassed by policemen and cheated by the subsidized dailies, who begs *La Guacamaya*'s editor for papers to sell because ". . . tiene más fama / Y cuenta con mas lectores / Porque a todos les agrada" (it is the best known / and has the most readers / because it pleases everyone). Canuto Godines (Mimi), "Un escándalo: Romance callejero," *La Guacamaya*, May 25, 1905, 2–3.

21. *El Periquito*, August 2, 1895. Reprinted in Soler and Avila, *Posada*, 37.

22. For newspaper prices and other useful information, see Toussaint Alcaraz, *Escenario*, 76–108.

23. The didactic tone of the mainstream working-class press was set early. See, e.g., Illades, *Las otras ideas*, 205–29.

24. Elisa Speckman Guerra makes a similar argument for the pamphlets and broadsides produced by Antonio Vanegas Arroyo, his family, and colleagues in "De amor," 70–71. Vanegas Arroyo broadsides figure prominently in the chapters to come.

25. There are several excellent works on Posada's prints, including Tyler, *Posada's Mexico*; Carrillo Azpeitia, *Posada*; Soler and Avila, *Posada*; Frank, *Posada's Broadsheets*; and Barajas Durán, *Posada*. Political analyses of the satiric penny press include Díaz, "Satiric Penny Press," and Lear, *Workers, Neighbors*, 91–106.
26. Important studies of working-class radicalism before, during, and immediately following the Revolution include Salazar and Escobedo, *Las pugnas*; Huitrón, *Orígenes*; Araiza, *Historia*; Ruiz, *Labor*; Hart, *Anarchism*; Bracho, *De los gremios*; and Leal, *Del mutualismo*. Salazar, Escobedo, and Huitrón were all labor organizers with connections to the radical Casa del Obrero Mundial. *Regeneración* lasted less than a year in Mexico but appeared sporadically in different parts of the United States until 1918. Cockcroft, *Intellectual Precursors*, 250–57.
27. The mobilization of the "red battalions" lasted only a year. Concerned about the growing radicalism and influence of the *Casa*, President Venustiano Carranza decommissioned and disarmed the battalions in January 1916. See Clark, *Organized Labor*, 23–56; Ruiz, *Labor*, 47–72; and Hart, *Anarchism*, 140. Some historians have interpreted the workers' alliance with the Constitutionalists against the more "radical" Zapata (and to a lesser extent Villa) as evidence of false consciousness or expediency. See Carr, "Obrero Mundial," 603–32.
28. Anderson, "Mexican Workers," 95. The italics are in the original. *La Reforma* refers to the mid-nineteenth-century liberal movement associated with the 1857 Constitution and President Benito Juárez. See also Anderson, *Outcasts*, 323. The "revisionist" perspective is prefigured but not explicitly articulated in González Navarro, *El Porfiriato*, 280–380, and Cosío Villegas, *Historia moderna*, 705–83. Cosío Villegas, e.g., notes that before the Revolution workers' political actions were most often motivated by "very concrete grievances, suffered in the flesh and for a long time and [were] only vaguely political much less doctrinaire" (705).
29. Knight, "Working Class," 71. For a useful analysis of Porfirian labor policy that supports Knight's argument about workers as reluctant revolutionaries, see Walker, "Porfirian Labor Politics," 257–89.
30. Lear, *Workers, Neighbors*, 130.
31. See, e.g., Illades, *Las otras ideas* and *Estudios*. For a useful take on the workers or artisans question, see Novelo, "Los trabajadores," 15–51.
32. Illades, *Hacia la República*, 204.
33. Díaz, "Satiric Penny Press," 516.
34. Díaz, "Satiric Penny Press," 512–13. Díaz's rankings make good sense. And Porfirian authorities appear to have shared her assessment: *El Diablito Bromista*'s editor, Antonio de P. Escárcega, spent time in Mexico City's notorious Belén jail in the company of distinguished colleagues like Filomeno Mata and Daniel Cabrera. Arenas Guzmán, *El periodismo en la Revolución*, 16. At the same time, she points out that the relatively conservative *El Diablito Rojo* was one of the first papers to openly criticize Porfirio Díaz. Díaz, "Satiric Penny Press," 522.
35. Díaz, "Satiric Penny Press," 499, 525.

36. Barajas Durán, *Posada*, 396

37. Illades, *Hacia la República*, 201–5, examines the complexities of working-class class formation in 1870s Mexico City.

38. Lear, *Workers, Neighbors*, 101–3, analyzes the role of the satiric penny press in the formation of urban working-class culture. According to Michael Warner, "the notion of a public enables a reflexivity [mutual awareness and interaction] in the circulation of texts among strangers who become, by virtue of their reflexively circulating discourse, a social entity"; Warner, *Publics and Counterpublics*, 11–12. Although not explicitly political, this definition of a public has obvious affinities with the concept of class consciousness. "To address a public or to think of oneself as belonging to a public," Warner argues, "is to be a certain kind of person, to inhabit a certain kind of social world, to have at one's disposal certain media and genres, to be motivated by a certain normative horizon, and to speak within a certain language ideology" (10). In other words, even though members of a public don't know each other by name, they nonetheless expect to recognize fellow travelers by the (discursive) company they keep.

39. Piccato, "Public Sphere," 168.

40. Piccato, "Public Sphere," 191. Piccato argues that "although besieged by politics, geography, and class, Latin American public spheres continued to think of themselves as unitary, coterminous with the nation, and those who met in the public sphere felt entitled to use rational languages as part of a universalistic drive for coherence and clarity" (183).

41. Acevedo Rodrigo and López Caballero, "Introducción," 13–37. Acevedo Rodrigo and López Caballero define citizenship as "the multiplicity of practices that: a) are necessary in order that the subject (individual or collective) *might become* competent in a given moment and in a specific social and legal field so that they can speak or act in the name of the public, or in the name of what they see as their rights (legally recognized or not), and b) those practices through which they *negotiate the criteria* that define that competence" (22); italics in original.

42. Scott, *Seeing*, 89–90.

43. Scott, *Seeing*, 89. On Porfirian high modernism or "scientific politics," see Hale, *Transformation*.

44. Mexico City was not the only Mexican site for high modernist social engineering. See, e.g., French, *Peaceful and Working People*, and Overmyer-Velazquez, *Visions*.

45. Scott, *Seeing*, 81–82.

46. Scott, *Seeing*, 78.

47. On Porfirian attempts to produce a legible and modern capital city, see Piccato, *City of Suspects*, 17–33.

48. Piccato, *City of Suspects*, 43–49.

49. Mexican liberal populism (as distinct from popular liberalism) and its revolutionary implications are discussed in ch. 3.

50. Agostoni, *Monuments*, 38–43.

51. Guerrero, *Génesis del crimen*, 132–33.

52. Macedo, *La criminalidad*, 28.

53. Scott, *Seeing*, 88, includes French utopian socialist Henri de Saint-Simon—a particular favorite of nineteenth-century Mexican socialists—in his high modernist hall of fame along with Lenin, Trotsky, and twentieth-century urban planners Le Corbusier and Robert Moses. On Mexican socialists' plans to rehabilitate working-class men, see Illades, *Las otras ideas* and *Hacia la República*.

54. Scott, *Seeing*, 132–46.

55. Nick Mansfield notes that "although [self and subject] are sometimes used interchangeably, the word 'self' does not capture the sense of social and cultural entanglement that is implicit in the word 'subject': the way our immediate daily life is already caught up in complex political, social and philosophical—that is, shared—concerns"; Mansfield, *Subjectivity*, 2–3.

56. See esp. Butler, *Bodies That Matter*; also, *Gender Trouble, Psychic Life*, and *Excitable Speech*. Butler stresses the relentless, everyday work that goes into becoming and remaining culturally intelligible. In *Gender Trouble*, e.g., she argues that "to qualify as a substantive identity is an arduous task, for such appearances are rule-generated identities, ones which rely on the consistent and repeated invocation of rules that condition and restrict culturally intelligible practices of identity" (184).

57. Butler, *Gender Trouble*, 4.

58. Butler, *Psychic Life*, 29.

59. In most modern societies, gendering is initiated by the official pronouncement, "it's a girl/boy" and reinforced throughout the subject's life by everything from color-coded baby clothes to public bathroom signs.

60. Butler, *Gender Trouble*, 23.

61. Butler, *Gender Trouble*, 23. On gendered citizenship in general, see Fraser, "Rethinking," 59–60, and Parker et al., "Introduction," 1–18. Their *Nationalisms and Sexualities* includes several essays on gendered citizenship in Latin America. See also Chambers, "What Independence Meant," 37–44. For Mexico, see esp. Seed, *Love, Honor, and Obey*.

62. E.g., see "El feminismo se impone," *La Guacamaya*, July 25, 1907, 1. For an analysis of the image, see Buffington, "Homophobia," 217–18.

63. In his 1895 *Diccionario de mejicanismos*, e.g., Feliz Ramos i Duarte, "Professor de Instrucción Primeria, Elemental, i Superior," identifies *pelado* as Mexico City slang for "bergante, camastrón, belitre," all Spanish variants of "scoundrel" or "rogue," and cites Hernán Cortés on vagabonds as a colonial source for the term (397). Francisco J. Santamaría provides slightly less derogatory definitions in his 1959 *Diccionario de mejicanismos*: "Que está sin recursos; específicamente sin dinero . . . tipo popular de las clases bajas, harapiento, mísero e inculto, pero por lo común simpatico . . . en el sentido figurado, persona de mala educación

que acostumbra lenguaje o modales obscenos . . ." [Someone without resources, specifically money . . . a popular lower-class type, tattered, wretched, and uneducated, but generally sympathetic . . . in the figurative sense, a badly brought up person who is in the habit of obscene language or manners] (824). Santamaría's multiple definitions suggest the contested nature of the term nearly fifty years after the end of the Porfiriato.

64. Butler, *Excitable Speech*, 28.

65. Butler, *Excitable Speech*, 133.

66. Butler, *Excitable Speech*, 133.

67. The *doctrina psicológica* (psychological doctrine), which Porfirian judges used to prosecute defamation cases, especially when they involved journalists' attacks on public officials, represented an extreme form of judicial discretion "which held that the decision to typify and punish an act as a crime happened only in the mind of the judge and was not, therefore, subject to discussion by others." See Piccato, *Tyranny*, 161.

68. Butler, *Excitable Speech*, 163.

69. Butler, *Excitable Speech*, 163.

70. The phrase "nosotros los pelados" is frequently used by fictionalized popular orators in the patriotic speeches that penny press editors wrote to mock official speechifying.

71. The desire of penny press editors to work for the rehabilitation and reeducation of working-class men echoes penal approaches to disciplining the "dangerous" (lower) classes, seen by criminologists as prone to criminal acts. Despite the similarities, penny press editors sought to teach by example and humor rather than through prescription and coercion, and they rejected criminologists' assumptions about the inherent criminality of their constituents. On the attitude of Porfirian criminologists toward the lower classes, see Buffington, *Criminal and Citizen*, 38–63.

72. See esp. Giddens, *Transformation*.

73. On the shifting fortunes of artisans, see Brachio, *De los gremios*.

74. Illades, *Las otras ideas*, 205. Marxist theorist Antonio Gramsci used the term "organic intellectual" to distinguish self-taught working-class intellectuals (organic to their class) from traditionally educated intellectuals, who tend to downplay any class affiliation.

75. Huitrón, *Orígenes*, 33–77, 101–10. His jobs as an ironworker included producing security grillwork for the mansion of Porfirio Díaz's influential Interior Minister, José Yves Limantour (77). A serious labor organizer, Huitrón makes no mention of the less overtly political satiric penny press.

76. According to biographers, Celada learned to write poetry while he was setting type for the literary pages of prominent journals. His poetry began to appear in 1898 in the opposition journal *El Diario del Hogar*, where he also worked as poetry editor, traveling correspondent, and copy editor; Sergio Cordero Espinoso,

"La obra literaria de Fernando Celada Miranda," 27–32. See also Lear, *Workers, Neighbors*, 97–101. Chs. 2 and 3 discuss Celada's poetry in more detail.

77. Rancière, *Proletarian Nights*, ix.

78. "Actual Cuerpo de Redacción," *La Guacamaya*, August 23, 1906, 1. In the poem, "psicología" refers to the judicial rationale for press censorship; the quip about "varias personas muy distintas / y un solo y verdadero redactor" references Catholic interpretations of the Holy Trinity (God, Jesus, the Holy Spirit) as three distinct beings that are also the one, true God.

79. This process is analyzed in detail in Bracho, *De los gremios*.

80. Piccato, *Tyranny*, 63–95. According to Piccato, contemporaries used the term *periodismo de combate* to identify "writers' political engagement but also their disposition to conflict" with other journalists and prominent political figures (64).

81. On the homoerotic undercurrents of penny press disputes, see Buffington, "Homophobia," 196–97.

82. Quoted in Campos, *El Bar*, 126. The Spanish original reads "querubes para el presidio y serafines para el burdel."

83. Thompson, *English Working Class*, 9–10.

84. "A los obreros," *El Chile Piquín*, January 12, 1905. This short blurb included a call for reader submissions and ran regularly on the second page of the paper. Antonio Negrete's patriotic poetry is discussed in chs. 2 and 3.

85. "Letter to Mademoiselle Leroyer de Chantepie, October 4, 1864," in Flaubert, *Letters*, 78.

CHAPTER 1. WORKING-CLASS HEROES

1. We know considerably less about popular conservatism in Mexico City. The 1891 papal encyclical *Rerum Novarum* sparked an interest in "the social question" among Mexico City Catholics, including the need to reach out to workers who might otherwise turn to socialism. By 1910, the Unión Católica Obrera (UCO) was serving as the umbrella organization for nine Mexico City *círculos* (circles), most of them connected to local parishes, and publishing its own newspaper, *El Grano de Mostaza*, edited by Father José Troncoso, who had been appointed by the archbishop to head worker-outreach efforts in the capital. While UCO and its newspaper, along with a series of recreational centers (also founded by Father Troncoso), openly sought the moralization of Mexico City workers through religious instruction, they also provided other educational and recreational services. It's not clear whether activist priests like Father Troncoso or the workers who participated in the different parish *círculos* considered Catholic "social action" a conservative movement, despite its antisocialist slant. Ceballos Ramírez, "La encíclica," 24–27. See also Ceballos Ramírez, *El catolicismo social*. In contrast to Mexico City, popular conservatism was widespread in rural areas. See, e.g., Smith, *Roots of Conservatism*.

2. Williams, *Marxism*, 132.

3. Weeks, *Juárez Myth*, 33. The Gran Círculo was founded in 1872, the year of Juárez's death, and represented as many as 8,000 workers. Included in this inaugural commemoration were speeches by a baker and a tailor. Chapter 3 examines popular patriotic oratory.

4. Guerra, *México*, 9–143, provides a detailed account of the rise of opposition liberal clubs and elite factions during the late Porfiriato.

5. Marxist theorist Antonio Gramsci distinguished "wars of maneuver," which involve direct confrontations between openly antagonistic blocs, from "wars of position," which seek to reconfigure hegemony from within. Lipsitz, *Life in the Struggle*, 232–33, explains that "In this 'war of position,' radicals do not storm the barricades, but try to engage in practical activity that undermines the legitimacy of existing power and builds a taste for something better. When grounded in the real structural tensions and antagonisms of social life, these acts of contestation can lay the groundwork for profound change." Roseberry, "Hegemony," 355–66, provides a lucid exposition of Gramsci's thoughts on hegemony, resistance, and popular culture. Especially useful is his definition of hegemony as "a common material and meaningful framework for living through, talking about, and acting upon social orders characterized by domination" (361).

6. Pérez Vejo, "Se puede," 26.

7. Pérez Vejo, "Pintura," 73. On the role of artistic images in the construction of a national imaginary in late nineteenth- and early twentieth-century Mexico, see El Consejo Nacional para la Cultura y las Artes, *Los pinceles*.

8. "En Honor de Juárez," *La Guacamaya*, July 18, 1907, 1, and "¡VIVA la LIBERTAD!," *La Guacamaya*, September 12, 1907, 1.

9. There are several excellent works on Posada and his work including Posada, *José Guadalupe Posada*; Tyler, *Posada's Mexico*; Carrillo Azpeitia, *Posada*; Soler and Ávila, *Posada*; Frank, *Posada's Broadsheets*; and Barajas Durán, *Posada*.

10. A liberal opposition newspaper, *El Hijo del Ahuizote*, coined the title "El Indispensable Caudillo" in a parody of an official decree extending the presidential term indefinitely or "for as long as God wills it." *El Hijo del Ahuizote*, October 2, 1892. Quoted in Cosío Villegas, *Historia moderna*, 321.

11. In 1880, on the eighth anniversary of his death, the tomb of Benito Juárez was installed in the Panteón de Hombres Ilustres (Pantheon of Illustrious Men) in Mexico City. The statue was sculpted by the brothers Juan and Manuel Islas from imported Carrara marble taken from the same quarry that supplied the material for Michelangelo's *La Pietà*. The mausoleum that houses the statue is modeled on the Parthenon in Athens.

12. See, e.g., "Tomb of President Benito Juárez, Mexico City—covered with wreaths from all the Mexican states," photographic print on stereo card (New York: Underwood and Underwood, c. 1901), LoC call number STEREO FOREIGN GEOG

FILE—Mexico—Mexico City, 93507288; and C. B. Waite (photographer), "Tomb of Juárez, Mexico City, December 1, 1904, Box 1, Folder 1, Rene d'Harnoncourt Photography Collection, Benson Latin American Collection, University of Texas at Austin. The images can be viewed on the websites of their respective archives. Political cartoons depicting the defilement of Juárez's tomb by hypocrites and scoundrels date back at least to the 1880s. See, e.g., El Consejo Nacional, *Los pinceles*, 202–4.

13. *Pulquerías* served pulque, a mildly alcoholic drink made from the fermented juice of the maguey cactus. Despite the drink's low alcohol content and nutritional benefits, the alleged social dangers associated with lower-class pulque drinking were an elite obsession. See, e.g., Piccato, "El Paso de Venus," 203–41, and Mitchell, *Intoxicated Identities*. Although all the penny press editors acknowledged the potential dangers of alcoholism for workingmen, only *El Diablito Rojo's* editor shared the obsessive concerns of elite social critics about lower-class drunkenness. Working-class leisure activities, including social drinking, are explored in ch. 4.

14. The official ceremony surrounding the annual *Grito* has remained virtually unchanged since 1896, the year Porfirian authorities brought the "liberty" bell to Mexico City from the Dolores church where Father Hidalgo had first assembled his followers. Since then, every September 15 at 11 PM, the president has emerged onto a balcony of the presidential palace, rung the liberty bell, repeated the official version of Hidalgo's speech, and ended it with the collective cry "¡Viva México! ¡Viva la Independencia!" For more on the history of Independence Day celebrations, see the essays in Beezley and Lorey, *Viva México*. The actual words of Hidalgo's *Grito* are unknown but probably included references to the Virgin of Guadalupe and a condemnation of "bad government"; official reconstructions have added *vivas* for an independent Mexico and a condemnation of *gachupines* (a derogatory term for Spaniards). See Fernández Tejedo and Nava Nava, "Images of Independence in the Nineteenth Century," in Beezley and Lorey, *Viva México*, 10. On popular rituals in general, see the introduction and essays in Beezley et al., *Rituals of Rule*. In a definitive (if deeply flawed) essay on Mexican national identity, philosopher-poet Octavio Paz argues that the defiant popular version of the *Grito*—"¡Viva México! ¡Hijos de la chingada!" (Long live Mexico! Sons of the Fucked Woman!)—represents an aggressive verbal challenge to an undefined (male) "other" that might or might not include Mexicans themselves as the "sons" of La Malinche, Hernán Cortés's Indian translator and concubine. Paz, "The Sons of La Malinche" in *Labyrinth of Solitude*, 75. The Spanish word *hijos* more accurately translates as "children," but Paz's English was excellent, and he allowed the translation "sons" to stand.

15. *Albures* are still popular in Mexican working-class culture (including in the US). They tend to work at several different levels, at least one of which typically carries a sexual connotation. Sexual innuendo isn't obvious in this particular

example, unless we read "¡la mar!" as "¡la madre!" which would open up a wide range of hard-to-prove but intriguing interpretive possibilities. On the interpretive problems presented by *albures* and translation of popular language in general, see Paredes, "Ethnographic Work," 73–112. Paredes points out that "the use of indirect language has been refined in the wordplay of the *albur* to double or triple levels of meaning . . . not to soften the force of an insult but rather to heighten its effect" (84).

16. Penny press appropriation of popular speech is addressed in some detail in later chapters.

17. Original: "DEL PUEBLO Y POR EL PUEBLO//SEMANARIO INDEPENDIENTE DEFENSOR DE LA CLASE OBRERA."

18. See, e.g., Adorno, *Guaman Poma*, and Adorno et al., *Guaman Poma de Ayala*. While Guaman Poma's art mixed European and Andean styles; Posada and other penny press artists worked mainly within the European tradition. For that reason, penny press illustrations read much more straightforwardly than hybrid colonial documents like Guaman Poma's.

19. The viewer's left is the "conceptual" right-hand side of the frame, or stage right. This reflects long-standing prejudices against the conceptual left, as, e.g., in the association of left-handedness with moral deviance and witchcraft. To keep things simple, I give directions from the viewer's perspective throughout. As we will see, the active/passive dichotomy is also heavily gendered.

20. Frank, *Posada's Broadsheets*, 174.

21. Beezley, *Judas*, 70–71, discusses the importance of manhood and hats in Porfirian Mexico.

22. The Spanish word *pueblo* connotes everything from a small town to the general population (i.e., "the populace") to the citizenry of a nation ("the people"). This web of connotations gives the word a grounded-in-the-land, intimate feel that is missing from English translations.

23. A Porfirian-era dictionary of "Mexicanisms" defines *roto* as "petimetre del pueblo, indio ó mestizo vestido á la europea" (popular dandy, Indian or mestizo dressed in European style); Ramos i Duarte, *Diccionario de mejicanismos*, 445. This is the meaning behind the nickname of the infamous Porfirian bandit Chucho el Roto (Chucho the Dandy). In the image for *La Guacamaya*, however, the *rotos'* deliberate rejection of working-class culture—symbolized by their fashionable clothes—marks them as class traitors eager to sell out their compatriots for personal gain. In this sense, the *roto* functions as a "constitutive other," an abject figure against which working-class men constructed their class identities. See Santamaría, *Diccionario de mejicanismos*, 948. Santamaría notes in his definition that "the woman of the people calls a young lady of the middle classes who lives like a rich person, a *rota*."

24. The feminization of bourgeois men is analyzed in depth in Buffington, "Homophobia."

25. On the symbolic role of women, including the Virgin of Guadalupe in the working-class imaginary, see Buffington, "Modern Sacrificial Economy."

26. On popular politics in Mexico City during the independence era, see Warren, *Vagrants and Citizens*. The links between consumption and citizenship are explored in ch. 4.

27. On early nineteenth-century Mexico City civic festivals, see Garrido Asperó, *Fiestas cívicas*, and Curcio-Nagy, *Great Festivals*. Mexico City also had (and continues to have) a rich tradition of religious festivals. The distinction between civic and religious festivals is complicated for the colonial period because of the close links between church and state. On the tensions between civic and religious festivals in late colonial Mexico City, see Viquiera Albán, *Propriety and Permissiveness*.

28. Garrido Asperó, *Fiestas cívicas*, 20.

29. See Beezley and Lorey, *Viva México*, and Beezley et al., *Rituals of Rule*.

30. For brief overviews of late nineteenth- and early twentieth-century liberal historiography, see Florescano, *Historia*, 317–74, and Hale, *Transformation*, 9–10. On the making and significance of *México a través de los siglos*, see Ortiz Monasterio, *México eternamente*. Among other things, liberal historians hoped to diminish the influence of conservative Lucas Alamán's well-known *Historia de México* and present the nation as unified after "centuries of turmoil" (Florescano, *Historia*, 353).

31. For a useful typology/genealogy of the main currents of Mexican liberalism, see Knight, "El liberalismo mexicano," 59–91.

32. According to Jiménez Marce ("La creación," 33), "liberal genealogy configured three archetypes that linked three key moments in history, conceived as a grand myth. Cuauhtémoc is converted into the archetype of the myth of origin, Miguel Hidalgo into the archetype of the myth of liberation, and Benito Juárez was the archetype of the myth of the golden age [of *puro* liberalism]."

33. On the history of the Cuauhtémoc cult and the late nineteenth-century archeological forgery that helped perpetuate it, see Gillingham, *Cuauhtémoc's Bones*. For an examination of nineteenth-century uses of Cuauhtémoc and pre-Hispanic history, see Pérez Vejo, "Los hijos," 1–15.

34. On the Juárez cult in his home state of Oaxaca (also the home state of Porfirio Díaz), see McNamara, *Sons of the Sierra*.

35. "El Credo Político," *El Diablito Bromista*, October 13, 1907, 4. First promulgated in 325 AD, the Nicene Creed, in one version or another, is the fundamental statement of belief for most Christian sects. The traditional English version from the *Book of Common Prayer* begins: "I believe in one God, the Father Almighty / Maker of heaven and earth, and of all things visible and invisible . . ." (Original: "Creo en Dios Miguel Hidalgo y Costilla todopoderoso, creador de la Independencia y de la Libertad; Creo en José María Morelos, digno hijo de esos principios, defensor nuestro que fue concebido por la obra del Sitio de Cuautla, nació de Santa Valladolid, virgen, padeció bajo el poder de los Domínicos Jesuitas, fue fu-

silado, muerto, y sepultado en San Cristóbal Ecatepec, descendió á los infiernos de la inquisición, resucitó de entre los muertos del Estado de Guerrero, subió á los cielos de Cuauhtémoc y está sentado á su diestra; Creo que desde ahí ha de venir á juzgar á los liberales y mochos [conservadores]; Creo en el Espíritu Santo de la Reforma, en el progreso de los liberales, el castigo de los traidores, la resurrección de Don Benito Juárez y el cumplimiento de la Constitución de 1857. Amén.") During the siege of Cuautla (now in the state of Morelos), Morelos and his men held off a superior royalist force for two months and then successfully escaped through enemy lines. Morelos was born in Valladolid (now Morelia) and attended seminary there under the rectorship of Father Hidalgo. He was defrocked and executed in San Cristóbal Ecatepec. His chief lieutenant, Vicente Guerrero, continued fighting after his death and eventually became president of Mexico (1829). The state of Guerrero carries his name. (This creed also appeared as "Credo patriótico" in *El Diablito Rojo*, September 14, 1908, 3.)

36. A larger French army returned the next year and succeeded in taking Mexico City—making Cinco de Mayo yet another celebration of Mexican heroism in the face of eventual defeat.

37. To supplement the literary efforts of liberal propagandists, the Porfirian city planners envisioned an impressive sequence of civic monuments—to Cuauhtémoc, Hidalgo, Juárez, Zaragoza—that would "progress" down the capital's principal boulevard, Paseo de la Reforma, to Chapultepec Castle, the residence of President Porfirio Díaz (Barbara Tennenbaum, "Streetwise History," in Beezley et al., *Ritual of Rule*, 127–50). This monumental history lesson began in 1886 with the inauguration of a massive monument to Cuauhtémoc and culminated in 1910 with the completion of the Angel of Independence (surrounded by statues of Hidalgo, Morelos, and other independence heroes) and a monument to Juárez in the *Alameda* (Central Park); Tenorio-Trillo, "1910 Mexico City," 167–97. Despite their steadfast opposition to his regime, penny press editors acknowledged Porfirio Díaz's status as a liberal war hero by including his image in Cinco de Mayo commemoratives; they even accorded him an occasional commemorative issue of his own. See, e.g., *El Hijo del Fandango*, September 23, 1901, 1; *La Guacamaya*, March 31, 1904, 1; *La Guacamaya*, April 6, 1905, 1.

38. On the role of women in the Mexican national imaginary and liberal efforts to diminish the contributions of independence-era heroines, see Gutiérrez, "Mujeres," 209–43. Gutiérrez adds that "it's interesting to note how women linked to some facet of nationalism are located first of all in their place of origin, the region, the province, before they're allowed to think or act as agents of national integration" (219).

39. McNamara, "Private Ramírez," 35–49. McNamara argues that male domination of the discourse on republican motherhood explains its failure to represent women's interests in Mexico (36) and notes that "with the exception of symbolic representations to Lady Liberty—El Angel de la independencia—and a naked

Diana la cazadora [Diana the Huntress], women are not present in the narrative of Paseo de la Reforma" (42).

40. On "republican motherhood" in Mexico, see Arrom, *Women of Mexico City*, 14–52; Franco, *Plotting Women*, 79–101; and Tuñón Pablos, *Women in Mexico*, 45–62. On gendered citizenship, see Fraser, "Rethinking," 56–60, and Parker et al. "Introduction," 1–18. *Nationalisms and Sexualities* includes several essays on gendered citizenship in Latin America. See also Chambers, "What Independence Meant," 37–44.

41. Quoted in Tuñón, *Women in Mexico*, 52–53.

42. The role of women in the working-class male imaginary is explored in Buffington, "Modern Sacrificial Economy."

43. For an overview of Prieto and his influence on Mexican letters, see McLean, *Guillermo Prieto*.

44. Prieto, *Colección*, 313.

45. Forment, *Democracy*, xii. Forment explains further that "citizens used the same religious terms—reason, passion, free will, and so on—but pronounced them slightly differently. Whether these terms acquired democratic or authoritarian connotations in everyday life was the result of 'pragmatic usage' rather than 'semantic meaning'" (25).

46. Ceballos Ramírez, "La Encíclica," 21. For more on working-class religious attitudes in Porfirian Mexico City, see Lear, *Workers, Neighbors*, 92–94.

47. Forment, *Democracy*, 401.

48. Jiménez Marce, "La creación," 29.

49. Cabera, Martínez Carrión, and Pérez Fernández all worked closely with and often published editorials written by the Flores Magón brothers (Ricardo and Enrique), editors of the opposition newspaper *Regeneración*. The Flores Magón brothers were forced into exile in the United States, where they continued to agitate for the overthrow of the Díaz regime.

50. Barajas Durán, *Posada*, 91. Jacobins were the most intransigent and anticlerical of the principal French revolutionary factions. On the linkage between secular heroes and Old Testament biblical figures, see Jiménez Marce, "La creación," 31.

51. "Situación de la clase obrera: De Herodes á Pilatos," *La Guacamaya*, August 11, 1902, 1. This image and the one that follows were illustrated by Posada, who also provided anticlerical images for *El Padre Padilla*, *El Padre Cobos*, and *La Patria Ilustrada*. Both images are discussed in Barajas Durán, *Posada*, 222–25.

52. "Calvario moderno," *La Guacamaya*, December 5, 1902, 1. In the New Testament, Longinus is the Roman soldier who stabbed the crucified Christ in the side.

53. The quotation is from Juárez's famous July 15, 1867, speech marking the restoration of the republic after the defeat of Maximilian. The longer excerpt sets the oft-quoted phrase in context: "Mexicans: let us now turn all our strength to obtaining and consolidating the benefits of peace. Under its auspices, the pro-

tection of the laws and of the authorities will work to the benefit of all the inhabitants of the Republic. May the people and the government respect the rights of all. Among individuals as among nations, peace means respect for the rights of others."

54. Hidalgo was a well-read aficionado of European Enlightenment thought, but his political vision remained vague. In contrast, his successor and former student, Morelos, convened a constitutional convention that, among other things, advocated universal male suffrage, abolished slavery and the caste system, and put an end to judicial torture.

55. The biggest dilemma was that Mexico finally achieved independence in 1821 under the auspices of General Agustín de Iturbide, a former loyalist commander who had fought for Spain against Morelos, Guerrero, and Victoria before turning against an increasingly liberal Spanish government. Iturbide had strong ties to conservative interests, and to make matters worse, he had himself declared emperor of Mexico within a year of independence. That controversial decision, coupled with a failing economy and an increasingly autocratic approach to governance, led to his ouster and exile soon thereafter. When he returned to Mexico in 1824, he was executed as a traitor. Despite their military failures, idealistic martyrs like Hidalgo and Morelos made better national heroes than Iturbide, especially from the perspective of liberal historians. On the early debates over these two distinct "national projects," see Garrido Asperó, *Fiestas cívicas*, 139–64. Hidalgo, Morelos, and their compatriots were declared national heroes by congressional decree shortly after Iturbide's abdication in 1823 (162).

56. "Después de las fiestas," *Don Cucufate*, September 25, 1906, 1.

57. Shedding tears of grief or shame (usually for "Mexico") on public occasions has been common practice for Mexican political leaders. Despite his strongman image, Porfirio Díaz often wept publicly on appropriate occasions, which led some opposition journalists to coin the nickname, "The Crybaby of Icamole," after the city where he began the Revolution of Tuxtepec that overthrew the government of President Sebastián Lerdo y Tejada and initiated the Porfiriato. See Barajas Durán, *El país*, 54–67. The most notorious example in more recent years is President Miguel López Portillo's 1982 presidential address to Congress during which he ostentatiously wiped away a tear while bemoaning Mexico's sudden (and humiliating) financial collapse and promising to defend the value of the peso "like a dog" by nationalizing the nation's banks.

58. The association of specific symbols or attributes with religious figures—i.e., St. Francis with doves—is ubiquitous in Mexican Catholicism and common elsewhere.

59. In the pre-smog era, Popcatépetl and Iztaccíhuatl were dramatic and instantly recognizable features of the Mexico City landscape. As potent and potentially dangerous natural wonders, the two volcanoes have long been used as symbols of Mexico's slumbering but nonetheless explosive national character.

60. See, e.g., the covers of *La Guacamaya*, August 6, 1903; *La Palanca*, September 18, 1904; *Don Cucufate*, September 17, 1906; *El Diablito Bromista*, September 16, 1907; *El Diablito Rojo*, September 14, 1908.

61. See, e.g., Posada's poster of Hidalgo for the 1899 Independence Day commemoration in Posada, *José Guadalupe Posada*, 356. Posada also produced many poster-sized images of religious figures like the Virgin of Guadalupe, Jesus, and Santo Niño; see, e.g., Posada, *José Guadalupe Posada*, 181–219.

62. "Dos bellísimas alegóricas patrias," *El Diablito Rojo*, August 29, 1910, 4. A similar ad appeared in *El Diablito Rojo*, November 7, 1910, 4.

63. "¡Libertad!," *La Guacamaya*, September 13, 1906, 1. Berets were associated with Spanish storekeepers—an unpopular group with working-class Mexicans, who were often in their debt. The fact that Posada bothered to sign the Hidalgo prints also suggests their commercial potential. At the same time, the print's informal, cartoonlike quality makes it somewhat exceptional. Posada also produced more conventional patriotic images, including portraits of Hidalgo and Juárez. See Posada, *José Guadalupe Posada*, 355–71.

• 64. "Himno a Hidalgo," *La Palanca*, September 18, 1904, 1; Felipe Debray, "Excelsior," *El Diablito Rojo*, September 14, 1908, 1.

65. See, e.g., "Glorias de la Patria," *El Diablito Rojo*, February 14, 1910, 4.

66. "Fusilamiento de Don Miguel Hidalgo y Costilla," *La Guacamaya*, July 30, 1902. The image is modeled loosely on Francisco Goya's famous painting, *The Third of May, 1808 in Madrid: The Execution on Príncipe Pío Hill*, which probably inspired several of Posada's firing squad images (see, e.g., Posada, *José Guadalupe Posada*, 262–63). Goya's painting depicts an event in Spain's popular uprising against the French puppet Joseph Bonaparte (Napoléon's brother). The French occupation of Spain set the stage for independence movements throughout Latin America, including Father Hidalgo's revolt. Although both images depict the moment the shots are fired, Posada plays with Goya's placement of the principle figures. In Posada's image the representatives of the state—firing squad, accompanying officers, and soldiers—appear on the (active) left; the representatives of the church, Hidalgo and attending priests, are on the (passive) right. There is also a touch of irony in the reversal of positions and roles: in Goya's painting the firing squad is French, the victims are Spanish insurgents; in Posada's print, the firing squad is Spanish, the victim is a Mexican insurgent. Another twist: the struggle against the French occupation of Mexico later defined Benito Juárez's political career. Yet another twist: Goya's picture also inspired Edouard Manet's *The Execution of Maximilian* (1867). The "infamous Elizondo" refers to rebel-turned-loyalist Ignacio Elizondo, who captured Hidalgo and his entourage and turned them over to the colonial authorities. Other issues commemorating Hidalgo's execution include *La Guacamaya*, August 6, 1903, and *El Diablito Bromista*, July 31, 1904. The latter includes the legal text of Hidalgo's death sentence, "Acta de la ejecución de la sentencia de muerte de Hidalgo" (2).

67. "La Sociedad Mano Amiga Hidalgo" and "Interesante a los obreros," *La Gua-camaya*, September 15, 1904, 2; "La Sociedad 'Mano Amiga Hidalgo,'" *La Gua-camaya*, October 20, 1904, 2; and "El Centenario," *La Guacamaya*, December 8, 1904, 2. Another penny press, *El Papagayo*, is listed among the subscribers. "Importante," *La Guacamaya*, September 15, 1904, 3.

68. "Excitativa á los obreros," *La Guacamaya*, July 28, 1902, 3. (Original: "Les su-plicamos á los obreros que nos han honorado con sus composiciones, nos las remitan con la mayor brevedad posible.")

69. "Al inmortal Hidalgo en el 91° aniversario de su muerte," *La Guacamaya*, July 30, 1902, 4. (Original: "¡Loor eterno! / Al noble anciano, / Al que mi Patria / Supo librar / Del férreo yugo, / Del cruel tirano.") The Spanish word *anciano* is often translated "old man" but carries connotations of respect missing from that translation. The Spanish word *patria* is also difficult to translate. The root is masculine and "patriarchal," but the noun itself is feminine. The English equiva-lents "fatherland" and "motherland" are too exclusively gendered, while "home-land" seems too neutered. A frequent penny press contributor, in 1904 Negrete became the editor of the relatively short-lived *El Papagayo*.

70. "Homenaje al inmortal Hidalgo," *La Palanca*, October 2, 1904, 3. (Original: "Grito santo de Dolores / Que derrocando virreyes / Y tiranos y opresores / Nos dio libertad y honores, / Nos dio independencia y leyes.")

71. Pascual Mendoza, Obrero, "A Hidalgo," *La Palanca*, September 25, 1904, 4. (Original: "[Poesía leída] por su autor la noche de 15 de Septiembre, en la velada literaria que en honor de nuestro libertador tuve verificativo en la Fábrica El Molino de Enmedio.") The opening is the same as the Latin Ave Maria, or Hail, Mary prayer in praise of the Virgin and used as a form of penance by Catho-lics. Other penny press writers used the Spanish version "salve," as in "¡Salve, oh padre del pueblo mexicano" (Hail, oh Father of the Mexican people!), the opening line of editor Antonio de P. Escárcega's "A Hidalgo," *El Diablito Brom-ista*, September 16, 1907, 2.

72. Martiniano Raso (obrero), "Homenaje á Hidalgo," *El Diablito Rojo*, November 15, 1909, 3. Like many others, Raso also invokes Hidalgo's religious background, contritely beginning his poem with "Pardon, oh Father," after the manner of a confession. In an essay in honor of Hidalgo's birthday, "a worker" even com-pared Hidalgo's "light of liberty" to the Star of Bethlehem. Un obrero, "8 de mayo de 1753," *La Guacamaya*, May 11, 1905, 3.

73. Lempérière, "Los dos centenarios," 325. Hidalgo's successor-in-struggle, More-los, posed a similar problem.

74. "Después de un siglo," *El Diablito Rojo*, September 20, 1909, 1.

75. "La voz del Pueblo," *El Diablito Bromista*, August 11, 1902, 3; reprinted as "La voz del pueblo," *La Guacamaya*, August 29, 1907, 2.

76. In a classic study from the same era, the German sociologist Max Weber (*Prot-estant Ethic*, 25) argued for an "elective affinity" between "the rational ethics of

ascetic Protestantism" and "the spirit of capitalism." He also noted that "it is a fact that the Protestants . . . both as ruling classes and as ruled, both as majority and as minority, have shown a special tendency to develop economic rationalism which cannot be observed to the same extent among Catholics . . ." (39–40).

CHAPTER 2. THE ONE TRUE JUÁREZ

1. See fig. 1.1.
2. This holds true for all the mid-July issues that I could locate: *La Guacamaya*, July 21, 1902; *La Guacamaya*, July 1903 (número extraordinario); *La Guacamaya*, July 18, 1904; *La Guacamaya*, July 18, 1907; *La Guacamaya*, July 23, 1908. The last two issues are only partially dedicated to Juárez, but he is featured on both covers.
3. "El respeto al derecho ageno [*sic*] es la paz," *La Guacamaya*, July 21, 1902, 1. The same portrait and quotation appear on the 1903 and 1904 *La Guacamaya* covers with slightly different framing. The motto comes from Juárez's 1867 speech reestablishing the republic after the defeat of Maximilian. See n. 27. The print is unsigned. Posada produced a nearly identical image for a 1906 Vanegas Arroyo broadsheet (even the shading is similar). See Posada, *José Guadalupe Posada*, 371. Parallels between representations of Juárez and the Virgin of Guadalupe— dark skin, benefactors of "the Americas," objects of popular veneration—are striking but hard to prove.
4. "¡Salve Juárez!," *El Pinche*, July 21, 1904, 1; "5 de Febrero de 1857," *El Chile Piquín*, February 16, 1905, 1; and "A Juárez," *El Chile Piquín*, July 20, 1905, 1. Both penny press titles have vulgar and self-deprecating connotations in Mexican Spanish. As an adjective *pinche* translates roughly as "shitty" (in a stingy sort of way); while a *chile piquín* suggests a little but potent penis. The cook's hat and its *El Pinche* label have been etched out of the *El Chile Piquín* illustrations. The corpulent kitchen worker appears on the *El Pinche* masthead plucking and cooking "the bourgeoisie" and "bad government" and represents its editor's public persona.
5. "Homenaje," *La Tranca*, July 22, 1906, 1.
6. "¡Juárez!," *La Guacamaya*, July 21, 1902, 2. Original: "la figura prepotente de nuestra Historia Patria." Creoles, or *criollos*, were people of Spanish descent born in the Americas. They were considered white and under colonial law enjoyed privileges denied to Indians, blacks, and people of mixed race. Because Creoles were born outside the metropolis, however, they had fewer legal privileges than whites born in Spain. This "racial" distinction between Creoles and Peninsulars (people born in Spain) was a source of colonial resentment that contributed to the independence movement.
7. "¡Juárez!," *La Guacamaya*, July 21, 1902, 2. Most sources give Juárez's birthplace as the nearby town of San Pablo Guelatao, Oaxaca. (Original: "nuestro gran Juárez, el indio de raza pura, el que nace en el pequeño pueblo de Ixtlán, confundido con

las masas populares, crece, se desarrolla, á la vez que su inteligencia toma proporciones gigantescas, para ocupar después el lugar que le era reservado por la mano del Creador, y semejanza del ave fénix se levanta de la nada para difundir sus doctrinas y sacudir el yugo de la tiranía.")

8. Juan G. Millán, "A Juárez," *La Guacamaya*, July 21, 1902, 2. (Original: "Los hombres como tú, se elevan desde la más ínfima clase social hasta donde tú te elevaste, merecen el respeto, admiración y cariño de todos sus conciudadanos, máxime, cuando ejecutan y ponen en práctica leyes que han venido á implantar el progreso y civilización.")

9. Reconciling the apparent disjunction between working-class racism and workers' adulation of Juárez isn't as hard as it might appear. In Mexico, as in most of Latin America, perceptions of cultural difference have played a key role in eliciting and sustaining racist attitudes. Because Juárez was well spoken, well educated, and well credentialed by the standards of the dominant culture, his Indianness served as reminder of his humble origins rather than as a marker of cultural inferiority.

10. "¡¡A los obreros!!," *La Guacamaya*, June 23, 1904, 4; and "El centenario de Juárez," February 15, 1906, 2. The latter call is for the March 21 birthday edition.

11. Some workers declined to identify themselves as such; so it's impossible to determine the number of worker submissions with any accuracy.

12. Antonio Negrete, "Al Benemérito de las Américas, Benito Juárez, en el 30° aniversario de su muerte," *La Guacamaya*, July 21, 1902, 4; Negrete, "Al Benemérito de las Américas, Benito Juárez, en el 31° aniversario de su muerte," *La Guacamaya*, July, 1903 (número extraordinario), 2–3; Negrete, "18 de Julio de 1872," *La Guacamaya*, July, 1903 (número extraordinario), 2. Although the titles are practically identical, the two poems are quite different.

13. Negrete, "Al Benemérito de las Américas, Benito Juárez, en el 31° aniversario de su muerte," 2. Original: "México, ¡Oh Patria mía! . . . si el Gran Juárez viviera; ¡Otra tu suerte sería!" Negrete's phrasing recalls the popular 1930s *danzón* "Juárez no debió de morir" [Juárez should never have died], which includes the lines "Porque si Juárez no hubiera muerto todavía viviría / otro gallo cantaría, / la patria se salvaría, / México sería felíz" [Because if Juárez hadn't died / he'd still be alive / another rooster would be singing, / the homeland would be saved, / and Mexico would be happy]. On *danzón* as a popular art form in mid-twentieth-century Mexico City, see Buffington, "La 'Dancing' Mexicana."

14. Celada, *Bronces*. This title [*Bronzes*] connotes both heroic statues (often made of bronze) and Juárez's race: in the racial typology of the time, Indians were labeled "the bronze race." The ad for *Bronces* appeared in *El Diablito Bromista*, August 7, 1904, 4. More of Celada's patriotic poems can be found in Cordero Espinosa et al., *Fernando Celada Miranda*, 441–519. Like many other anticlerical liberal *letrados*, including the renowned romantic poet Guillermo Prieto, Celada also wrote quite a bit of religious poetry (321–37).

15. "5 de Febrero de 1857," *El Chile Piquín*, February 16, 1905, 1; and "Á Juárez," *El Chile Piquín*, July 20, 1905, 1, 4. The first poem is the first stanza of "Á Juárez" from *Bronces* (26–30); the second is the complete version of another "Á Juárez" poem from *Bronces* (15–17). Both poems had been published earlier in *El Diario del Hogar*, an opposition paper aimed at the middle class and Celada's principal publisher. While neither Posada nor Celada would have been considered famous at the time, both men were at the top of their respective professions and a commemorative edition that featured both artists must have held considerable appeal. This probably explains why *El Chile Piquín* reran the same cover with a different poem by the same poet just six months later.

16. "Á Juárez," *El Chile Piquín*, July 20, 1905, 4. The English translation makes no attempt to reproduce Celada's rhyme scheme (*ababccb*), syllabification (four lines of eleven syllables, one of seven, two of eleven), and meter (accents mostly on the sixth and tenth syllables). His careful but playful attention to rhyme, rhythm, and meter probably reflects the influence of romantic and modernist poets like Guillermo Prieto, Manuel Gutiérrez Nájera, and Salvador Díaz Mirón.

17. The reform law that bears his name, *Ley Juárez*, abolished the use of ecclesiastical courts for civil and criminal offenses. It was later written into the 1857 constitution.

18. Celada, "Á Juárez," *Bronces*, 13–14. (Original: "Jesucristo es un símbolo, un sagrario / Y tú eres Patria, convertido en Hombre! [. . .] ¡La iglesia te calumnia . . . no eres reo, / No eres un miserable ni un ateo, / Eres de Dios reflejo y de su gloria!")

19. Partly in response to its merciless personal attacks, a period of relative freedom of the press came to an end when in 1884 Porfirio Díaz took up the presidency again after the Manuel González interregnum. See Barajas Durán, *El país*. After 1884, the journalist Daniel Cabrera, editor of the satirical *El Hijo de Ahuizote*, and his illustrator Jesús Martínez Carrión, who were less circumspect than most, especially with regard to Díaz himself, spent time in prison as a consequence. For examples of political caricatures mocking the president directly, see Pruneda, *La caricature*, 255–68.

20. Luzbel, "Por el pueblo y para el pueblo," *El Diablito Rojo*, March 23, 1908, 2. The sarcastic comment about paper from the San Rafael Factory refers to the government's monopoly on newsprint, which it provided at reduced cost and in ample supply to *El Imparcial* and other "subsidized" papers, which were staffed by "bribe-taking" journalists. On the subsidized press, see Smith, "Contentious Voices," 89–119.

21. "Al Museo de Antigüidades," *El Diablito Rojo*, February 8, 1909, 1. As early as 1908, *El Diablito Rojo* had incorporated the 1857 constitution into its masthead, which also included caricatures of several prominent Porfirians, among them Porfirio Díaz and his *científicos*.

22. "El capital y los brazos," *La Guacamaya*, July 2, 1903, 2. (Original: "hay una Constitución que ampara y favorece á todo ciudadano, sin distinción de clase ni

de categoría.") Other prominent constitutional critiques include covers for *La Guacamaya* (February 11, 1904; February 8, 1906; July 18, 1906) and *El Diablito Bromista* (September 19, 1907; July 21, 1907; May 10, 1909).

23. His crime was to have slandered a Porfirian official. Arenas Guzmán, *El periodismo*, 16.

24. "Al Sr. Presidente de la República Mexicana General Díaz," *El Diablito Bromista*, February 7, 1904, 1. (Original: "Llamamos su atención sobre el atentado anticonstitucional de que han sido víctimas seis obreros de la Fábrica 'La Colmena' consignados arbitrariamente al servicio de las armas por el Jéfe Político de Tlatnepantla. ¿Se hará justicia? Así lo esperamos.")

25. "Un matrimonio desafortunado," *El Diablito Bromista*, November 26, 1908, 1. The paper's more confrontational editorial tone is reflected in a new masthead that includes the slogan "[*El Diablito Bromista*] neither asks for nor gives quarter [i.e., mercy]" (*ni pide ni da cuartel*), and depicts the "joking devil" with a pitchfork in one hand and a *matraca* (noisemaker) in the other. The *matraca* is used in traditional Easter celebrations to scare away "sins" and "evil spirits."

26. In all likelihood the young bride also references Díaz's second wife, Carmen Romero Rubio, the daughter of a prominent Mexico City politician, whom he married in 1881, when she was just seventeen and he was fifty-one. Because the Romero Rubios were staunch Catholics, many historians see this second marriage as the first step in Díaz's gradual rapprochement with the Church—a situation that *puro* liberals (including most penny press editors) considered untenable. "Doña Carmen" played an active role in Mexico City society, and there is no evidence that their marriage involved spousal abuse of any kind.

27. The reform laws—*Ley Juárez*, *Ley Lerdo*, and *Ley Iglesias*—provided a foundation for the 1857 constitution. They were especially concerned with issues of legal equality and restrictions on the special privileges (*fueros*) of the Church and the military. Title 1 of the 1857 constitution, "Of the Rights of Man," lays out the individual guarantees typical of a liberal bill of rights, including freedom of the press (Article 7).

28. This depiction of intimate partner violence as a political act by a threatened male subject reflects an important shift in the social meaning of violence against women. See esp. Buffington, "Modern Sacrificial Economy."

29. "La Constitución de 1857," *El Diablito Rojo*, November 2, 1910, 1. (Original: "[. . .] sudan, temen y pujan, / mas no te matan . . . te estrujan / ó te arrancan unas hojas!")

30. For a detailed account of the Bulnes polemic, see Weeks, *Juárez Myth*, 54–70.

31. The phrase "good dictator" is from Bulnes's nomination speech. The complete sentence reads thus: "The good dictator is an animal so rare, that the Nation that possesses one should prolong not only his power but his very life" (El dictador bueno es un animal tan raro, que la Nación que posee uno debe prolongarle no sólo el poder, sino hasta la vida). Quoted in Cosío Villegas, *Historia moderna*, 292.

32. Hale, *Transformation*, 133–36.

33. Weeks, *Juárez Myth*, 62.

34. Bulnes, *El verdadero Juárez*, 844. (Original): "Juárez es ciertamente un ídolo de la veneración liberal, pero ídolo subjetivo, formado pieza por pieza con subterfugios políticos y material legendario extraído de los volcanes de nuestras ilusiones siempre encendidas, nunca para iluminarnos sino para calcinar nuestro espíritu. El molde en que hemos fundido la figura de Juárez es el inmenso vacío de nuestras ignorancias y en consecuencia la escultura ha resultado colossal. Juárez está en camino de ser un Boudha zapoteca y laico, imponente y maravilloso, emanado del caos intellectual, siempre tenebroso por la ausencia de criterio en nuestras clases ilustradas, por la exuberancia de vanidad de nuestras masas, por la necesidad de catolicismo residual, que busca siempre una imagen, un culto, una piedad para la emoción social desprendida del sentimiento religioso."

35. For a detailed history of the controversy over Bulnes's books (and other related polemics), see Jiménez Marce, *La pasión*. See also Weeks, *Juárez Myth*, 54–70.

36. Weeks, *Juárez Myth*, 63–65; Jiménez Marce, *La pasión*, 136–41. Jiménez Marce provides an extensive overview of Bulnes's allegations, opponents' rebuttals, and Bulnes's responses (129–206). On the struggles between the *científicos* and the *reyistas* (supporters of Bernardo Reyes) over the nomination of vice president and successor to Díaz in the 1904 elections, see Guerra, *México*, 79–143.

37. "Díaz injuriando a Juárez," *Regeneración*, November 5, 1904, 3. (Original: "no solo es el producto de un cerebro demente y de un espíritu corrompido; es el producto de la tiranía; es el florecimiento de la abyección; es el aborto del despotismo porfirista, que después de haber ultrajado á los mexicanos en sus derechos y en sus personas, los ultraja en sus afectos, en sus veneraciones, en sus glorias!")

38. "Díaz injuriando a Juárez," *Regeneración*. (Original: "El autócrata, que siempre odió á Juárez; que se rebeló contra él y fue vencido; que quiso levantarse y fue humillado; que guardó siempre en el alma la hiel de sus despechos y sus derrotas, no pudo sufrir que fuera tan entusiastamente glorificado el hombre á quien él detestó, ni pudo contemplar tranquillo que la gratitud nacional agobiara con infinitos laureles la frente del inmortal Benemérito, mientras que él, Díaz, sólo contaba con los homenajes comprados á peso de oro y con las aclamaciones de lacayos bien retribuidos.)

39. See fig. 1.2. The alert reader will note other iconographic conventions at work in this image as well: the actors and action move "impulsively" from right to left on the horizontal axis, right-handedness and hats signify activeness, and a higher position on the vertical axis marks the moral superiority of Juárez and the pursuing workers.

40. *La Guacamaya*, September 15, 1904, 1. (Original: "el denigrador Francisco Bulnes . . . son indignos de pisar el territorio Nacional [y] debemos clavarles los hirientes dardos de nuestro desprecio y maldición.") The *El Diablito Bro-*

mista cover for September 11, 1904, "Los Evangelistas de Zoquipan," featured Bulnes as an *evangelista*, or writer for hire, duping a gullible worker. The image is unsigned.

41. Fernando García, "¡Viva Juárez! Los Obreros en Acción," *La Palanca*, October 9, 1904, 2–3. (Original: "una manifestación pública . . . protestar contra el libelo infamante que en mala hora escribío el Diputado D. Francisco Bulnes.") In January 1907 a bloody strike at Río Blanco would result in the deaths of several workers and their wives and children at the hands of government troops; this and other atrocities helped undermine the legitimacy of the Porfirian regime.

42. "Lo del día: el escándalo de Bulnes," *El Diablito Bromista*, September 11, 1904, 2. (Original: "el futuro yankee de Bulnes.")

43. *La Guacamaya*, September 29, 1904, 1. In this instance, the artist uses the upper right-hand corner to indicate distance or horizon rather than moral superiority. The image is unsigned but in the style of Posada. The caricature of Bulnes, with its balding head and buckteeth, indicates that the same artist did the *El Diablito Bromista* illustration cited in the previous note.

44. Martín Rosas, "Ridículo," *La Guacamaya*, November 24, 1904, 4. (Original: "guarda tu libro dentro de un costal / y vete a Nueva York con tío Samuel.")

45. "Enzaladillas Satánicas," *El Diablito Bromista*, September 11, 1904, 3. (Original: "dicen que Bulnes es Guatemalteco y á ser cierta la noticia conviene decirle de, nó no muela á los nuestros, favor de ir a moler á la madre patria.")

46. Plutón, "La conquista pacífica yankee," *El Diablito Bromista*, January 31, 1904, 2. (Original: "¿Entonces á que viene [la inversión yankee en México]? A apoderarse de una manera lenta pero segura de los mejores negocios, á establecer más fábricas, y á aminorar más los sueldos para sujetarnos con más facilidad.") Complaints like this one about U.S. domination of the Mexican economy and its impact on Mexican workers were ubiquitous in all the penny presses.

47. "Guate . . . mala," in *La Guacamaya*, July 11, 1907, 4. (Original: "Conmueve al universo y lo exaspera / la actitud expectante y resignada / de toda una Nación tan estimada / que soporta el gobierno de Cabrera." Criticism of Guatemala and Cabera was a recurring theme in the penny press. See, e.g., Buffington, "Homophobia and the Mexican Working Class," 215–16.

48. Federíco Pérez Lomelí, "A gran reformador Benito Juárez," *La Guacamaya*, October 6, 1904, 4. (Original: "aquel que lo intente [insultar a Juárez] es un canalla y debe abandonar los patrios lares.")

49. "Lo del día: el escándalo de Bulnes," *El Diablito Bromista*, September 11, 1904, 2; and "¿Quien es Bulnes?," *La Guacamaya*, October 20, 1904, 2. (Original 1: "periódico horriblemente grosero, difamador, y no recuerdo si támbien calumniador." Original 2: "el actual presidente [Díaz], sus amigos, sus Generales, sus Magistrados, [. . .] todo el mundo." Original 3: "todos los que me han agredido han tenido razón: si me hubieran matado, hubieran hecho bien.") Apparently

two articles were involved: an initial report in *El Correo Español* and Bulnes's confession/response in *El Mundo*. The 1904 version appears to have circulated widely; although its story is nearly identical to the *El Diablito Bromista* version, *La Guacamaya* credits *El Obrero* of León, Guanajuato, as its source. *La Palanca* also reprinted excerpts from Bulnes's confession, citing a Durango paper, *La Nueva Era* (de Hidalgo de Parral), "Bulnes pintado por si mismo," *La Palanca*, October 9, 1904, 2. That article compared Bulnes to Leonardo Márquez, a conservative general notorious for executing liberal civilians during the War of the Reform (1858–61) and considered a traitor by liberals for supporting the French Intervention and Maximilian's short-lived empire.

50. "Lo del día: el escándalo de Bulnes," *El Diablito Bromista*, September 11, 1904, 2. (Original: "el hombre del porvenir, el hombre de la paz, la gloria nuestra, ¡nuestro ídolo!")

51. "Lo del día: el escándalo de Bulnes," *El Diablito Bromista*, September 11, 1904, 2. (Original: "ese fantoche que mueve manos ocultas, á pesar de su talento, de su pluma afiligranada, no es mas que un cínico y un cobarde, que en su debilidad y falta de valor civil, insulta á los inertes, y lame los pies de los vivos.")

52. "El que ha nacido en zalea . . . ," *El Diablito Bromista*, September 11, 1904, 2–3. (Original: "¡El que ha nacido en zalea, siempre anda jediendo [*sic*] a chivo!")

53. On the implications of abjection for male subjectivity, see Buffington, "Modern Sacrificial Economy."

54. *La Guacamaya*, September 15, 1904, 1. (Original: "Bulnes ha caído en el fango confundido entre los miserables de su especie.")

55. Pito Real, "Juárez Victrix," and José Muñoz Lumbier, "Juárez y Bulnes," *La Guacamaya*, September 29, 1904, 4. (Original 1: "[Bulnes] es un reptil cobarde que se azota en las charcas inmundas del pantano." Original 2: "[Bulnes es] el reptil más sucio y más mezquino [. . .] del fango, de la charca, de la escoria.")

56. "Bulnes.—Su entrada triunfal al país de la Fama," *La Palanca*, September 11, 1904, 1. The headline translates as "BULNES—his triumphal entrance into the country of Fame."

57. K. Chiman, "Solemne protesta de La Palanca," *La Palanca*, September 11, 1904, 2. Infanticide and abortion cases—widely reported by such mainstream dailies as *El Imparcial* and the tabloids—often noted the discovery of aborted fetuses and murdered infants in public latrines. A more conventional denunciation appeared in the following issue. Celedonio S. Gómez, "Para La Palanca," *La Palanca*, September 18, 1904, 2.

58. *El Diablito Bromista*, November 2, 1904, 3; and *La Guacamaya*, November 2, 1904, 2. The less elaborate Day of the Dead issue of *La Palanca* included an unillustrated Bulnes *calavera* poem. "Fosa común," *La Palanca*, November 4, 1904, 2. Upset about what he considered inappropriate language in *La Guacamaya*, *La Palanca*'s editor included a *calavera* poem for its editor, Rafael R. y Rodríguez, just below the poem about Bulnes.

59. *La Guacamaya*, November 2, 1904, 2. (Original: "al fin entre desprecios la muerte arrebató [a Bulnes], y se lee sobre su tumba 'aquí se oculta un traidor.'")

60. *El Diablito Bromista*, November 2, 1909, 2. (Original: "En castigo de su audacia / De poner de oro y azul / Al que nos dió democracia, / ¡Le dieron una curul! . . . / ¡Allí murió en desgracia!")

61. Maravelo, "Ave, Juárez," *La Guacamaya*, October 27, 1904, 4.

62. M. Rosas, "Bochornos [Hot Breezes]," *La Guacamaya*, October 20, 1904, 4. The final Francisco Bulnes y Judas resembles a typical Spanish *apellido* (last name), which often strings together family names and thus joins the two betrayers in fictive kinship.

63. Over the course of several issues, *La Palanca*'s editor attacked *La Guacamaya* for its use of "street talk." For example, one editorial included a letter from workers in Toluca complaining that "unfortunately some newspapers of the penny press, in the guise of defending the interests of the Working Class, inadvertently slander and dishonor us in the eyes of our oppressors, with certain articles that they publish with the title of *contestas callejeras* or *desde la estaca*, etc., through the vulgar and indecorous dialect used in their production." (Original: "desgraciadamente algunos periódicos de la Prensa pequeña, proponiéndose defender los intereses de la Clase Obrera, inadvertidamente nos perjudican y nos deshonran ante nuestros opresores con ciertos artículos que publican con el título de *contestas callejeras* ó *desde la estaca*, etc., por el dialecto tan soez y nada decoroso conque se producen.") "La Prensa Pequeña," *La Palanca*, September 25, 1904, 2. See also K. Chimán, "Defensores," *La Palanca*, October 2, 1904, 2; "Primera exhibición de un pe . . . riodísta claudicante," *La Palanca*, October 23, 1904, 1; "A memoria de dos . . . defensores (!) del Obrero," *La Palanca*, October 30, 1904, 1; and "Fosa común," *La Palanca*, November 6, 1904, 2. "Fosa común" (common grave) paired Day of the Dead *calaveras* for *La Guacamaya* editor Rafael R. de Rodríguez and Francisco Bulnes! Despite its vigorous defense of working-class propriety, *La Palanca* lasted less than six months. In contrast, *La Guacamaya* appeared on and off from 1902 to 1911 and in its heyday claimed to have sold as many as 29,000 copies of a single issue. *La Guacamaya*, December 5, 1907, 2.

64. The declaration is from the masthead of *El Diablito Bromista*: "Organo de la clase Obrera, Azote del mal Burgués, y COCO DEL MAL GOBIERNO [Organ of the Working Class, Scourge of the Bad Bougeoisie, and BOGEYMAN TO BAD GOVERNMENT]." The reference to "bad government" echoes the famous *Grito de Dolores*, which called for "death to bad government" (¡*Muera el mal gobierno!*), a colonial-era slogan that appeared prominently in independence revolts throughout Latin America, including the rebellion of Túpac Amaru II in Peru (1780–82) and the revolt of the Comuneros in New Granada (1781).

65. Papagayo, "Desde la estaca," *La Guacamaya*, September 15, 1904, 3. Papagayo is the nom de plume used by the editor for the "street talk" columns. Although not identified in this particular column, the two friends are most likely Pitacio and

Chema, the principal personalities for "Desde la estaca." Chema is a common nickname for José María, while Pitacio likely comes from the phrase *"enredar la pita"* (to foul up the works), which is the cantankerous Pitacio's role in most dialogues. The verb *pitar* can mean "to blow a whistle" or "to boo someone off the stage"; either meaning fits with the character's personality.

66. The *La Palanca* cover analyzed earlier, in which a worker kicks Bulnes into an open toilet, suggests that this was a typical response. "Bulnes.—Su entrada triunfal al país de la Fama," *La Palanca*, September 11, 1904, 1.

67. Use of *tú* among casual acquaintances is much more common in Mexico these days; its use as a marker of social distinction—someone of the upper classes using *tú* to address a servant for example—is in decline. In this dialogue between equals, *tú* marks social intimacy rather than social distinction.

68. The feature illustrations mentioned earlier provide visual confirmation of the link between Bulnes, buckteeth, donkeys, and mules. The excerpt mentions burros, while the illustration refers to mules. All things being equal, the sterile, stubborn mule seems the better fit. However, "güey y burro" sounds better than "güey y mula" and was probably chosen for that reason.

69. *La Guacamaya*, October 13, 1904, 3. (Original: "Pos olle [oye] manito no me lagas [la hagas] de gorgús [garrocha], ni miandes [me andes] con cacayacas por que ya sabes que yo soy yo y no me parezco a Bulnes.")

70. The use of popular vernacular in Mexican literary texts dates from at least the celebrated essays that José Joaquín Fernández de Lizardi (1776–1827) wrote for his independence-era newspaper, *El Pensador Mexicano*. Lizardi's intent, however, was to mock popular speech and its lower-class practitioners for the amusement of well-educated readers. The same is true of penny press newspapers aimed at the middle class, like the short-lived *El Periquillo Sarniento* (The Mangy Parrot), which took its name, appropriately enough, from Lizardi's great picaresque novel and titled its first street talk section "Between Drunks." "Entre ebrios," *El Periquillo Sarniento*, October 12, 1902, 3. Although subsequent issues attempted to reach out to working-class readers, the paper lasted only four months. In contrast to these condescending appropriations of the popular vernacular for middle-class audiences, the much more colloquial working-class penny press style, although highly literate in its own right, was intended for popular consumption and quite possibly oral performance. Some working-class advocates, like the editors of *La Palanca*, considered the style demeaning to workers, but the considerable popularity and greater longevity of papers like *La Guacamaya* suggests that these critics were a distinct minority.

71. Fraser, "Rethinking," 61.

72. Scott, *Domination*, 107.

73. Fraser, "Rethinking," 67.

74. Warner, *Publics*, 120.

CHAPTER 3. THE APOTHEOSIS OF THE WORKING MAN

1. See fig. 1.2.
2. For an analysis of the different discursive strategies used to criminalize the Mexican lower classes, see Buffington, *Criminal and Citizen*.
3. Butler, *Psychic Life*, 16.
4. Reyes got the idea for the Second Reserve from Antonio Ramos Pedrueza, a congressional deputy and prominent jurist, who hoped that it might also function as a political-military counterweight to the troublesome regular army. It was one of Reyes's most popular initiatives during his brief tenure as defense minister (1900–1902). Reyes's political problems with other members of Porfirio Díaz's inner circle, esp. the influential Finance Minister José Ives Limantour, resulted in temporary exile to his home state of Nuevo León. Díaz abolished the Second Reserve by presidential decree shortly thereafter. Niemeyer, *El General*, 103–9. Reyes remained popular with the Mexico City working class, and several penny press editors supported his later vice presidential aspirations. For an historical photograph of the Second Reserve on parade during the 1902 Independence Day celebrations, see Niemeyer, *El General*, 104; and Cosío Villegas, *Historia moderna*, 512.
5. "La Segunda Reserva del Ejército Nacional," *La Guacamaya*, August 18, 1902, 1.
6. *La Guacamaya*, August 18, 1902, 1–2. (Original: "Para muchos el obrero es el ser vicioso, que huye del taller los lunes, que dilapida el pan de sus hijos en la taberna y esgrime el cuchillo por vaso más ó menos de pulque, nada más exacto . . . Hoy el obrero va á la tumba de Juárez y deja su humilde ofrenda; hoy el obrero da una gran prueba de civismo aplicándose á la segunda reserva.") Monday absenteeism—the infamous *San Lunes* or Saint Monday "holiday"—as a longstanding problem among Mexican workers is dealt with in the next chapter. The reference to humble offerings at Juárez's tomb predates the "En Honor de Juárez" illustration by nearly five years and conveys some sense of the ritual's importance for the Mexico City working class.
7. *La Guacamaya*, August 18, 1902, 2. (Original: "[. . .] una institución meritísma que tiene por objeto hacer del ciudadano un soldado, soldado digno y pundonoroso que sabrá defender palmo á palmo a su querida patria, que sabrá morir por su bandera!")
8. "Los Reservistas. Paso Doble," *La Guacamaya*, October 5, 1902, 1. The editor attributes the music and lyrics to Messrs. Rosales y Murillo, advises readers that they can buy recordings (*fonogramos*) of the piece at "the phonographic establishment [*la casa fonográfica*] of Mr. Joaquín Espinosa," and notes that "all the ambulant phonographers are exploiting this piece with magnificent results [*todos los fonógrafos ambulantes explotan esta pieza con magníficos resultados*]." The paso doble is a musical form, usually in 2/4 time, that resembles a march.

NOTES TO CHAPTER 3

—

247

The Second Reserve also inspired an issue of the middle-class penny press *El Periquillo Sarniento*, which headlined the inauguration of the "official" hymn (lyrics by Heriberto Barrón, music by Luis Jordá) at a public ceremony presided over by Finance Minister José Ives Limantour. The cover illustration includes cameos of Reyes and Limantour. Despite this appeal to the working class, the editor's decision to pair the despised *científico* Limantour with the popular Reyes—who had temporarily fallen out of favor with the regime—could hardly have attracted many workers. *El Periquillo Sarniento*, November 30, 1902, 1–4.

9. *La Guacamaya*, August 18, 1902, 2. (Original: "¡Uno!¡Dos!¡Uno!¡Dos!¡Dos! De frente, ar[mas] . . . Por la derecha, conversión á la izquierda, paso redoblando, ar[mas] . . . por la derecha á linearse, descansen, ar[mas] . . . tercien, ar[mas] . . . presenten arrrr[mas].")

10. *La Guacamaya*, August 18, 1902, 3. (Original 1: "pos ya sabes que nosotros los obreros, no lo tenemos miedo ni á la muerte en zancos, ni á los chocos en bicicleta." Original 2: "¿pos qué tiene que ver el as de oros con las témporas? pos allí se queren hombres que tengan pechos en los pelos, digo, de pelo en pecho, que no sean gallinas y que se sepan sacudir con los yankes [*sic*] cuando vengan a visitarnos, pos alcabo á cada uno dan su Mauser y no a peliar [pelear] á mordidas, ni estamos en la época de su alteza serenísima, en que tenían que morder los cartuchos.") Note esp. that the comparison of the ace of spades (ace of gold coins, or *oros*, in the Spanish deck) to army reservists—apples to oranges—is much cleverer in the original Spanish, which (loosely) inverts "as de oros" to produce the palindrome-like "témp-or-as" (literally: temporaries).

11. Santa Anna served as president on eleven different occasions between 1833 and 1855. He began his career as a liberal but had switched sides by 1836. Over the course of a long military and political career, he commanded armies against conservatives, liberals, Spain, France, Texas insurgents, and the United States. Liberal historians—and most everyone else—blame him for the loss of Texas, Mexico's defeat in the U.S.-Mexican war, and the sale of national territory in the Gadsden Purchase.

12. The Mauser was the basic German infantry rifle until 1945 and was exported in great numbers. Pitacio is contrasting the modern Mauser with the muzzle-loading rifles used by Santa Anna's army, which required that the soldier tear open the cartridges with his teeth and pour the contents down the barrel of his rifle. During this period, armies typically required soldiers to have at least four matching teeth (two on top, two on the bottom)—hence Chema's comment about losing his teeth in a fight. (My thanks to Jim Rose for this information.)

13. "El Servicio Militar Obligatorio," *La Guacamaya*, April 11, 1907, 1. The image is unsigned; the style is Posada's.

14. For more on penny press feminization of bourgeois men, see Buffington, "Homophobia," 204–20.

15. "El Pípila," *La Guacamaya*, October 10, 1907, 4. The poem is paired with another poem, "A Hidalgo" (to Hidalgo), by the same unidentified author—possibly director-editor Fernando P. Torroella.

16. Although the cadets have names in the official story, little is known about any of them. Anderson, *Imagined Communities*, 9–11, discusses the symbolic function of the Tomb of the Unknown Soldier.

17. For an historical analysis of the *Niños Héroes* story, see Plansencia de la Parra, "Conmemoración," 241–79.

18. Plansencia de la Parra, "Conmemoración," 252–53.

19. Plansencia de la Parra, "Conmemoración," 254. The quotation is from the title of Amando Nervo's 1903 poem "Los niños mártires de Chapultepec."

20. See, e.g., Jesús Urbina de Hernández, "A los héroes de Chapultepec," *La Guacamaya*, September 29, 1902, 4 (repr. March 23, 1905, 4); *El Diablito Bromista*, September 8, 1907, 2; *El Diablito Rojo*, September 12, 1910, 2; "Hoja de diamante," *Don Cucufate*, September 10, 1906, 2.

21. "8 de Septiembre de 1847," *La Araña*, September 8, 1904, 1. The image is signed by José Guadalupe Posada. September 8 was the traditional date for celebrating various heroic acts associated with the American assault on Mexico City during the U.S.-Mexican War. (Original: "[. . .] sacrificaron de a manera más bestial a un puñado de niños que apenas traspasían los umbrales de la pubertad.") In the image, Chapultepec Castle, as might be expected, occupies the position of moral superiority on the vertical axis. And the sun's superior position heightens the effect of moral disapproval (from on high) conveyed by its shrouded visage. The same image appeared in "8 de Septiembre de 1847," *La Guacamaya*, September 7, 1905, 1–2. Fernando Torroella was an editor at both papers and the author of the accompanying poem (which appears in both editions). The charge of "bestial" child sacrifice references the medieval Christian "blood libel," which accused Jews of killing Christian children and using their blood in religious rituals, and reinforces the anti-Semitic nature image of Uncle Sam.

22. "8 de Septiembre de 1847," *La Guacamaya*, September 7, 1905, 2. (Original: "[. . .] la humilde ofrenda de un pueblo abnegado y trabajador que sabe respetar, bendecir [y] venerar a aquellos que no midiendo peligros, á aquellos que abandonando hogar, familia y bienestar, sacrifican su vida en aras de la patria que los vio nacer, que les dio nombre y abrigo [. . .]")

23. "¡Es cuestion . . . americana!" (It's an American question!), *La Guacamaya*, September 6, 1906, 1.

24. Other iconographic conventions in the image include active right-handedness (Uncle Sam) vs. passive left-handedness (Díaz, workers), active right profiles (Uncle Sam), and hats to indicate power (Uncle Sam wears a hat, Díaz and the blacksmiths are bareheaded).

25. "8 de Septiembre," *La Guacamaya*, September 6, 1906, 2.

26. For a discussion of Civic Catholicism as the public language in nineteenth-century Latin America and its appropriation by penny press editors and contributors, see ch. 1.

27. "El Aniversario de Churubusco," *El Diablito Bromista*, August 16, 1903, 3. (Original: "El *Diablito*, que en eso del patriotismo no es de los arriados, los invita el 20 de este mes á que se reunan en el histórico pueblo de Churubusco, á las 10 ½ de la mañana, hora en que tendrá verificativo el acto patriótico que la Agrupación Patriótica 'Gratitud' llevará a cabo en conmemoración de los olvidados patriotas obreros que sucumbieron allí, peleando vigorosamente contra la invasion gringa.")

28. "Discurso que apronució un valedor ante la tumba de los héroes de Churubusco," *El Diablito Bromista*, August 23, 1903, 3. (Original 1: "Queridas [*sic*] valedores del riño [riñon] suave: afeituosas [afectuosas] jaranas [damas] de la brigade descalza: plebe en general." Original 2: "[. . .] si no juera [fuera] por los riatotas obreros que se pelaron [murieron] aquí defendiendo á la patria, nuestro honor hubiera quedado como larpa [la harpa] del tortugo, rechinando por falta de cuerdas y abriéndose por la muchagua [mucha agua].")

29. "Discurso que apronució un valedor ante la tumba de los héroes de Churubusco," *El Diablito Bromista*, August 23, 1903, 3. (Original: "[. . .] porque la gratitud de los grandes hombres, nomás son ronquidos.") The apathy of the privileged—often represented metaphorically as napping/snoring—was a recurring theme in working-class culture (see chs. 1, 2, and esp. 4).

30. "Discurso que apronució un valedor ante la tumba de los héroes de Churubusco," *El Diablito Bromista*, August 23, 1903, 3. (Original: "Si pudiera chillar con todas mis ganotas, les aseguro astededes [a ustedes] que derramaría toda lalberca [la alberca] Pane y me sobaría gas.")

31. The binary opposition between Apollo and Pan also breaks down along urban/rural lines. This opposition works less well than the class division but still appears with some regularity in the penny press, as, e.g., with the campesino/*rotos* contrast in the "En Honor de Juárez" illustration analyzed in ch. 1.

32. The etymology is the same in English (Pan→panic) and Spanish (Pane→pánico).

33. See, e.g., the covers and illustrations that José Guadalupe Posada produced for the prolific printing house of Antonio Vanegas Arroyo in Barajas Durán, *Posada*; Berdecio and Appelbaum, *Posada's Prints*, 102–23; and Posada, *José Guadalupe Posada*, 155–79.

34. "Desde la estaca," *La Guacamaya*, August 27, 1903, 3. (Original: "[. . .] yo ni modelo [modo] de acompañarte, pos en el taller donde le adoy [doy] á la chamba [trabajo], tenemos un maestro medio redrojo [andrajo], que ese, tiene la patria en la barriga y que si falto, me quita la chamba, y se riña mi fierrado [dinero] y después no tengo conque darle el moque [comida] á mis chilpayates [hijos].")

35. "Desde la estaca," *La Guacamaya*, September 3, 1903, 3.

36. Apache raids into northern Mexico were still a problem at the turn of the century. The label "apaches" was also commonly applied to urban gangs during this period, even in European cities like Paris. The terms *jaraño* and *jaraña* appear frequently in the street talk columns as informal words for "wife" or "steady girlfriend," as in the English phrase "my old lady." In this instance (possibly in general usage as well) *jaño* may also derive from *janos*, an Apache tribe from Chihuahua.
37. The *El Diablito Bromista* speech also ends with "he dicho."
38. The different connotations of *pelado* are examined in Santamaría, *Diccionario*, 824. A 1906 *La Cagarruta* cover, e.g., depicts José Ives Limantour literally shaking down a worker as Porfirio Díaz looks on and their minions scramble for the failing coins. The caption explains that "entre D. Porfi y D. Lima han pelado el pueblo á rape" ("between Díaz and Limantour they have shaved the people bald"). "Leyenda de . . . los Limones," *La Cagarruta*, December 1, 1906, 1.
39. Legal and cultural authorities considered duels affairs of honor appropriate only to upper-class men, who had honor to lose—a position not shared by lower-class men. See Piccato, *City of Suspects*, 80–92.
40. "La Fiesta en Churubusco," *El Diablito Bromista*, August 28, 1904, 2–3. (Original: "La animación en el pueblo fué grande y á fé que tenía razón, pues ya se había relegado al olvido esa significativa y patriótica fiesta.") In the 1907 report, the editor informs readers that the Patriotic Group "Gratitude" initiated the Churubusco ceremony in 1902. "La fiesta patriótica de Churubusco," *El Diablito Bromista*, August 25, 1907, 3.
41. "Simpático festival," *La Guacamaya*, September 5, 1907, 3. (Original: "[. . .] infinidad de obreros y respetables familias de los pueblos circunvecinos.") Carlos Ezeta later directed and edited the short-lived *El Chango* (1912).
42. "Simpático festival," *La Guacamaya*, September 5, 1907, 3. (Original: "[. . .] reinó el órden más completo y demostró ese pueblo al que se le juzga analfabeta y altanero, que su civilización naciente y su respeto á las autoridades, pueden servir de ejemplo á muchas naciones más cultas aun de la nuestra.") On the same festival, see "La fiesta patriótica de Churubusco," *El Diablito Bromista*, August 25, 1907, 3.
43. Antonio Negrete, "20 de Agosto de 1847," *La Guacamaya*, August 27, 1903, 2. (Original: "Luchaisteis con un valor sobrehumano contra las huestes invasoras que querían imponer la fuerza por la ley, la vida disteis en aras de la Patria, por amor á ella, si la victoria no quiso ceñiros la frente con sus laurels, la Patria agradecida; os cubre cariñosa con su manto y os arrulla con cánticos celestials para que durmáis tranquilos el sueño de la inmortalidad. ¡Héroes de Churubusco! Yo os saludo.") The following year, Negrete wrote an editorial for his own short-lived penny press, *El Papagayo*, which explicitly linked Churubusco and *Niños Héroes*. Antonio Negrete, "8 y 13 de Septiembre de 1847," *El Papagayo*, September 11, 1904, 2.

44. Fernando Celada, "Churubusco," *El Diablito Bromista*, August 23, 1903, 4.

45. Carlos Ezeta, "Por los muertos," *El Diablito Bromista*, September 1, 1907, 3.

46. Antonio de P. Escárcega, "Comparemos," *El Diablito Bromista*, July 21, 1907, 2. (Original [1]: "El capital huye de las convulsiones armadas, no reconoce los sentimientos de patriotismo, no posee una patria determinada: es cosmopolita.") (Original [2]: "Poco menos que una bestia de carga [. . .] [el obrero] ha desempeñado y cumplido los deberes que impone el patriotismo, abandonando intereses y familia para lanzarse á la defensa nacional.") Escárcega's bitter critique of "cosmopolitan" capital came in the wake of a series of bloody strikes, including Cananea and Río Blanco. See Anderson, *Outcasts*.

47. Antonio de P. Escárcega, "¡Despierta Pueblo obrero!," *El Diablito Bromista*, November 21, 1909, 2. (Original: "¡Despierta! el porvenir es tuyo: tú eres el poderoso brazo con que cuenta nuestra adorada México, para llegar al fin de sus aspiraciones, y tú que siempre has demostrado valor y grandeza en épocas dolorosas, debes dar un ejemplo más de tu heroísmo y tu grandeza, acercándote por medio de tu trabajo y tus energías, al gran festín de las Naciones civilizadas: A la Libertad, al Progreso y al lebre [*sic*] ejercicios de tus indiscutibles Derechos.")

48. Escárcega, "¡Despierta Pueblo obrero!," *El Diablito Bromista*, November 21, 1909, 2. (Original: "esos lazos que encadenan tu apatía y la falta de cumplimiento en tus deberes de ciudano [*sic*].")

49. The street vernacular of Mexico City's working classes was (and continues to be) an ongoing source of concern, amusement, fascination, and grudging admiration on the part of the educated classes, including penny press editors, as evidenced by Porfirian-era slang dictionaries, such as Ramos i Duarte's *Diccionario* and criminologist Carlos Roumagnac's guide to criminal argot in *Los criminales*, 376–82.

50. "¡Orden . . . y nos amanecemos," *El Diablito Rojo*, March 30, 1908, 2. (Original: "Los que amamos á esta Patria nobilísima y grande, nos brota por todos los poros del alma el regocijo y el orgullo, cuando vemos una manifestación pública en que el elemento obrero forma parte principal, y que da realce y color, honra y animación á un acto cívico.")

51. "El regaño de mama" (Mama's scolding), *El Diablito Rojo*, March 16, 1908, 1; and "¡Fué el pueblo el domingo y no!" (It was the people on Sunday and it wasn't), *El Diablito Rojo*, May 10, 1909, 1. (Original: "Las fiestas 'sin pueblo' son falso oropel y cantares sin sentido.") In the 1909 version, Mother Mexico's criticism is directed at that year's Cinco de Mayo celebration in honor of the 1862 defeat of an invading French army outside Puebla, the victory that first thrust then Brigadier General Díaz into the national limelight. She also holds a steaming cup with the words "perpetual presidency" floating above it, a reference to Díaz's decision not to honor a pledge—made to American journalist James Creelman in a widely distributed 1908 interview—to remove himself from the 1910 presidential race.

52. On the Porfirian repression of popular festivals, see Beezley, *Judas*. On Porfirian concerns about Independence Day in particular, see Pérez-Rayón, "Capital Commemorates," 141–66.

53. Pedro Arnal Frontelo, "Las Fiestas Patrias," *La Guacamaya*, October 3, 1907, 2. (Original: "[. . .] la *cuasi* hermosa Anáhuac, cuyas calles invadidas por algunos centenares de patriotas que temerosos lanzando el acostumbrado grito de ¡Viva México! se verían al poco tiempo completamente desiertas, pues la policía echaba grandes *rialadas* de entusiastas ciudadanos, llevando la consigna usual de 'ebrios escándalosos.'")

54. Cotorrón, "Desde la estaca," *La Guacamaya*, October 3, 1907, 2–3. (Original 1: "Patadas no más nos dan y eso que somos mexicanos revalsadores [valerosos] y no escandalosos, como nos dicen los estrangis [extranjeros]." Original 2: "Mira Pitacio, más mejor que no me hables deso [. . .] si ansina va estar el día del centenario, mecho de cabeza de mi petate al suelo onque me rompa la maceta.") Pitacio's use of the anglicized "estrangis" (strangers) instead of the Spanish "extranjeros" for "foreigners" mocks both American attitudes toward lower-class Mexicans and the much-lamented Americanization of Mexican Spanish. Used colloquially here in place of *cabeza*, "maceta" also signifies "flowerpot"; hence the reference to falling off the bed and breaking open.

55. "Las fiestas Patrias," *Don Cucufate*, September 25, 1906, 2. (Original: "En cambio de la ausencia del público, se *dotó* á la ciudad de un aumento considerable de policía, pública y secreta.") One of a host of less successful penny press papers, *Don Cucufate* appeared from July through October 1906.

56. "Las fiestas Patrias," *Don Cucufate*, September 25, 1906, 2. (Original: "Como al pueblo le prohibieron *ponerse* una *trompeta*, se dedicó á tocar *trompetas* de barro; pero, eso,—lo de tocar—constituyó una infracción extra, que ameritó que muchos *trompeteros* pasaron á la Inspección de Policía respectiva, acusados de turbar el silencio nocturno y atentados contra los órganos auditivos de los transeúntes.")

57. Santamaría, *Diccionario*, 1089.

58. "Las fiestas Patrias," *Don Cucufate*, September 25, 1906, 2. (Original: "Los extranjeros circularon tranquilamente por calles y plazas, sin ser molestados por nadie.")

59. "Crónicas color de Hormiga," *El Diablito Rojo*, May 24, 1909, 2. (Original: "El obrero es crédulo, sencillo, generoso y patriótico. Va á donde lo invita el entusiasmo ó lo engaña la ilusión.")

60. "Crónicas color de Hormiga," *El Diablito Rojo*, September 6, 1909, 2. (Original: "Cuando el Primer Magistrado aparece con sus arreos militares, la bunda tricolor terciada al pecho cuajado de áureas condecoraciones, tremolando la bandera de México, glorifica á la Patria, toca el esquilón de Dolores, y da el 'grito de Hidalgo,' símbolo del heroísmo y de victoria, veinte mil espectadores tiemblan del estampido del cañón, miríadas de luces multicolores y el himno triunfal de

la torre, cuyas lenguas metálicas llevan á los habitantes de la urbe oleadas de patriótico entusiasmo.")

61. "Crónicas color de Hormiga," *El Diablito Rojo*, September 6, 1909, 2. (Original: "[. . .] sirve para excitar las pasiones populares que se desbordan en insultos, mueras destemplados y otras manifestaciones con que la plebe estalla su odio contra los ricos y los pudientes [. . .].") In Spanish, *mueras* (death to . . .) are the opposite of *vivas* (long live . . .); both are included in Hidalgo's famous *grito*, including "Death to Bad Government!"

62. "Crónicas color de Hormiga," *El Diablito Rojo*, September 6, 1909, 2. (Original: "[. . .] el pueblo [. . .] circula por todas partes gritando como salvaje, apedrando, y pernocta en parques y jardines públicos, haciendo de aquellos lugares un sitio en donde parece que vivaqueó una horda de salvajes.")

63. Laclau, *Populist Reason*, 21–64, provides a concise analysis of the major works on crowd psychology. For an in-depth discussion of crowd theory, see Barrows, *Distorting Mirrors*.

64. Porfirian "scientific politics" are analyzed in depth in Hale, *Transformation*. The dissemination of European criminology into Mexico and the popularization of criminological theories are addressed in Buffington, *Criminal and Citizen*.

65. "Crónicas color de Hormiga," *El Diablito Rojo*, September 6, 1909, 2. (Original: "[. . .] la supresión esa sería antipatriótica é inoportuna.") For elite concerns about crowd control for the 1910 centenary, see Tenorio-Trillo, "1910 Mexico City," 167–97.

66. "¡15 de Septiembre!," *La Guacamaya*, September 20, 1906, 1. (Original: "No obstante que varios gringos / soltaron el notición / de que el 15 de Septiembre / iba a ver revolución, / Todo el pueblo mexicano/en amigable reunión, / canta, goza, come y grita/y mira la formación.")

67. "¡¡El Grito!!," *La Guacamaya*, October 4, 1906, 1.

68. The policeman's passing resemblance to Porfirio Díaz is probably no accident. Among other things, the president's nephew Félix Díaz was the Mexico City chief of police at the time.

69. The *rurales* were touted by the Porfirian regime as fierce bandits turned policemen. In reality, most *rurales* were typical police recruits. See Vanderwood, *Disorder*.

70. Papagayo, "Desde la estaca," *La Guacamaya*, October 1, 1903, 2–3. The area around Chapultepec, at the "other" end of Mexico City's major boulevard (Paseo de la Reforma) from the older downtown, included swanky new neighborhoods for the Porfirian bourgeoisie.

71. La Redacción, "Nuestras Fiestas Patrias y Nuestras Autoridades," *La Guacamaya*, September 29, 1904, 2. (Original: "[. . .] agente del orden público en el 2° período de embriagez escandalizaba [. . .] amenazando con pistola en mano á sus compañeros y á todo el que tenía la desgracia de pasar por ahí.")

72. La Redacción, "Nuestras Fiestas Patrias y Nuestras Autoridades," *La Guaca-maya*, September 29, 1904, 2. (Original: "[. . .] no defendemos el odioso vicio de la embriaguez, puesto que no ignoramos que está penado en el art. 840 de nuestro código penal que ha la letra dice: El que públicamente defienda un vicio ó delito, graves como lícitos, ó haga la apología de ellos ó de sus autores, será castigado con arresto mayor y multa de segunda clase.")

73. Often used to describe the popular response to the *Grito*, the phrase *correr el gallo* translates more exactly as "let the rooster loose" and thus includes a strong element of male posturing, crowing, and sexual aggressiveness. It also refers to bands of men and women roaming the streets singing songs and playing instruments as part of the celebration of the *Grito*.

74. "Preparativos para el grito," *La Guacamaya*, September 5, 1907, 1.

75. Santamaría, *Diccionario*, 333.

76. *Hijos de la chingada* translates loosely as "motherfuckers" and literally as "sons of the fucked mother." For the classic analysis of the phrase, see Paz, "The Sons of La Malinche," in *Labyrinth of Solitude*, 65–88. According to Paz, "this phrase is a true battle cry, charged with a particular electricity; it is a challenge and an affirmation, a shot fired against an imaginary enemy, and an explosion in the air" (74).

77. Cotorrón, "Desde la estaca," *La Guacamaya*, September 27, 1908, 2. In this context, "*taribel*" might be "*caribal*," the hunting lodge or hidden place in the forest to which Caribbean Indians (*caribes*) often retreated in the face of Spanish persecution. See Santamaría, *Diccionario*, 217.

78. Cotorrón, "Desde la estaca," *La Guacamaya*, September 27, 1908, 3. (Original: "No más arrigule [arguye] que yo iba pasando con mi garrote [mujer] y que me lo coje el choco [policía] y por más que li [sic] averiguaba que estaba malo de la pata, me echó á palos y mejor, pa no estrenar el chero [cárcel] nuevo me jui [fui] al taribel [caribal?], porque dialitiro [de todo] son muy abusadores algunos.") Pitacio's colloquial reference to his female companion as my "garrote"—a cord, rope, or wire used to strangle someone from behind—serves here as a more extreme version of the common word substitution of "esposas" (wives) for "manillas" (handcuffs). Men's displacement of acts of domestic violence onto women is explored in Buffington, "Modern Sacrificial Economy."

79. See fig. 1.2.

80. Laclau, *Populist Reason*. In contrast to most previous accounts of populism, Laclau insists that "by 'populism' we do not understand a *type* of movement—identifiable with either a special social base or a particular ideological orientation—but a *political logic*" (117; italics in original).

81. Laclau, *Populist Reason*, 74.

82. Laclau, *Populist Reason*, 83.

83. Laclau, *Populist Reason*, 17.

84. Laclau, *Populist Reason*, 17–18.

85. Laclau, *Populist Reason*, 18.

86. Laclau, *Populist Reason*, 70, argues that a "signifier" becomes "empty" when "its body is split between the particularity which it is and the more universal signification of which it is the bearer." Our discussion of Hidalgo and Juárez as working-class heroes (chs. 1–2) explores this emptying process in some detail. The liberal slogan "effective suffrage, no reelection" also functioned as an empty signifier throughout this period and into the revolutionary era. The Zapatista motto "Land and Liberty" became an important revolutionary addition. In an argument too complex to reproduce here, Laclau also explains how empty signifiers become "floating signifiers" when links in the equivalential chain are appropriated by "a rival hegemonic project" (131).

87. Laclau, *Populist Reason*, 110.

CHAPTER 4. *RUMBO PERDIDO*

1. The introduction defines terms and provides a theoretical framework for understanding the gendered nature of human subjectivity.

2. Elias, *Civilizing Process*. Elias doesn't explicitly address the colonial implications of his thesis, but they are obvious enough, and an argument could be made that the colonial experience with native peoples intensified the process as colonizers and "civilized" local elites sought to differentiate themselves, culturally and racially, from the colonized masses of subaltern subjects. The tradition of British colonial administrators dressing up for dinner in the tropics is the absurd extreme of a spectrum of "civilized" behaviors that set them (and those that shared their values) apart from the natives.

3. Elias, *Civilizing Process*, 370.

4. Prerevolutionary French society was divided into three estates with distinct privileges and duties: the First Estate was composed of aristocrats, the Second Estate of clergy, the Third Estate of everyone else. Although less codified in other places, similar legally sanctioned social divisions characterized most European societies at least through the eighteenth century. As the "middle" classes became wealthier, better educated, and more influential, so did the "need" to separate themselves from the "lower" classes of the Third Estate. Adopting and adapting aristocratic refinements thus served to set them above the rabble and justify their claims to social superiority. The civilizing of bourgeois sensibilities in western Europe and the United States is explored in depth in Gay, *Education* and *Tender Passion*.

5. Carmen Romero Rubio (age 17) married President Porfirio Díaz (age 51) in 1881. Her father was the prominent liberal lawyer Manuel Romero Rubio and her godfather, former president Sebastian Lerdo de Tejada. In addition to helping to "civilize" the president, Doña Carmen has been credited with reconciling his nominally liberal (and thus anticlerical) regime with the conservative Catholic Church.

6. Tilly, *Durable Inequality*, analyzes the structural causes behind persistent social inequalities.

7. Piccato, *City of Suspects*, 48–49, notes that the urban poor in early twentieth-century Mexico City "associated their community with a rumbo, a geographical destination for their wanderings around the city."

8. As explained in the Introduction, the phrase *nosotros los pelados* (we the pelados) seeks to resignify *pelado*, a derogatory term for a lower-class person (usually gendered male), by having it stand in for *pueblo*, as in "we the people." The term *roto* (literally, "broken one") refers to a formerly working-class person (usually gendered male) who aspires to higher status *and* denies/rejects/betrays his class origins. The term *catrín* (dandy) refers to a bourgeois and upper-class man, a type penny press editors generally portrayed as vain, lazy, corrupt, selfish, and effeminate. See, e.g., Buffington, "Homophobia," 204–20.

9. For the hegemonic definition of "hegemonic masculinity," see Connell, *Masculinities*, 76–86. Connell and Messerschmidt, "Hegemonic Masculinity," 829–59, convincingly defends and refines the concept. In the latter, Connell and Messerschmidt note that the concept of "hegemonic masculinity was not assumed to be normal in the statistical sense; only a minority of men might enact it. But it was certainly normative. It embodied the currently most honored way of being a man, it required all other men to position themselves in relation to it, and it ideologically legitimated the global subordination of women to men" (832). Connell explains "protest masculinities" in *Masculinities*, 109–18. For overviews and critiques of current research, see Broude, "Protest Masculinity," 103–22, and Walker, "Disciplining," 5–22.

10. For an influential modern interpretation of the links between criminality and masculinities, see Messerschmidt, *Masculinities*.

11. Judith Butler's concept of "cultural intelligibility" and its connection to citizenship are discussed in the Introduction.

12. See, e.g., the cover of *El Diablito Bromista*, July 14, 1907, which depicts a policeman hauling a working-class man out of a bar (fig 4.1). His friend, El Peladito, asks: "Listen Mr. Cop, why are you taking my friend Squirrel when he's less wasted than this *roto*?" El Roto responds: "Don't be stupid, because the thread always breaks at its thinnest point."

13. The exact meaning of "desde la estaca" is unclear, but it probably refers, among other things, to the *estaca de gallo*, the stake used to restrain roosters so they don't wander off and get into fights. Given the *La Guacamaya* editors' affinity with raucous, disruptive birds, this is likely one of the phrase's principal connotations. The illustration that accompanies most "Desde la estaca" columns, esp. in its early years, depicts two men drinking and talking at a bar—quite possibly the *estaca*, or stake, of the title.

14. On "hidden transcripts," see Scott, *Domination*.

15. Most penny press offices were located within a few blocks of the Zócalo in downtown Mexico City.

16. The *jarana* is a small guitar used in traditional music from Veracruz. In this context, the word stands in for woman, probably because the *jarana*, like the larger guitar, is shaped like a woman's torso. A more literal translation of *sazona*, "ripe," reinforces the image of a shapely woman. The common idiom *meterse en jaranas*, "to get into scrapes," adds a misogynistic twist to the usage that also acknowledges the fun to be had with female companions, despite the often undesirable consequences. The masculine counterpart *jarano* or *jaño* is sometimes used to refer to men as it is in the following excerpt. A *jarano* is a hat, also from Veracruz, with a high crown and wide brim often worn by musicians (who might play the *jarana*).

17. Although pool halls have a slightly unsavory reputation, turn-of-the-century billiard academies ("parlors" in English) attracted a mostly bourgeois clientele that came either to play or to attend exhibitions by professionals, which often involved gambling.

18. On the allure of consumer culture in Porfirian Mexico, see Bunker, *Creating*.

19. *Hacerse la chaqueta* is the complete phrase. In this instance, Chema figuratively "jerks off" Pitacio. (Thanks to Pablo Piccato for catching this reference.) For an analysis of the homoerotics of male bonding among working-class Mexican men on the border, see Limón, "Carne, Carnales, and the Carnivalesque," in *Dancing*, 123–40.

20. "Tuna" connotes several things here, including the rosy fruit of the prickly pear cactus, the slang word used by *rateros* (petty thieves) for informants, and a longstanding association of street minstrels with tricksters. For example, Saus et al., *Cancionero*, 300, records the following medieval minstrel song, which resembles Pitacio's phrasing in this vignette: "La tuna con no ser tuna / la tuna que he de correr / pero saben engañar / a los muchachos cada vez" (The tuna not being tuna / the tuna that has to run / but knows how to deceive / the boys every time). References to "tuna" also appear in Mexican folk songs—e.g., "me he de comer esa tuna / aunque me espine la mano" (I have to eat that cactus fruit / even if it pricks my hand)—and in the title of the 1944 Jorge Negrete film *Me he de comer esa tuna*. The literal translation of *plagiarios* is plagiarists.

21. Michel Foucault addresses the productive tension between punishable crimes and tolerated illegalities in *Discipline*. "Penality would then appear to be a way of handling illegalities, of laying down the limits of tolerance, of giving free rein to some, of putting pressure on others, of excluding a particular section, of making another useful, of neutralizing certain individuals and of profiting from others. In short, penality does not simply 'check' illegalities; it 'differentiates' them, it provides them with a general 'economy'" (272).

22. On the Porfirian bourgeoisie's obsession with bathing and the culture of public bathhouses, see Macías-González, "Bathhouse," 25–52.

23. On the proliferation of authoritarian public health campaigns in Porfirian Mexico City, see Agostoni, "Discurso médico," 1–22; "Los infinitamente," 167–89; and *Monuments*. It can hardly come as a surprise that the more coercive aspects of these campaigns focused on the unsanitary practices of the urban poor—a sore point for penny press editors.

24. González Navarro, *El porfiriato*, 462–63, and Agostoni, *Monuments*, 69. According to González Navarro, on St. John's Day the middle classes crowded into pools, while "the poor made do with muddy water from the ditches that surrounded the Capital" (463).

25. *Las de burro* translates awkwardly as "those of the burro," a pack animal known for its big ears and capacity for hard work.

26. Austrian Hapsburg Archduke Maximilian was installed as emperor of Mexico in 1864 with the support of Mexican monarchists, including generals Miguel Miramón and Tomás Mejía, and a French expeditionary force supplied by Napoleon III. Under pressure from the United States, which had just emerged from the Civil War, Napoleon III withdrew the French army. In 1867 republican forces led by deposed president Benito Juárez defeated the royalists. Maximilian, Miramón, and Mejía were captured, court-martialed, convicted, and executed by firing squad. Despite his patriotic fervor, Pitacio manages to confuse things by mixing up *tirar* (to shoot) and *restaurar* (to restore), and changing the site of the execution from *Cerro de las campanas* (Hill of the Bells) to *Cerro de las esquilas* (Hill of the Sheepshearers), a reference to his earlier comments about San Juan and sheep. The point here is that Pitacio and his "old lady" are intensely and spontaneously patriotic despite their lack of proper instruction.

27. Translated here as "old shotgun," the muzzle-loading *trabuco* resembles a blunderbuss with a wide muzzle and has an exceptionally loud retort, which explains Pitacio's loss of hearing. It was traditionally used for crowd control and still plays a prominent role as a prop in popular religious festivals.

28. In defense of Chema and municipal authorities, turn-of-the-century Mexico City was an extraordinarily unhealthy place, esp. in the poorer barrios. See Agostoni, *Monuments*, 65–76.

29. The word *desaforado* suggests loss of self-control in general and religious passion in particular.

30. English uses "sheep" (rather than "lamb") in a similar way: a sheep is someone without a will of his or her own, and a wolf in sheep's clothing is a predator who feigns harmlessness.

31. The use of "sheepskin" or "lambskin" condoms—usually made from sheep or lamb cecum, a section of the intestine—to prevent pregnancy and venereal disease was widespread in Europe and the Americas by the nineteenth century, esp. among the middle and upper classes. While it is not clear that ordinary workers in Porfirian Mexico City would have been able to afford condoms, they would certainly have known about them. Moreover, sheep cecum condoms

are not difficult or expensive to manufacture. See, e.g., Sally Pointer and Gareth Risborough, "Animal Gut Condoms," http://sallypointer.com/animal-gut-condoms. Accessed December 17, 2014.

32. See François, *Culture*.

33. The refrain, apparently quite popular, shows up in several different contexts. See, e.g., Pérez Monfort, *Cotidianidades*, 98–99, and Sánchez, "Nueve sones," 194–215. The catchy refrain survived the Revolution, providing the title of a major musical review of popular Mexican music, *Upa y Apa*, put together by members of the influential Contemporáneos literary group, including Xavier Villaurrutia, Celestino Gorostiza, and Salvador Novo. Retitled *Mexicana*, the review had a short run on Broadway. Ortiz Bullé Goyri, "Presencia del teatro de arte en el teatro de revista mexicano de los años treinta," in Pellettieri, *Huellas escénicas*, 119–26.

34. The phrase "mestá haciendo trampolin el gusto en la caja de los requiriosos ayocotes" translates literally as "This desire [to eat] is making a trampoline in my necessary bean box [stomach]." Here as in most instances, Pitacio carefully distinguishes among the different types of beans he's eating or fantasizing about. *Ayocotes* are large scarlet runner beans with special appeal for a hungry man coming off an involuntary fast. A staple of the preconquest Mexican diet, *ayocotes* were considered more Indian and working class than smaller, more "refined" beans.

35. *Parraleños* are small, reddish beans associated with Parral, Chihuahua, but cultivated and eaten all over Mexico.

36. The exact meaning of *chumbanba*, translated here as "gathering," is unclear. One possibility is that the word should be *chumbanda*, which mixes *chumbando*, the barking of a dog about to attack, and *banda*, a gang or a musical group. If this is the case, a better translation might be "howling" or "shrieking."

37. An alert reader will recognize the phrase from the first story, where it also had sexual connotations.

38. The inspiration for Zorrilla's *Don Juan Tenorio* (1844) is Tirso de Molina's 1640 play *El burlador de Sevilla y convivado de piedra* (The Trickster of Seville and the Stone Guest). Both plays directly or indirectly inspired several masterworks, including Molière's 1665 play *Dom Juan ou le Festin de pierre* (Don Juan, or the Stone Statue's Feast), Byron's poem *Don Juan* (1818–23), and Wolfgang Amadeus Mozart's opera *Don Giovanni* (1787). The pivotal role of Don Juan in the construction of "modern" Mexican masculinities is the subject of ch. 5.

39. José Zorrilla, *Don Juan Tenorio: Drama religioso-fantástico en dos partes*, part 2, act 1, scene 6; part 2, act 3, scene 2. http://www.gutenberg.org/etext/5201 (with English translation). Accessed December 17, 2014.

40. On colonial notions of honor and shame, see the essays in Johnson and Lipsett-Rivera, *Faces of Honor*. For aristocrats in particular, honor involved patriarchs protecting their women from the predations of other men and taking prompt

action to redress any perceived slight, as Don Gonzalo and Don Luis attempt to do in "calling out" Don Juan.

41. Gordon, *Ghostly Matters*, xvi.

42. In addition to the conventional translation given above, the phrase "no se quen; pero mian jalado los pelos . . . de la cabeza" suggests that Pitacio's *jaña* thinks that she's been tricked somehow. The common Spanish-language expression *tomar el pelo* can mean either "to pull hair" or "to pull someone's leg" (i.e., trick someone). The ellipsis between "*pelo*" and "*de la cabeza*" hints at hair in other, more intimate places, a connotation that supports this interpretation. Pitacio is the most obvious source of her agitation, but the third-person plural "*mian jalado el pelo*" (*me han jalado*), "they have pulled my hair," could refer to either the children or a collective "they" as the culprit.

43. Although focused on Pitacio's personal experience in this particular story, the author hints at a more sustained satirical critique. For example, at the end of this chat with Chema, Pitacio asks after one of the column's recurring characters, D. Grabiel el titiritero (Don Grabiel the Puppeteer), whose profession was well known for its merciless mocking of the status quo. On the subversive power of laughter, see Bakhtin, *Rabelais*, 59–144. According to Bakhtin, for low-status people in the Middle Ages, "laughter showed the world anew in its gayest and most sober aspects. . . . This is why laughter could never become an instrument to oppress and blind people. It always remained a free weapon in their hands" (94).

44. Derrida, *Specters of Marx*, 135.

45. This is not to deny that violence against women was a serious problem among the working (and other) classes in early twentieth-century Mexico City. See, e.g., Buffington, "Modern Sacrificial Economy."

46. Elias, *Civilizing Process*, 370.

47. Giddens, *Modernity*, 70. In theoretical and historical terms, the traditional/ modern binary often distorts more than it explains. As an ideological construct, it works to validate some behaviors as modern and dismisses others as traditional in order to establish who is and who isn't on the cutting edge of social change. Despite serious conceptual flaws, it's useful here (in a specific historical circumstance) because that same binary permeates Porfirian discourses about social class and progress.

48. Giddens, *Modernity*, 54; italics in original.

CHAPTER 5. DON JUAN AND THE TROUBLED BIRTH OF MODERN LOVE

1. Ortega y Gasset, "Para una psicología del hombre interesante," 468–69. The essay was first published in 1925. Translation: "The whole world believes it has the real truth about him—about Don Juan, the most secret, most abstruse, most acute problem of our time. And it is that, with few exceptions, men can be divided into

three categories: those who believe they are Don Juan, those who believe they once were, and those who believe they could have been, but chose not to. These last are the ones who tend to attack Don Juan and perhaps decree his demise."

2. The playwright's eleven-year residence in Mexico City (1854–66; the dates include a year spent in Cuba), allegedly to escape an unhappy marriage, likely contributed to the play's popularity, especially after Maximilian named him court poet and made him director of the *Teatro Nacional* in 1864. Zorrilla returned to Spain in 1866 after his wife's death and Maximilian's execution.

3. *Día de los muertos* (Day of the Dead) combines two Catholic feast days, All Saints' Day (November 1) and All Souls' Day (November 2). The custom of staging *Don Juan Tenorio*, usually on the evening of All Saints' Day, is a common practice all over the Spanish-speaking world, from Spain to the Americas to the Philippines. In Mexico, the festival's pagan roots (Native American and European) are especially strong.

4. "La calavera de don Juan Tenorio" (Mexico City: Antonio Vanegas Arroyo, 1909–17). A literal translation of *calavera* would be "skull," but in this instance the word also refers to satirical Day of the Dead poems, *calaveras*, usually directed at the earthly pretensions of real and fictional individuals or groups. A literal translation of "no lo babosea cualquiera" would be "no one drools over him." The broadside reuses an image by Manuel Manilla from an earlier Don Juan Tenorio *calavera*, "Levantaos de sus fosas, calaveras / Que aquí se halla el mayor de los troneras" (Mexico City: Antonio Vanegas Arroyo, 1904). The date of the image itself is unknown, but Manilla worked for Vanegas Arroyo from 1882 to 1892; so it was likely made during that period. The regular reuse of Manilla's images of Don Juan Tenorio for several years after the artist's death (ca. 1900) suggests that Vanegas Arroyo, penny press editors, and their customers saw Manilla's traditional woodcut style as especially well suited to a paragon of traditional (protest) masculinity. For other Manilla images of Don Juan, see López Casillas, *Monografía*, 36–37.

5. "Yo soy Don Juan Tenorio y sin Quimeras / haré platos de sus calaveras" (Mexico City: Antonio Vanegas Arroyo, n.d.). Posada probably etched the plate around 1910, but Vanegas Arroyo reprinted the broadside several times over the next ten years.

6. See, e.g., the illustration, in the style of Manilla, in *El Duende*, November 15, 1904, 3.

7. Dabove, *Nightmares*, 6.

8. Pamphlets and broadsides produced by Antonio Vanegas Arroyo and his collaborators, including printmakers Manual Manilla and José Guadalupe Posada, sometimes acknowledged the humor in modern love but mostly proffered practical advice for negotiating courtship. See Speckman Guerra, "De amor," 68–101.

9. "Don Juan al cadalso," in Franco Sodi, *Don Juan*, 8.

10. "Don Juan al cadalso," in Franco Sodi, *Don Juan*, 11.

11. "Los flores que ofenden: la mujer en la calle," *El Diablito Rojo*, September 21, 1908, 4.

12. Original: "En la capital azteca—el centro culto—la manía donjuanesca se extralimita. Aquí el catrín 'florea' y el pelado 'agarra.' Cada quien hace el amor a su manera, pero ambos del mismo modo encantadoramente ridículo." The distinction between *florea* and *agarra* in the original Spanish is impossible to capture in English. *Echar flores* or *florear*—literally, to throw flowers—suggests a more refined form of verbal harassment, while *agarrar* (literally, to grab) implies a cruder approach. In this instance, the author is noting the different approaches of upper class *catrines* and lower-class *pelados*.

13. Adelina Patti, known as "la Patti," was one of Porfirian Mexico City's most celebrated sopranos. The pun on *sí* plays on the Spanish word for "yes" and the solfège note si. Although si would technically be high B in the fixed solfège system in use in Mexico at the time, the high note for virtuoso sopranos and tenors is most often C—hence the translation above.

14. "Crónica color de Hormiga," *El Diablito Rojo*, November 9, 1908, 2.

15. Original: ". . . con alegría, con entusiasmo, con fruición. Es un calavera, un perdulario, pero tiene tres cualidades: es riquísimo, es valiente, y es amigo nuestro."

16. Original: ". . . racimo de horca. Mata a 34 víctimas, seduce a 73 mujeres, y emplea 'Un día para enamorarlas, / otro para conseguirlas, / otro para abandonarlas, / dos para sustituirlas, / y una hora para olvidarlas." The phrase "racimo de horca" is nearly identical in meaning and imagery to the English phrase "gallows fruit." It appears most prominently in Spanish as the title of an 1874 short story by Peruvian writer Ricardo Palma, written for the second installment of his well-known collection of *Tradicciones peruanas*. The Don Juan quote is from Zorrilla's *Don Juan Tenorio*, act 1, scene 12. The exact quotation suggests that the *El Diablito Rojo* editor knew the play quite well—and perhaps had a copy in his hand when he wrote the editorial.

17. Original: "Vivan, pues, los Tenorios; pero que nadie invoque después los codigos. Eso es." An editorial from the previous week criticized a recent theater production of *Don Juan Tenorio* in which the lead actor invoked the ghost of "el Cura Hidalgo" to save him from hell and then danced a *jarabe* with Doña Inés who was dressed as a *china poblana*. The audience responded with tumultuous applause and thus, in the editor's view, made a mockery of "actors, art, and Mexico." "Oratorio popular," *El Diablito Rojo*, November 14, 1908, 2.

18. Pedro Trujillo de Miranda, "Noviembre," *El Diablito Rojo*, November 29, 1909, 3. Calisto, Melibea, and Celestina are the principal characters in Fernando de Rojas's 1499 *Tragedicomedia de Calisto y Melibea y de la puta vieja Celestina* (Tragicomedy of Calisto and Melibea and the Old Whore Celestina), one of the classic works of Spanish literature.

19. Original: "Hoy los caballeros no galantean las damas y las seducen, las engañan. Tenorio no roba á su amor, la explota. Doña Inés era antes doncella pulcra, en convent, soñadora y pura. Hoy las Ineses, son las mujeres de los démas."

20. Original: ". . . la muchedumbre va á ver á 'Don Juan Tenorio. En día de difuntos. Porque el 'Tenorio' ha muerto."

21. *Romance* is one of the oldest poetic forms in Spanish language literature and one of the least rigid. In general, a *romance* has eight-syllable lines, lots of assonance (internal rather than end rhymes), and tells a story of some kind.

22. Pérez Monfort, *Estampas*, 47. *Costumbrismo* served much the same function throughout Latin America.

23. Pérez Monfort, *Estampas*, 51.

24. The picaresque novel chronicles the life of its protagonist antihero, the *pícaro*, or rogue. Although most provide moralistic commentary on the failings of the *pícaro* and the society that produced him, their appeal has more to do with carnivalesque immersion in the seamier side of popular culture than sanctimonious interludes. Some literary critics have argued that Mexican writer José Joaquín Fernández de Lizardi's *El periquillo sarniento*, written in 1816 and published in 1831, was the last great picaresque novel. For Pérez Monfort, the heyday of Mexican *costumbrismo* begins with its publication and lasts until 1870.

25. Pérez Monfort, *Estampas*, 50. As might be expected, the emphasis on social types is especially apparent in Mexican lithography. See, e.g., Pérez Salas C., *Costumbrismo*.

26. Pérez Monfort, *Estampas*, 58.

27. Pérez Monfort, *Estampas*, 62. For an analysis of elite fears of lower-class political participation in the years following independence, see Warren, *Vagrants*.

28. Prieto, *Musa callejera*. The prologue notes that "the man of the *Musa Callejera* is astute, jealous, tenacious, and frequently cruel; the woman, self-denying, brave, quick with a witty retort. One and the other recognize their failings and know how to find, in the midst of economic misery, the means to satisfy their caprices, to pay for their small pleasures, to forget their poverty, with improvised festivities" (xv–xvi). The third section of *Musa Callejera* consists of romances, including the extremely popular "Romance de la Migajita," about an abused woman who dies from distress when she discovers that the man who had stabbed her has died (196–99). For an overview of Prieto's popular poetry, see McLean, *Vida y obra*, 85–92. Along with his *puro* liberalism and popular poetry, Prieto was also beloved by old-school liberals for having saved Benito Juárez from a firing squad when they were imprisoned together during the Reform War (1857–61).

29. Sommer, *Foundational Fictions*, 24. Overt homosocial bonding and covert homosexual desire in foundational fictions are explored in Irwin, *Mexican Masculinities*, 1–49.

30. There are other, incidental connections. Sommer's Mexican example is Ignacio Altamirano's *El Zarco*, probably written in the 1860s but not published until

1901. Like Juárez, Altamirano was of Indian descent and a hero in the liberal pantheon.

31. Riva Palacio, *Páginas*, 75–77. Vicente Riva Palacio, "Romances nacionales," *El Diablito Bromista*, July 10, 1904, 3. *Páginas* includes another *chinaco* poem, "El Chinaco (Romance Nacional)," that may have inspired the name change in the reprint. Riva Palacio was one of the most respected *letrados* of the nineteenth century. He was also a liberal general in the struggle against Maximilian, founded the influential liberal newspaper *El Ahuizote*, wrote one of the great histories of Mexico (*México a través de los siglos*), and served as governor of two states. A well-known poet, he wrote under his own name and as a woman under the pseudonym Rosa Espino. For more on Riva Palacio as a woman poet, see Easterling, "Gender and Poetry Writing," 115–17. *Chinacos* were rural horsemen (like gauchos in Argentina) who often served as mercenary soldiers during armed conflicts. They were especially renowned as liberal guerrilla fighters in the struggle against Maximilian. The *charro* stereotype is a direct descendent of the *chinaco*.

32. The original Spanish reads "Que ni precia de valiente / Ni es de amores un rayo / Ni le *gustan los amigos* / Ni tiene horror al trabajo"; italics in original.

33. The original Spanish reads "Tan *picuda* me la pone / Que de seguro no alcanzo / Pues pide más imposible / Que una vieja en el rosario"; italics in original.

34. One likely source for many of these unattributed romances was *El Diablito Bromista* editor Antonio de P. Escárcega.

35. "El baile de la Petra," *El Diablito Bromista*, May 17, 1908, 4. The original Spanish reads ". . . seis cubos / De fermentador tlamapa, / Aparte de diez botellas / De *amarte sin esperanzas*, / y de una ollota de ponche / Llena de chínguere y agua." Tlamapa is a small town just southeast of Mexico City known for its fine pulque.

36. "El santo de la casera," *El Diablito Bromista*, September 27, 1903, 3. The romance was published later as "No fumen masquen tabaco" (Don't Smoke Anything but Tobacco), *El Diablito Bromista*, July 21, 1907, 4. The author doesn't specify which of Mexico City's four *tívoli* the celebrants visit, but the Tívoli de San Cosme was the largest, most popular, and least likely to need further introduction.

37. "Corriendo gallo," *El Diablito Bromista*, September 20, 1903, 3. An author identified as El Pato (the duck) wrote another romance about *corriendo gallo* for *El Diablito Bromista*, July 31, 1904, 2–3. For more on working-class participation in patriotic celebrations, see chs. 2 and 3.

38. "El muerto resucitado," *El Diablito Bromista*, August 25, 1907, 2–3. The original Spanish description of the dead man reads ". . . un pobre diablo, / Sin hogar y sin familia, . . . Uno de aquellos gitanos / De la bohemia peridida / Que siempre amanecen crudos / Con calambres en las tripas." The original Spanish for the dead man's comments to the doctor reads "Ya no me tronchen tan verde / Por que se seca la milpa" and "Pues por la chamba tan fina / A que un jefe tan charro / Que ni las botas se quita."

39. Gabriel Villanueva, "La Garbancera," *El Diablito Bromista*, May 3, 1908, 4. The original Spanish description of the maid reads "Era morena, con su cutis suave / y sus mejillas de color de grana, / ojos muy negros y provocativos." The market woman's comments read ". . . no deje por nada de servirle / su cenita, ó lo que él tome, en la cama." A *cuentachiles* is a man obsessed with tracking household expenses, as in the popular saying: "no es peor marido el ladrón, sino el cuentachiles" (the worst husband isn't the thief but the miser). Pérez Martínez, *Refranero*, 290.

40. "Hay te van de canto," *El Diablito Bromista*, December 22, 1907, 3. The description of the female singer as a *grulla*, "crane," suggests both the piercing cry of the bird and the common phrase *grulla baleada* for a deceitful or lost woman (as an adjective *grullo* means "uncouth"). Zaid, "Divagación," 24. La Merced, the huge street market just east of the Zócalo in downtown Mexico City, has long been associated with low-end prostitution, a connection also implied in the description of the singer's clothing and hairdo, including the comment about the pomade containing either lard (from pigs) or tallow (from cows). "Temamatlá" refers to the site of a massive 1895 train wreck. Matthews, *"De Viaje,"* 251–89, argues that media representations of train wrecks, especially Temamatlá, reflected (and fed) widespread ambiguity about the unintended consequences of Porfirian development.

41. *Coime* generally refers to card dealers, pimps, waiters, and other "hustlers." It is no coincidence that thirty years later both the character types described in this *romance callejero* (and others) would show up in the *cabaretera* (cabaret) films of directors like Emilio Fernández.

42. *Embalsamada* usually means "embalmed" but is used here to mean "perfumed" or "infused." *Furriel*, "quartermaster," is also a word play on *furris*, Mexican slang for "ugly" or "despised." The double meaning implied in this usage—women supply men's basic needs and are despised for it—is clear enough.

43. "Macetita embalsamada." The song also appears in Ausucua, *El Ruisenor*, 4–6. The two versions vary slightly, mostly in punctuation. (The Yucatecan songbook can be found at www.bibliotecavirtualdeyucatan.com.mx). Another version of the song, titled "El Pañuelo," appears in Kuri-Aldana and Mendoza Martínez, *El Cancionero popular mexicano*, 234. "Macetita embalsamada" has maintained its popularity. The first lines from the second verse appear in Juan Rulfo's *Pedro Páramo*, and a copy of the song's lyrics was discovered among his papers (www .clubcultura.com/clubliteratura/clubescritores/juanrulfo/03.pdf). The most recent recording is probably the one by Mercedes Castro on her 2007 album *Maldita miseria* (Musart-Balboa).

44. The final verse uses two common Spanish verbs for "to love"—*querer* and *amar*—probably to avoid excessive repetition but perhaps also using the more formal *amar* for men to indicate that men need to take love more seriously. For this reason, in the final line *querer* is translated as "to care for."

45. "El rapto de Dorotea," *El Diablito Bromista*, October 4, 1908, 3.

46. "La güera del cantero," *El Diablito Bromista*, February 8, 1908, 3.

47. "Romance callejero," *El Diablito Bromista*, August 9, 1903, 3.

48. "Así me gusta agarrarlos," *El Diablito Bromista*, May 10, 1909, 4.

49. "La Verbena de los Angeles," part 1, *La Guacamaya*, August 18, 1902, 3. The *verbena* for the Assumption is celebrated every year on August 15 at the Metropolitan Cathedral on the Zócalo in Mexico City.

50. "La Verbena de los Angeles," part 2, *La Guacamaya*, August 25, 1902, 3.

51. "La Verbena de los Angeles," part 3, *La Guacamaya*, September 1, 1902, 3.

52. Hague, "Five Dances from Mexico," 384–85.

53. For an in-depth analysis of representations of male violence against women, see Buffington, "Modern Sacrificial Economy."

54. On male poets writing as women, see Easterling, "Gender and Poetry Writing," 97–142.

55. Canuto Godines (Mimi), "No Judas mejor Matraca," *La Matraca de La Guacamaya*, special edition, April 1905, 3–4. The title is difficult to translate but refers to the Mexican custom of using loud wooden or metal clappers (*matracas*) to celebrate the burning of Judas figures on Easter Sunday. The implication is that it's better to celebrate the death of the great betrayer (Judas) than to betray.

56. Canuto Godines (Mimi), "¿Pero de qué . . . ?," *La Guacamaya*, September 20, 1906, 2–3.

57. Magdalena's practical approach to romance mirrors the advice for women in the Vanegas Arroyo pamphlets and broadsheets. Speckman Guerra, "De amor y desamor," 97.

58. Canuto Godines (Mimi), "Para que la cuña apriete," 2 parts, *La Guacamaya*, May 30, 1905, 2–3; April 13, 1905, 4. The title is the opening of the popular adage "Para que la cuña apriete, ha de ser del mismo palo" (For the wedge to stick it must be from the same piece of wood), which means that for a venture to succeed everyone needs to work together. It appears most often these days with regard to team sports, but the reference here is to a successful marriage.

59. *Fra diablo* in Mexican cooking refers to seafood dishes that are hot and spicy.

60. Her uncle is a *chinampero*, one who farms a *chinampa* (a garden plot in one of Mexico City's lakes), an occupation associated with certain indigenous groups.

61. Canuto Godines (Mimi), "Juventina," 7 parts, *El Diablito Bromista*, October 25, November 15, November 22, November 29, December 20, and December 27, 1903; January 3, 1904.

62. Illouz, *Why Love Hurts*, 48.

63. For more on consumption and identity in Porfirian Mexico City, see Bunker, *Creating*.

64. Canuto Godines, "¡Que pobre!," *El Diablito Bromista*, July 14, 1907, 3–4.

65. Canuto Godines, "¡Adultera!," *La Guacamaya*, February 1, 1905, 2.

66. Canuto Godines (Mimi), "De mala raza!!!," *La Guacamaya*, March 16, 1905. The title might be a reference to the 1886 play of the same name by Spanish dramatist

(among other things) José Echegaray, who had won the Nobel Prize for Literature the previous year. Echegaray also wrote about the hereditary evils of *donjuanismo*, symbolized by venereal disease passed from father to son, in *El hijo de Don Juan* (1892). His plays were staged all over Latin America, including Mexico City. González Navarro, *El Porfiriato*, 792–95, 800–803.

67. A similar romance by an anonymous poet tells the story of another sincere young man who ends up in jail after he attempts to rob a jewelry store for a gift for his fiancée. The sensible young woman, who never asked for jewels, moves on. "El amor de Nacha," *La Guacamaya*, August 22, 1907, 2–3.

68. Canuto Godines (Mimi), "Pero . . . que zapatos!," *La Guacamaya*, November 10, 1904, 2.

69. Mixcalco is a *rumbo* (road/direction) in downtown Mexico City, a few blocks north and east of the Zócalo.

70. Canuto Godines (Mimi), "El Aguila de Oro," *La Guacamaya*, April 20, 1905, 2–3.

71. The original Spanish reads "Será lo que á ti te plazca, / Pues sabes que no me opongo, / Pero escucha, si he venido / Anoche cual nunca beodo/Voy á explicarte el motive / Y después piensa á tu modo."

72. The original Spanish reads "—¡Que tonto! / Prefieres gastar tus fierros / En tomar, ¿y yo qué como? / Siempre estás con que me quieres / Me quieres y te haces sordo."

73. The ellipsis alerts the reader that "la . . . China" is standing in for *la . . . chingada*, hence the translation "go fuck yourself." *Tostadas de horno* are sweet cornmeal biscuits or cookies.

74. Canuto Godines (Mimi), "¡Qué viva la Independencia!," *La Guacamaya*, October 4, 1906, 2. For more on popular patriotism, see chs. 1–3.

75. According to traditional Catholic belief, the Holy House was transported by angels from the Holy Land to Loreto, Italy, in the late thirteenth century. The Basilica della Santa Casa has been a pilgrimage site ever since. Loreto is also the name of a prominent Mexico City church, Templo de Nuestra Señora de Loreto, near Mixcalco, where the young woman in the poem lives. Mixcalco, a few blocks northeast of the Zócalo, is mentioned in several Godines romances.

76. Conrado Palido, "Romance modernista," *Don Cucufate*, September 10, 1906, 3.

77. Padilla et al., "Introduction," xv.

78. Hirsch, "'Love Makes a Family,'" 94–95. See also Hirsch, *Courtship*.

79. *El Chile Piquin*, January 12, 1905, 1. The Posada image was popular in its day and is still considered one of his finest.

80. "Entre Cotorras," *La Guacamaya*, November 12, 1903, 2–3. The *cotorra* is recalling the opening lines of act 3, scene 2, from *Don Juan Tenorio*, where the Statue of the Comendador addresses Don Juan before taking him to hell (until Doña Inés intercedes): "Aquí me tienes, don Juan, / y he aquí que vienen conmigo / los que tu eterno castigo / de Dios reclamando están."

1. "Coplas de Don Simón" (Mexico City: Antonio Vanegas Arroyo, 1912 [1910 for Getty Research Institute]), cited in Speckman Guerra, "De amor," 90. (Translation: "There are traps a man avoids / but these modern ones, no . . .")

2. La Tricolor 96.5, www.965tricolor.com/show/erazno-y-la-chokolata/. Accessed December 17, 2014.

3. García Peña, *El fracaso de amor*, 15, implicates liberal ideas about gender relations, especially the division of the social world into public and private spheres, for intensifying patriarchal domination of women and increasing male domestic violence against women.

4. The spelling of Doggie/Doggy varies in the show's promotional literature. As listener comments make clear, the name Doggie references "doggie style," a sexual position in which a dominant male mounts a woman (or another man) from behind—a crude symbol of male sexual mastery.

5. "Erazno" references *el asno*, "the ass," which has the same pejorative connotations as its English counterpart. "Chente" is a common nickname for mariachi great Vicente Fernández but in this case probably refers in a derogatory way to someone (usually of Hispanic rather than Indian origin) who has no idea what's going on, in this instance a blustery former president who once called his political opponent a *mariquita* (little sissy).

6. Szasz, "Sexualidad y género," 90. In the paragraph that follows, Szasz cites anthropologist Jennifer Hirsch on the prevalence of this type of humor among working-class Mexican men. Hirsch, "Missionaries' Positions."

7. La hora del Doggie, "Llamada de radio escucha enojada por La hora de Doggy," July 28, 2011. This particular show was still receiving blog responses in fall 2013. www.youtube.com/watch?v=PS6jzlNbPXo. Accessed December 17, 2014.

8. The show's promotional blurb notes that "La Chokolata es toda una diva (según ella), es una dama que no tiene pelos en la lengua, da a expresar sus opiniones en un estilo fresco por que ella no es 'Naca' y le encanta poner a Erazno en su lugar" (La Chokolata is a real diva [according to her], she's a lady who doesn't hold back, she expresses her opinions in a fresh style because she's not an 'idiot' and she loves putting Erazno in his place). The strategic deployment of multiple personas, including drag personas, has a long and distinguished history in Mexican letters and includes several writers mentioned in earlier chapters: liberal statesman Vicente Riva Palacio (a.k.a. Rosa Espina), modernist poet Manuel Gutiérrez Nájera, and the do-everything editor of *La Guacamaya*, Fernando Torroella. La Chokolata refers to chocolate, the character's dark skin, and her lack of class. This last trait emerges in Choko's ongoing obsession with who is and who isn't *naco*, a derogatory term in Mexican Spanish for people considered stupid, uncultured, working class, tacky, and too Indian—much like *pelado* and akin to

the English term "white trash" but with different racial connotations. The show's website, www.elerazno.com/, includes a link to a page of *nacadas*, with photos of everything from a dashboard cup holder made from a role of packing tape to a Vespa outfitted with stirrups, reins, and saddlebags.

9. Octavio Paz explores the meaning of masks, *albures*, and "hermetic" Mexican men in "Máscaras mexicanas," in *Laberinto de soledad*, 26–41.

10. Halberstam, *Queer Art*, 4.

11. A similar theme is evident in a three-part YouTube "La hora del Doggie" episode entitled "Hombres ¿buenos or tontos?" [Men, good or stupid?], during which Doggie admits that some women have accused him of being a gay woman-hater but swears that "yo soy hombre que gustan a las mujeres *buenas*" [I'm a man who enjoys *good* women]. Erazno y la Chokolata, "La hora del doggy-hombres buenos o tontos, parte 1," uploaded November 22, 2011. www.youtube.com /watch?v=Hzpc3TSSD70. Accessed December 17, 2013.

12. The argumentative suffix in "Chokolat*azo*" indicates a powerful blow or strike and conveys the intense emotional blow to the betrayed partner and the shock of exposure to the betrayer produced by the phone call.

13. For an explanation of how gender scripts shape subjectivity in working-class men and women in contemporary Mexico City, see Gutmann, *The Meanings of Macho*, 1–10. Channeling the spirits of masculine and feminine archetypes, like revolutionary leader Pancho Villa, is common in Mexican popular culture. See, e.g., Behar, *Translated Women*, 203–24, and the popular film *Entre Pancho Villa y una mujer desnuda* (Between Pancho Villa and a Naked Woman; 1996, directed by Sabina Berman and Isabelle Tardán), in which the commitment-phobic male protagonist channels Pancho Villa to win back his alienated fiancée.

14. Reliance on a commonsense female expert like Dr. Contreras is common in Spanish-language media for both sex education and immigration advice.

15. For an explanation of "unexpected citizens," see ch. 1. The term comes from Acevedo Rodrigo and López Caballero, "Introducción," 13–37.

BIBLIOGRAPHY

PERIODICALS

La Araña	*El Imparcial*
El Cabezón	*El Padre Cobos*
La Cagarruta	*El Padre Padilla*
El Chango	*La Palanca*
El Chile Piquín	*El Papagayo*
El Colmillo Público	*La Patria Ilustrada*
El Diablito Bromista	*El Periquillo Sarniento*
El Diablito Rojo	*El Periquito*
Diario del Hogar	*El Pinche*
Don Cucufate	*Regeneración*
El Duende	*Revista Azul: el domingo*
La Guacamaya	*de "El Partido Liberal"*
El Hijo de Ahuizote	*San Lunes*
El Hijo del Fandango	*La Tranca*

BROADSIDES

"La calavera de Don Juan Tenorio." Mexico City: Antonio Vanegas Arroyo, n.d.

"Coplas de Don Simón." Mexico City: Antonio Vanegas Arroyo, 1912.

"Levantaos de sus fosas, calaveras/Que aquí se halla el mayor de los troneras." Mexico City: Antonio Vanegas Arroyo, 1904.

"Macetita embalsamada." Mexico City: Antonio Vanegas Arroyo, 1905.

"María la del cielo (*danza*)." Mexico City: Antonio Vanegas Arroyo, 1911.

"Yo soy Don Juan Tenorio y sin Quimeras/haré platos de sus calaveras" (Manuel Manilla, illustrator). Mexico City: Antonio Vanegas Arroyo, n.d.

"Yo soy Don Juan Tenorio y sin Quimeras/haré platos de sus calaveras" (José Guadalupe Posada, illustrator). Mexico City: Antonio Vanegas Arroyo, n.d.

PUBLISHED SOURCES

Acevedo Rodrigo, Ariadna, and Paula López Caballero. "Introducción: Los ciudadanos inesperados," in *Ciudadanos inesperados: Espacios de formación y de la ciudadanía ayer y hoy*. Mexico City: Colegio de México, 2012, 13–37.

Adorno, Rolena. *Guaman Poma: Writing and Resistance in Colonial Peru*. Austin: University of Texas Press, 1986.

Adorno, Rolena, et al., eds. *Guaman Poma de Ayala: The Colonial Art of an Andean Author*. New York: American Society, 1992.

Agostoni, Claudia. "Discurso médico, cultura higiénica y la mujer en la ciudad de México al cambio del siglo (XIX–XX)." *Mexican Studies/Estudios Mexicanos* 18, no. 1 (Winter 2002): 1–22.

Agostoni, Claudia. "Los infinitamente pequeños: Debates y conflictos en torno a la bacteriología (Ciudad de México, siglos XIX al XX)," in Elisa Speckman Guerra and Claudia Agostoni, eds., *De normas y transgresiones: Enfermedad y crimen en América Latina (1850–1950)*. Mexico City: Universidad Nacional Autónoma de México, 2005, 167–92.

Agostoni, Claudia. *Monuments of Progress: Modernization and Public Health in Mexico City, 1876–1910*. Calgary, AB: University of Calgary Press, 2003.

Anderson, Benedict. *Imagined Communities: Reflections on the Origin and Spread of Nationalism*, rev. ed. New York: Verso, 1991.

Anderson, Rodney D. "Mexican Workers and the Politics of Revolution, 1906–1911." *Hispanic American Historical Review* 54, no. 1 (1974): 94–113.

Anderson, Rodney D. *Outcasts in Their Own Land: Mexican Industrial Workers, 1906–1911*. DeKalb: Northern Illinois University Press, 1976.

Araiza, Luis. *Historia del movimiento obrero mexicano*, vol. 1. Mexico City: Ediciones Casa del Obrero, 1975.

Aréchiga Córdoba, Ernesto. "Lucha de clases en la ciudad: La disputa por el espacio urbano, ca. 1890–1930," in Carlos Illades and Mario Barbosa, eds., *Los trabajadores de la Ciudad de México, 1860–1950: Textos en homenaje a Clara E. Lida*. Mexico City: El Colegio de México/Universidad Autónoma Metropolitana Unidad Cuajimalpa, 2013, 19–50.

Arenas Guzmán, Diego. *El periodísmo en la Revolución Mexicana (de 1876–1908)*. Mexico City: Biblioteca del Instituto Nacional de Estudios Históricos de la Revolución Mexicana, 1966.

Arrom, Silvia Marina. *The Women of Mexico City: 1790–1857*. Stanford, CA: Stanford University Press, 1985.

Ausucua, Juan, ed. *El Ruisenor Yucateco*, part 2: *Collección de canciones de todos los géneros*. Mexico City: Editor "El Parnaso Mexicano," 1902.

Bakhtin, Mikail. *Rabelais and His World*. Translated by Hélène Iswolsky. Bloomington: University of Indiana Press, 1984.

Barajas Durán, Rafael. *El país de "El Llorón de Icamole": Caricatura mexicana de combate y libertad de imprenta durante los gobiernos de Porfirio Díaz y Manuel González*. Mexico City: Fondo de Cultura Económica, 2007.

Barajas Durán, Rafael. *Posada, mito y mitote: La caricatura política de José Guadalupe Posada y Manuel Alfonso Manilla*. Mexico City: Fondo de Cultura Económica, 2009.

Barrón Gavito, Miguel Ángel. "El baile de los 41: La representación de lo afeminado en la prensa porfiriana." *Historia y Grafía* 34 (2010): 47–76.

Barrows, Susanna. *Distorting Mirrors: Visions of the Crowd in Late Nineteenth-Century France*. New Haven, CT: Yale University Press, 1981.

Beezley, William H. *Judas at the Jockey Club and Other Episodes of Porfirian Mexico*. Lincoln: University of Nebraska Press, 1987.

Beezley, William H., and David E. Lorey, eds. ¡*Viva México! ¡Viva la Independencia!: Celebrations of September 16*. Wilmington, DE: Scholarly Resources, 2001.

Beezley, William H., Cheryl English Martin, and William E. French, eds. *Rituals of Rule, Rituals of Resistance: Public Celebrations and Popular Culture in Mexico*. Wilmington, DE: Scholarly Resources, 1994.

Behar, Ruth. *Translated Woman: Crossing the Border with Esperanza's Story*. Boston: Beacon Press, 1993.

Berdecio, Robert, and Stanley Appelbaum, eds. *Posada's Popular Mexican Prints*. New York: Dover, 1972.

Berlant, Lauren, and Michael Warner. "Sex in Public," in Lauren Berlant, ed., *Intimacy*. Chicago: University of Chicago Press, 2000.

Bracho, Julio. *De los gremios al sindicalismo: Genealogía corportiva*. Mexico City: UNAM, 1990.

Broude, Gwen J. "Protest Masculinity: A Further Look at the Causes and the Concept." *Ethnos* 18, no. 1 (March 1990): 103–22.

Buffington, Robert M. *Criminal and Citizen in Modern Mexico*. Lincoln: University of Nebraska Press, 2000.

Buffington, Robert M. "La 'Dancing' Mexicana: Danzón and the Transformation of Intimacy in Post-Revolutionary Mexico City." *Journal of Latin American Cultural Studies* 14, no. 1 (March 2005): 87–108.

Buffington, Robert M. "Homophobia and the Mexican Working Class, 1900–1910," in Robert McKee Irwin, Edward J. McCaughan, and Michelle Rocío Nasser, eds., *The Famous 41: Sexuality and Social Control in Mexico, 1901*. New York: Palgrave Macmillan, 2003, 193–225.

Buffington, Robert M. "Los Jotos: Contested Visions of Homosexuality in Modern Mexico," in Daniel Balderston and Donna Guy, eds., *Sex and Sexuality in Latin America*. New York: New York University Press, 1997, 118–32.

Buffington, Robert M. "Towards a Modern Sacrificial Economy: Violence against Women and Male Subjectivity in Turn-of-the-Century Mexico City," in Víctor M. Macías-González and Anne Rubenstein, eds., *Masculinity and Sexuality in Modern Mexico*. Albuquerque: University of New Mexico Press, 2012, 157–95.

Buffington, Robert M. "La violencia contra la mujer y la sujetividad masculine en la prensa popular de la ciudad de México en el cambio del siglo," in Elisa Speckman Guerra and Claudia Agostoni, eds., *De normas y transgresiones: Enfermedad y crimen en América Latina (1850–1950)*. Mexico City: Universidad Nacional Autónoma de México, 2005, 287–325.

Buffington, Robert M., and Pablo Piccato. "Tales of Two Women: The Narrative Construal of Porfirian Reality." *The Americas* 55, no. 3 (January 1999): 391–424.

Buffington, Robert M., and Pablo Piccato, eds. *True Stories of Crime in Modern Mexico*. Albuquerque: University of New Mexico Press, 2009.

Bulnes, Francisco. *El verdadero Juárez y la verdad sobre la intervención y el imperio*. Mexico City: Librería de la Viuda de C. Bouret, 1904.

Bunker, Steven B. *Creating Mexican Consumer Culture in the Age of Porfirio Díaz*. Albuquerque: University of New Mexico Press, 2012.

Butler, Judith. *Bodies That Matter: On the Discursive Limits of "Sex."* New York: Routledge, 1993.

Butler, Judith. *Excitable Speech: A Politics of the Performative*. New York: Routledge, 1997.

Butler, Judith. *Gender Trouble: Feminism and the Subversion of Identity*. New York: Routledge, 1990.

Butler, Judith. *The Psychic Life of Power: Theories in Subjection*. Stanford, CA: Stanford University Press, 1997.

Campos, Rubén M. *El Bar: La vida literaria de México en 1900*. Mexico City: Universidad Nacional Autónoma de México, 1996.

Carr, Barry. "The Casa del Obrero Mundial, Constitutionalism and the Pact of February 1915," in Elsa Cecilia Frost, Michael C. Meyer, Josefina Zoraida Vázquez, and Lilia Díaz, eds., *El trabajo y los trabajadores en la historia de México/Labor and Laborers through Mexican History*. México and Tucson: El Colegio de México/University of Arizona Press, 1979, 603–32.

Carrillo Azpeitia, Rafael. *Posada y el grabado mexicano*. Mexico City: Panorama Editorial, 1983.

Castillo, Alberto del. "Prensa, poder y criminalidad a finales del siglo XIX en la Ciudad de México," in Ricardo Pérez Monfort, ed., *Hábitos, normas y escándalo: Prensa, criminalidad y drogas durante el porfiriato tardío*. Mexico City: Centro de Investigaciones y Estudios Superiores en Antropología Social y la Editorial Plaza y Valdés, 1997, 15–74.

Ceballos Ramírez, Manuel. *El catolicismo social: "Rerum Novarum," la "cuestión social," y la movilización de los católicos mexicanos (1891–1911)*. Mexico City: El Colegio de México, 1991.

Ceballos Ramírez, Manuel. "La Encíclica *Rerum Novarum* y los trabajadores católicos en la ciudad de México (1891–1913)." *Historia Mexicana* 33 (1): 216–53.

Celada, Fernando. *Bronces: Cantos épicos á Juárez*. Mexico City: Tipografía Literaria de Filomeno Mata, 1904.

Chambers, Sarah C. "What Independence Meant for Women," in John Charles Chasteen and James A. Wood, eds., *Problems in Latin American History: Sources and Interpretations*. Wilmington, DE: Scholarly Resources, 2004, 37–44.

Clark, Marjorie Ruth. *Organized Labor in Mexico*. Chapel Hill: University of North Carolina Press, 1934.

Cockcroft, James D. *Intellectual Precursors of the Mexican Revolution, 1900–1913*. Austin: University of Texas Press, 1968.

Collado, María del Carmen, ed. *Miradas recurrentes: La ciudad de México en los siglos XIX y XX*, vol. 2. Mexico City: Instituto de Investigaciones Doctor José María Luis Mora/Universidad Autónoma Metropolitana–Azcapotzalco, 2004.

Connell, R. W. *Masculinities*, 2nd ed. Berkeley: University of California Press, 2005.

Connell, R. W., and James W. Messerschmidt. "Hegemonic Masculinity: Rethinking the Concept." *Gender and Society* 19, no. 6 (December 2005): 829–59.

Consejo Nacional para la Cultura y las Artes, El. *Los pinceles de la historia: La fabricación del estado, 1864–1910*. Mexico City: Patronato del Museo Nacional de Arte/Banco Nacional de México, 2003.

Cordero Espinosa, Sergio, et al., eds. *Fernando Celada Miranda y su obra poética*. Mexico City: EDAMEX, 1996.

Cosío Villegas, Daniel. *Historia moderna de México*, vol. 2: *El Porfiriato: La vida política interior*. Mexico City: Editorial Hermes, 1985.

Curcio-Nagy, Linda A. *The Great Festivals of Mexico City: Performing Power and Identity*. Albuquerque: University of New Mexico Press, 2004.

Dabove, Juan Pablo. *Nightmares of the Lettered City: Banditry and Literature in Latin America, 1816–1929*. Pittsburgh: University of Pittsburgh Press, 2007.

Derrida, Jacques. *The Specters of Marx*. Translated by Peggy Kamuf. New York: Routledge, 1994.

Díaz, María Elena. "The Satiric Penny Press for Workers in Mexico, 1900–1910: A Case Study in the Politicisation of Popular Culture." *Journal of Latin American Studies* 22 (1990): 497–525.

Easterling, Stuart. "Gender and Poetry Writing in Light of Mexico's Liberal Victory, 1867–ca. 1890." *Mexican Studies/Estudios Mexicanos* 27, no. 1 (Winter 2011): 97–142.

Elias, Norbert. *The Civilizing Process: Sociogenetic and Psychogenetic Investigations*, rev. ed. Translated by Edmund Jebhcott. London: Blackwell, 2000.

Ellis, Havelock. "Auto-eroticism: A Psychological Study." *Alienist and Neurologist* 19 (1898): 260–99.

Ellis, Havelock, and John Addington Symonds. *Sexual Inversion*. London: Wilson and MacMillan, 1897.

Fernández Aceves, María Teresa, Carmen Ramos Escandón, and Susie Porter, eds. *Orden social e identidad de género: México, siglos XIX y XX*. Mexico City: Centro de Investigaciones y Estudios Superiores en Antropología Social/Centro Universitario de Ciencias Sociales y Humanidades–Universidad de Guadalajara, 2006.

Fernández Tejedo, Isabel and Carmen Nava Nava. "Images of Independence in the Nineteenth Century: The *Grito de Dolores*, History and Myth," in William H. Beezley and David E. Lorey, eds. *¡Viva México! ¡Viva la Independencia!: Celebrations of September 16*. Wilmington, DE: Scholarly Resources, 2001, 1–41.

Flaubert, Gustave. *The Letters of Gustave Flaubert, 1857–1880*, vol. 2. Translated by Francis Steegmuller. Cambridge, MA: Harvard University Press, 1982.

Florescano, Enrique. *Historia de las historias de la nación mexicana*. Mexico City: Taurus, 2002.

Forment, Carlos A. *Democracy in Latin America, 1760–1900*. Vol. 1, *Civic Selfhood and Public Life in Mexico and Peru*. Chicago: University of Chicago Press, 2003.

Foucault, Michel. *Discipline and Punish: The Birth of the Prison*. Translated by Alan Sheridan. New York: Vintage Books, 1979.

Franco, Jean. *Plotting Women: Gender and Representation in Mexico*. New York: Columbia University Press, 1989.

François, Marie Eileen. *A Culture of Everyday Credit: Housekeeping, Pawnbroking, and Governance in Mexico City, 1750–1920*. Lincoln: University of Nebraska Press, 2006.

Franco Sodi, Carlos. *Don Juan delincuente y otros ensayos*. Mexico City: Ediciones Bota, 1952.

Frank, Patrick. *Posada's Broadsheets: Mexican Popular Imagery, 1890–1910*. Albuquerque: University of New Mexico Press, 1998.

Fraser, Nancy. "Rethinking the Public Sphere: A Contribution to the Critique of Actually Existing Democracy." *Social Text* no. 25/26 (1990): 56–80.

French, William E. *The Heart in the Glass Jar: Love Letters, Bodies, and the Law in Mexico*. Lincoln: University of Nebraska Press, 2015.

French, William E. *A Peaceful and Working People: Manners, Morals, and Class Formation in Northern Mexico*. Albuquerque: University of New Mexico Press, 1996.

French, William E., and Katherine Elaine Bliss, eds. *Gender, Sexuality, and Power in Latin America since Independence*. Lanham, MD: Rowman and Littlefield, 2007.

Freud, Sigmund. *Three Essays on the Theory of Sexuality*. Translated and edited by James Strachey. New York: Basic Books, 1962.

Gallo, Rubén. *Freud's Mexico: Into the Wilds of Psychoanalysis*. Cambridge, MA: MIT Press, 2010.

García Canclini, Néstor. *Hybrid Cultures: Strategies of Entering and Leaving Modernity*. Translated by Christopher Chiappari and Silvia López. Minneapolis: University of Minnesota Press, 1995.

García Peña, Ana Lidia. *El fracaso de amor: Género e indiviudalismo en el siglo XIX mexicano*. Mexico City: El Colegio de México/Universidad Autónoma del Estado de México, 2006.

Garrido Asperó, María José. *Fiestas cívicas históricas en la ciudad de México, 1765–1823*. Mexico City: Instituto Mora, 2006.

Gay, Peter. *Education of the Senses: The Bourgeois Experience: Victoria to Freud*. London: Oxford University Press, 1984.

Gay, Peter. *The Tender Passion: The Bourgeois Experience: Victoria to Freud*. London: Oxford University Press, 1986.

Giddens, Anthony. *Modernity and Self-Identity: Self and Society in the Late Modern Age*. Cambridge: Polity Press, 1991.

Giddens, Anthony. *The Transformation of Intimacy: Sexuality, Love, and Eroticism in Modern Societies*. Cambridge: Polity Press, 1992.

Gillingham, Paul. *Cuauhtémoc's Bones: Forging National Identity in Modern Mexico*. Albuquerque: University of New Mexico Press, 2011.

González Montes, Soledad, and Pilar Iracheta Cenegorta. "La violencia en la vida de las mujeres campesinas: El distrito de Tenango, 1880–1910," in Carmen Ramos Escandón et al., eds., *Presencia y transparencia: La mujer en la historia de México*. Mexico City: El Colegio de México, 1987, 111–61.

González Navarro, Moisés. *El Porfiriato: La vida social*. Mexico City: Editorial Hermes, 1985.

Gordon, Avery F. *Ghostly Matters: Haunting and the Sociological Imagination*, 2nd ed. Minneapolis: University of Minnesota Press, 2008.

Granillo Vázquez, Lilia. "Masculine and Political Imagery in Mexican Public Opinion, 1898–1900: The Dawn of the Famous 41," paper delivered to mark the centenary of *The Famous 41: Sexuality and Social Control in Latin America*, Tulane University, November 15–17, 2001.

Gretton, Thomas. "Posada and the 'Popular': Commodities and Social Constructs in Mexico before the Revolution." *Oxford Art Journal* 17, no. 2 (1994): 32–47.

Grimes, Larry M. *El tabú lingüístico en México: El lenguaje erótico de los mexicanos*. New York: Bilingual Press, 1978.

Guerra, François-Xavier. *México: Del Antiguo Régimen a la Revolución*, vol. 2. Mexico City: Fondo de Cultura Económica, 1991.

Guerrero, Julio. *La génesis del crimen en México: Estudio de psiquiatría social*. Mexico City: Consejo Nacional para la Cultura y las Artes, [1901] 1996.

Gutiérrez, Florencia, and Fausta Gantús, "Los pequeños voceadores: Prácticas laborales, censura y representaciones a finales del siglo XIX," in Carlos Illades and Mario Barbosa, eds., *Los trabajadores de la Ciudad de México, 1860–1950: Textos en homenaje a Clara E. Lida*. Mexico City: El Colegio de México/Universidad Autónoma Metropolitana Unidad Cuajimalpa, 2013, 81–116.

Gutiérrez, Natividad. "Mujeres Patria-Nación: Mexico, 1810–1920." *La Ventana* 12 (2000): 209–43.

Gutiérrez, Ramón A. "Conclusion: Mexican Masculinities," in Víctor M. Macías-González and Anne Rubenstein, eds., *Masculinity and Sexuality in Modern Mexico*. Albuquerque, NM: University of New Mexico Press, 2012, 262–71.

Gutmann, Matthew C., ed. *Changing Men and Masculinities in Latin America*. Durham, NC: Duke University Press, 2003.

Gutmann, Matthew C. *The Meanings of Macho: Being a Man in Mexico City*. Berkeley: University of California Press, 1996.

Habermas, Jürgen. *The Structural Transformation of the Public Sphere: An Inquiry into a Category of Bourgeois Society*. Translated by Thomas Burger and Frederick Lawrence. Cambridge, MA: MIT Press, 1989.

Hague, Eleanor. "Five Dances from Mexico." *Journal of Amerian Folk-Lore* 28 (1915–1916): 379–81.

Halberstam, Judith. *The Queer Art of Failure*. Durham, NC: Duke University Press, 2011.

Hale, Charles A. *The Transformation of Liberalism in Late Nineteenth-Century Mexico*. Princeton, NJ: Princeton University Press, 1989.

Hart, John M. *Anarchism and the Mexican Working Class, 1860–1931*. Austin: University of Texas Press, 1987.

Hirsch, Jennifer S. "Between the Missionaries' Positions and the Missionary Position: Mexican Dirty Jokes and the Public (Sub)Version of Sexuality." *Princeton Working Papers in Women's Studies* 5 (Spring–Summer 1990): 1–42.

Hirsch, Jennifer S. *A Courtship after Marriage: Sexuality and Love in Mexican Transnational Families*. Berkeley: University of California Press, 2003.

Hirsch, Jennifer S. "'Love Makes a Family': Globalization, Companionate Marriage, and the Modernization of Gender Inequality," in *Love and Globalization: Transformations of Intimacy in the Contemporary World*. Nashville: Vanderbilt University Press, 2007, 93–106.

Huitrón, Jacinto. *Origenes e historia del movimiento obrero en México*, 3rd ed. Mexico City: Editores Mexicanos Unidos, 1984.

Illades, Carlos. *Estudios sobre el artesanado urbano del siglo XIX*. Mexico City: El Atajo, 1997.

Illades, Carlos. *Hacia la república del trabajo: La organización artisanal en la ciudad de México, 1853–1876*. Mexico City: El Colegio de México/Universidad Autónoma Metropolitana–Iztapalapa, 1996.

Illades, Carlos. *Las otras ideas: El primer socialismo en México, 1850–1935*. Mexico City: Biblioteca ERA/Universidad Autónoma Metropolitana–Cuajimalpa, 2008.

Illouz, Eva. *Why Love Hurts: A Sociological Explanation*. Malden, MA: Polity Press, 2012.

Irwin, Robert McKee. "The Famous 41: The Scandalous Birth of Modern Mexican Homosexuality." *GLQ* 6, no. 3 (2000): 353–76.

Irwin, Robert McKee. *Mexican Masculinities*. Minneapolis: University of Minnesota Press, 2003.

Irwin, Robert McKee, Edward J. McCaughan, and Michelle Rocío Nasser, eds. *The Famous 41: Sexuality and Social Control in Mexico, 1901*. New York: Palgrave Macmillan, 2003.

Iturribarría, Jorge Fernando. *Porfirio Díaz ante la historia*. Mexico City: Carlos Villegas García, 1967.

Jiménez Marce, Rogelio. "La creación de una genealogía liberal." *Historias* 51 (2002): 27–49.

Jiménez Marce, Rogelio. *La passion por la polémica: El debate sobre la historia en la época de Francisco Bulnes*. Mexico City: Instituto Mora, 2003.

Johnson, Lyman L., and Sonya Lipsett-Rivera, eds. *The Faces of Honor: Sex, Shame, and Violence in Colonial Latin America*. Albuquerque: University of New Mexico Press, 1998.

Kimmel, Michael. *The Gendered Society*. New York: Oxford University Press, 2000.

Knight, Alan. "El liberalismo mexicano desde la Reforma hasta la Revolución (una interpretación)." *Historia Mexicana* 35, no. 1 (1985): 59–91.

Knight, Alan. "The Working Class and the Mexican Revolution, c. 1900–1920." *Journal of Latin American Studies* 16, no. 1 (1984): 51–79.

Kuri-Aldana, Mario, and Vicente Mendoza Martínez, eds. *Cancionero popular mexicano*, vol. 1. Segunda edición en Lecturas Mexicanas, Cuarta Serie. Mexico City: Consejo Nacional para la Cultura y las Artes, 2001.

Laclau, Ernesto. *On Populist Reason*. New York: Verso, 2005.

Laclau, Ernesto, and Chantal Mouffe. *Hegemony and Socialist Strategy*. New York: Verso, 1985.

Leal, Juan Felipe. *Del mutualismo al sindicalismo en México: 1843–1910*. Mexico City: Ediciones El Caballito, 1991.

Lear, John. *Workers, Neighbors, and Citizens: The Revolution in Mexico City*. Lincoln: University of Nebraska Press, 2001.

Lempérière, Annick. "Los dos centenarios de la independencia mexicana (1910–1921): De la historia patria a la antropología cultural." *Historia Mexicana* 45, no. 2 (1995): 317–52.

Lepidus, Henry. "The History of Mexican Journalism." *University of Missouri Bulletin* 29 (1928): 1–87.

LeVine, Sarah. *Dolor y Alegría: Women and Social Change in Urban Mexico*. Madison: University of Wisconsin Press, 1993.

Lewis, Oscar. *The Children of Sánchez: Autobiography of a Mexican Family*. New York: Vintage Books, 1961.

Lewis, Oscar. *Five Families: Mexican Case Studies in the Culture of Poverty*. New York: Basic Books, 1959.

Limón, José E. *Dancing with the Devil: Society and Cultural Poetics in Mexican American South Texas*. Madison: University of Wisconsin Press, 1994.

Lipsitz, George. *Life in the Struggle: Ivory Perry and the Culture of Opposition*. Philadelphia: Temple University Press, 1988.

López Casillas, Mercurio. *Monografía de 598 estampas de Manuel Manilla: Grabador mexicano*. Mexico City: Editorial RM, 2005.

Macedo, Miguel S. *La criminalidad en México: Medios de combatirla*. Mexico City: Oficina Tipografía de la Secretaría de Fomento, 1897.

Macías-González, Víctor M. "The Bathhouse and Male Homosexuality in Porfirian Mexico," in Víctor M. Macías-González and Anne Rubenstein, eds., *Masculinity and Sexuality in Modern Mexico*. Albuquerque: University of New Mexico Press, 2012, 25–52.

Macías-González, Victor M., and Anne Rubenstein, eds., *Masculinity and Sexuality in Modern Mexico*. Albuquerque: University of New Mexico Press, 2012.

Mansfield, Nick. *Subjectivity: Theories of the Self from Freud to Haraway*. New York: New York University Press, 2000.

Matthews, Michael. "*De Viaje*: Elite Views of Modernity and the Porfirian Railroad Boom." *Mexican Studies/Estudios Mexicanos* 26, no. 2 (Summer 2010): 251–89.

McLean, Malcolm D. *Vida y obra de Guillermo Prieto*. Mexico City: Colegio de México, 1998.

McNamara, Patrick J. "Saving Private Ramírez: The Patriarchal Voice of Republican Motherhood in Mexico." *Gender and History* 18 (1) (2006): 35–49.

McNamara, Patrick J. *Sons of the Sierra: Juárez, Díaz, and the People of Ixtlán, Oaxaca, 1855–1920*. Chapel Hill: University of North Carolina Press, 2007.

Messerschmidt, James W. *Masculinities and Crime: Critique and Reconceptualization of Theory*. Lanham, MD: Rowman and Littlefield, 1993.

Monsiváis, Carlos. *Escenas de pudor y liviandad*. Mexico City: Editorial Grijalbo, 1981.

Monsiváis, Carlos. "The 41 and the *Gran Redada*," in Robert McKee Irwin, Edward J. McCaughan, and Michelle Rocío Nasser, eds., *The Famous 41: Sexuality and Social Control in Mexico, 1901*. New York: Palgrave Macmillan, 2003, 139–67.

Monsiváis, Carlos. "El mundo soslayado (donde se mezclan la confesión y la proclama)," in Salvador Novo, ed., *La estatua de sal*. Mexico City: Consejo Nacional para la Cultura y las Artes, 1998, 11–41.

Niemeyer, E. V., Jr. *El General Bernardo Reyes*. Monterrey: Biblioteca de Nuevo León, 1966.

Novelo, Victoria. "Los trabajadores mexicanos en el siglo XIX: ¿Obreros o artesanos?," in *Comunidad, cultura y vida social: Ensayos sobre la formación de la clase obrera*. Mexico City: Seminario de Movimiento Obrero y Revolución Mexicana/Instituto Nacional de Antropología e Historia, 1991, 15–52.

Ortega y Gasset, José. *Obras completas*, vol. 4. Madrid: Revista de Occidente, 1962.

Ortiz Monasterio, José. *México eternamente: Vicente Riva Palacio y la escritura de la historia*. Mexico City: Instituto Mora/Fondo de Cultura Económica, 2004.

Overmyer-Velazquez, Mark. *Visions of the Emerald City: Modernity, Tradition, and the Formation of Porfirian Oaxaca, Mexico*. Durham, NC: Duke University Press, 2006.

Padilla, Mark, Jennifer Hirsch, Robert Sember, Miguel Muñoz-Laboy, and Richard Parker, eds. "Introduction: Cross-Cultural Reflections on an Intimate Intersection," in *Love and Globalization: Transformations of Intimacy in the Contemporary World*. Nashville: Vanderbilt University Press, 2007, ix–xxxi.

Paredes, Américo. "On Ethnographic Work among Minority Groups: A Folklorist's Perspective," in Richard Baumen, ed., *Folklore and Culture on the Texas-Mexican Border*. Austin: CMAS Books, University of Texas at Austin, 1993, 73–112.

Parker, Andrew, Mary Russo, Doris Sommer, and Patricia Yaeger, eds. Introduction to *Nationalisms and Sexualities*. New York: Routledge, 1992.

Paz, Octavio. *El Laberinto de la soledad*. Mexico City: Fondo de Cultura Económica, 1959.

Paz, Octavio. *The Labyrinth of Solitude and Other Writings*. Translated by Lysander Kemp, Yara Milos, and Rachel Phillips Belash. New York: Grove Press, 1985.

Pellettieri, Osvaldo, ed. *Huellas escénicas*. Buenos Aires: Galerna, 2007.

Pérez Martínez, Herón. *Refranero mexicano*. Mexico City: Lengua y Estudios Literarios, 2004.

Pérez Monfort, Ricardo. *Cotidianidades, imaginarios y contextos: Ensayos de historia y cultura en México, 1850–1950*. Mexico City: Centro de Investigaciones y Estudios Superiores en Antropología Social, 2008.

Pérez Monfort, Ricardo. *Estampas de nacionalismo popular mexicano: Ensayos sobre cultura popular y nacionalismo*. Mexico City: CIESAS, 1994.

Pérez-Rayón, Nora, "The Capital Commemorates Independence at the Turn of the Century," in William H. Beezley and David E. Lorey, eds. *¡Viva México! ¡Viva la Independencia!* Wilmington, DE: Scholarly Resources, 2001, 141–66.

Pérez Salas C., María Esther. *Costumbrismo y litografía en México: Un nuevo modo de ver*. Mexico City: Universidad Nacional Autónoma de México/Instituto de Investigaciones Estéticas, 2005.

Pérez Vejo, Tomás. "Los hijos de Cuauhtémoc: El paraíso prehispánico en el imaginario mexicano decimónico." *Araucaria* 5 (2003): 1–15.

Pérez Vejo, Tomás. "Pintura de historia e imaginario nacional: El pasado en imágenes." *Historia y grafía* 16 (2001). Accessed December 17, 2014. www.redalyc .org/articulo.oa?id=58901604.

Pérez Vejo, Tomás. "¿Se puede escribir historia a partir de imágenes? El historiador y las fuentes icónicas." *Memoria* 32, no. 16 (2012): 17–30.

Piccato, Pablo. "'El Chalequero' or the Mexican Jack the Ripper: The Meanings of Sexual Violence in Turn-of-the-Century Mexico City." *Hispanic American Historical Review* 81 (2001): 623–51.

Piccato, Pablo. *City of Suspects: Crime in Mexico City, 1900–1931*. Durham, NC: Duke University Press, 2001.

Piccato, Pablo. "Public Sphere in Latin America: A Map of the Historiography." *Social History* 35 (2): 165–92.

Piccato, Pablo. *The Tyranny of Opinion: Honor in the Construction of the Mexican Public Sphere*. Durham, NC: Duke University Press, 2010.

Piccato, Pablo. "Urbanistas, Ambulantes, and Mendigos: The Dispute for Urban Spaces in Mexico City, 1890–1930," in Carlos Aguirre and Robert Buffington, eds., *Reconstructing Criminality in Latin America*. Wilmington, DE: Scholarly Resources, 2000, 113–48.

Pilcher, Jeffrey M. *The Sausage Rebellion: Public Health, Private Enterprise, and Meat in Mexico City, 1890–1917*. Albuquerque: University of New Mexico Press, 2006.

Plansencia de la Parra, Enrique. "Conmemoración de la hazaña épica de los Niños Héroes: Su origin, desarrollo, y simbolismos." *Historia Mexicana* 45, no. 2 (1995): 241–79.

Poniatowska, Elena. *Hasta no verte Jesús mío*. Mexico City: Ediciones Era, 1969.

Posada, José Guadalupe. *José Guadalupe Posada: Ilustrador de la vida mexicana*. Mexico City: Fondo Editorial de la Plástica Mexicana, 1963.

Prieto, Guillermo. *Colección de poesías escogidas*. Mexico City: Tipografía de la Oficina Impresora de Estampillas, Palacio Nacional, 1895.

Prieto, Guillermo. *Musa callejera*. Edited by Francisco Monterde. Mexico City: Ediciones de la Universidad Nacional Autónoma de México, 1940.

Pruneda, Salvador. *La caricatura como arma política*. Mexico City: Biblioteca del Instituto Nacional de Estudios Históricos de la Revolución Mexicana, 1958.

Rabasa, Emilio. *El cuarto poder*. Mexico City: Editorial Porrúa, 1970.

Ramos, Samuel. *El perfil del hombre y la cultura en México*, 3rd ed. Mexico City: Espasa-Calpe, 2005.

Ramos i Duarte, Feliz. *Diccionario de mejicanismos: Colección de locuciones i frases viciosas*. Mexico City: Imprenta de Eduardo Dublan, 1895.

Rancière, Jacques. *Proletarian Nights: The Workers' Dream in Nineteenth-Century France*. Translated by John Drury. New York: Verso, 2012.

Rancière, Jacques. *Staging the People: The Proletarian and His Double*. Translated by David Fernbach. New York: Verso, 2011.

Riva Palacio, Vicente. *Páginas en verso*. Mexico City: Librería de Ilustración, 1885.

Rodríguez Kuri, Ariel. "Julio Guerrero: Ciencia y pesimismo en el 900 mexicano." *Historias* 44 (1999): 43–56.

Roseberry, William. "Hegemony and the Language of Contention," in Gilbert M. Joseph and Daniel Nugent, eds., *Everyday Forms of State Formation: Revolution and the Negotiation of Rule in Modern Mexico*. Durham, NC: Duke University Press, 1994, 355–66.

Roumagnac, Carlos. *Los criminales en México: Ensayo de psicología criminal*. Mexico City: Tipografía el Fénix, 1904.

Ruiz, Ramón Eduardo. *Labor and the Ambivalent Revolutionaries: Mexico, 1911–1923*. Baltimore: Johns Hopkins University Press, 1976.

Salazar, Rosendo, and José Escobedo. *Las pugnas de la gleba*. Mexico City: UNAM, 1978.

Sánchez, Rosa Virginia. "Nueve sones huastecos paralelísticos, II." *Revista de Literaturas Populares* 5, no. 2 (July–December 2005): 194–215.

Santamaría, Francisco J. *Diccionario de mejicanismos*, 6th ed. Mexico City: Porrúa, 2000.

Saus, Antonio Luis, José Manuel García Lagos, and Emigdio Cano Gómez, eds. *Cancionero de estudiantes de la tuna: El cantar estudiantil de la Edad Media al siglo XX*. Salamanca: Ediciones Universidad de Salamanca, 2001.

Scott, James C. *Domination and the Arts of Resistance: Hidden Transcripts*. New Haven, CT: Yale University Press, 1992.

Scott, James C. *Seeing like a State: How Certain Schemes to Improve the Human Condition Have Failed*. New Haven, CT: Yale University Press, 1998.

Secretaría de Economía. *Estadísticas sociales del porfiriato, 1877–1910*. Mexico City: Dirección General de Estadística, 1956.

Seed, Patricia. *To Love, Honor, and Obey in Colonial Mexico: Conflicts over Marriage Choice, 1574–1821*. Stanford, CA: Stanford University Press, 1988.

Silverman, Kaja. *Male Subjectivity at the Margins*. New York: Routledge, 1992.

Smith, Benjamin T. *The Roots of Conservatism in Mexico: Catholicism, Society, and Politics in the Mixteca Baja, 1750–1962*. Albuquerque: University of New Mexico Press, 2012.

Smith, Phyllis Lynn. "Contentious Voices amid the Order: The Porfirian Press in Mexico City, 1876–1911." PhD diss., University of Arizona, 1996.

Soler, Jaime, and Lorenzo Avila, eds., *Posada y la prensa ilustrada: Signos de modernización y resistencias*. Mexico City: Museo Nacional de Arte, 1996.

Sommer, Doris. *Foundational Fictions: The National Romances of Latin America*. Berkeley: University of California Press, 1991.

Speckman Guerra, Elisa. *Crimen y castigo: Legislación penal, interpretaciones de la criminalidad y adminstración de justicia* (Ciudad de México, 1872–1910). Mexico City: El Colegio de México/UNAM, 2002.

BIBLIOGRAPHY

—

Speckman Guerra, Elisa. "De amor y desamor: Ideas, imágenes, recetas y códigos en los impresos de Antonio Vanegas Arroyo." *Revista de Literaturas Populares* 1, no. 2 (July–December 2001): 68–101.

Speckman Guerra, Elisa, and Claudia Agostoni, eds., *De normas y transgresiones: Enfermedad y crimen en América Latina (1850–1950)*. Mexico City: Universidad Nacional Autónoma de México, 2005.

Stern, Steve J. *The Secret History of Gender: Women, Men, and Power in Late Colonial Mexico*. Chapel Hill: University of North Carolina Press, 1995.

Szasz, Ivonne. "Sexualidad y género: Algunas experiencias de investigación en México." *Debate Feminista* 9, no. 18 (1998): 77–104.

Tapia Ortega, Francisco. *Grito y silencio de las imprentas: Los trabajadores de las artes gráficas durante el porfiriato*. Mexico City: Universidad Autónoma Metropolitana–Xochimilco, 1990.

Tenorio-Trillo, Mauricio. *I Speak of the City: Mexico City at the Turn of the Twentieth Century*. Chicago: University of Chicago Press, 2012.

Tenorio-Trillo, Mauricio. *Mexico at the World's Fairs: Crafting a Modern Nation*. Berkeley: University of California Press, 1996.

Tenorio-Trillo, Mauricio. "1910 Mexico City: Space and Nation in the City of the Centenario." *Journal of Latin American Studies* 28, no. 1 (February 1996): 75–104

Thompson, E. P. *The Making of the English Working Class*. New York: Vintage Books, 1963.

Tilly, Charles. *Durable Inequality*. Berkeley: University of California Press, 1999.

Toussaint Alcaraz, Florence. *Escenario de la prensa en el Porfiriato*. Mexico City: Fundación Manuel Buendía, 1989.

Tuñón Pablos, Julia. *Women in Mexico: A Past Unveiled*. Translated by Alan Hynds. Austin: University of Texas Press, 1999.

Tyler, Ron, ed. *Posada's Mexico*. Washington, DC: Library of Congress, 1979.

Vanderwood, Paul J. *Disorder and Progress: Bandits, Police, and Mexican Development*, 2nd ed. Wilmington, DE: Scholarly Resources, 1992.

Viquiera Albán, Juan Pedro. *Propriety and Permissiveness in Bourbon Mexico*. Translated by Sonya Lipsett-Rivera and Sergio Rivera Ayala. Wilmington, DE: Scholarly Resources, 1999.

Walker, David W. "Porfirian Labor Politics: Working-Class Organizations in Mexico City and Porfirio Díaz, 1876–1902." *The Americas* 37, no. 3 (January 1980): 257–89.

Walker, George Wayne. "Disciplining Protest Masculinities." *Men and Masculinities* 9, no. 1 (2006): 5–22.

Warner, Michael. *Publics and Counterpublics*. New York: Zone Books, 2002.

Warren, Richard A. *Vagrants and Citizens: Politics and the Masses in Mexico City from Colony to Republic*. Wilmington, DE: Scholarly Resources, 2001.

Weber, Max. *The Protestant Ethic and the Spirit of Capitalism*. Translated by Talcott Parsons. New York: Dover, [1904–05] 2003.

Weeks, Charles A. *The Juárez Myth in Mexico.* Tuscaloosa: University of Alabama Press, 2005.

Williams, Raymond. *The Long Revolution*, rev. ed. New York: Harper and Row, 1961.

Williams, Raymond. *Marxism and Literature.* Oxford: Oxford University Press, 1977.

Zaid, Gabriel. "Divagación sobre las grullas." *Letras Libres* (January 2001): 22–25.

INDEX

f represents figure (image)